PATRIOTISM & PIETY

Jeffersonian America

JAN ELLEN LEWIS, PETER S. ONUF,
AND ANDREW O'SHAUGHNESSY, EDITORS

PATRIOTISM & PIETY

FEDERALIST POLITICS AND RELIGIOUS
STRUGGLE IN THE NEW AMERICAN NATION

Jonathan J. Den Hartog

UNIVERSITY OF VIRGINIA PRESS   CHARLOTTESVILLE AND LONDON

University of Virginia Press
© 2015 by the Rector and Visitors of the University of Virginia
All rights reserved
Printed in the United States of America on acid-free paper

First published 2015

9 8 7 6 5 4 3 2 1

LIBRARY OF CONGRESS CATALOGING-IN-PUBLICATION DATA
Den Hartog, Jonathan J.
   Patriotism and piety : Federalist politics and religious struggle in the new American nation / Jonathan J. Den Hartog.
      pages   cm
   Includes bibliographical references and index.
   ISBN 978-0-8139-3641-3 (cloth : acid-free paper) — ISBN 978-0-8139-3642-0 (e-book)
   1. United States—Politics and government—1783–1865. 2. Federal Party (U.S.)—History. 3. Christianity and politics—United States—History—18th century. 4. Patriotism—United States—History—18th century. 5. Piety—Political aspects—United States—History—18th century. 6. Political culture—United States—History—18th century. 7. Evangelicalism—United States—History—18th century. 8. United States—Religion—To 1800. I. Title.
   E302.1.D46 2014
   973.3'39—dc23

2014016344

For Jacqueline
and
For Abigail, Hannah, Caleb, and Lydia
S.D.G.

Contents

Illustrations

Acknowledgments

THE FEDERALISTS WHO POPULATE THESE PAGES WOULD REMIND ME that acknowledging those who have contributed to this book is a duty not to go unfulfilled. It is that, but it is also a joy and a privilege to thank those who have invested in this research.

This book began in a different form at the University of Notre Dame. There, it took shape under the sage guidance of George Marsden. Professor Marsden has shaped how I think about religion in American history, and for that I am grateful. The rest of my dissertation committee also saved me from many errors. James Turner contributed his customary erudition to reviewing the work, while Linda Przybyszewski added a viewpoint from the nineteenth century. Daniel Walker Howe deserves special thanks for graciously agreeing to serve as an outside reader and helping to refine the project. At Notre Dame, a number of additional people encouraged me as I wrote. David Waldstreicher helped me to conceptualize the project, and this book definitely bears his mark. A number of graduate students who have gone on to academic placements helped to nurture the work, especially the circle around Notre Dame's Colloquium on Religion and History: Thomas Kidd, Tom Bergler, Bryan Bademan, Neil Dhingra, Mark McCarthy, Kristin Kobes DuMez, Darren Dochuk, John Turner, Tim Gloege, David Swartz, and Andrea Turpin. I have especially benefited from extended conversations with Grant Brodrecht and Margaret Abruzzo.

Looking further back, the ideas on which this book builds were first nurtured by some outstanding undergraduate professors who taught me to read closely, think clearly, take historical actors seriously, and determine how ideas have consequences. I am deeply grateful for the investment of professors in both history and political science: Mark Kalthoff, John Willson, "Doc" Thomas Conner, David Stewart, Ted McAllister, Mickey Craig, and Robert Eden.

I am grateful for the organizations that have seen value in this project enough to provide financial support for research and writing. The history department at Notre Dame provided an initial research grant that allowed me to discover where best to invest my energies. The graduate school at Notre Dame provided a Zahm Research and Travel Grant. My research on the Jay family would have been impossible without a grant from the Gilder-Lehrman Institute of American History to do several months' work in New York City. A National Endowment for the Humanities Summer Stipend allowed for the drafting of chapters 5 and 6. The University of Northwestern provided several faculty development grants that helped in manuscript revision. I undertook final manuscript preparation as the Garwood Visiting Fellow in the James Madison Program in American Ideals and Institutions at Princeton University, which proved an extremely rich place to finish one project and begin working on several new ones.

In the archives, I benefited from the attention of archivists and librarians. I would especially like to thank Martha Foley at the American Bible Society and Elise Feeley at the Forbes Library in Northampton, Massachusetts. I would also like to express gratitude to the staffs at the New-York Historical Society; the Manuscripts Division of the Firestone Library at Princeton University; Columbia University's Rare Book and Manuscript Division; the Presbyterian Historical Society; the Historical Society of Pennsylvania; the Manuscripts and Archives Division of the New York Public Library; the Massachusetts Historical Society; the Manuscripts Division of the Library of Congress; Duke University's Rare Books, Manuscripts, and Special Collections; the Manuscripts and Special Collections Library at the University of North Carolina–Chapel Hill; the South Carolina Historical Society; the South Caroliniana Library at the University of South Carolina; the Houghton Library at Harvard University; the Connecticut Historical Society; Yale's Manuscripts and Archives at Sterling Memorial Library; and Yale's Beinecke Rare Book and Manuscript Library.

Speaking of academic debts, I gratefully acknowledge the University of Notre Dame Press for allowing me to use in chapter 1 some material that had previously appeared as "John Jay and the 'Great Plan of Providence'" in Daniel Dreisbach, Mark Hall, and Jeffry Morrison, eds., *The Forgotten Founders on Church and State* (Notre Dame, IN: University of Notre Dame Press, 2009), 145–170. I am also grateful to the collections that allowed me the use of the illustrations in this book.

While doing research, I encountered a great deal of hospitality, beyond what anyone could expect. Raymond Erikson showed great hospitality several times. In Philadelphia, Barry and Sharon Traver opened their home. David and Bethany Michelson showed amazing hospitality, in the best Princetonian tradition. Dan Schwartz welcomed me to his apartment, while David and Saskia Lewis hosted me for Thanksgiving dinner. Jack and Kristin Kobes DuMez opened their Albany, New York, home to me. At Duke, I benefited from the hospitality of David Yang and Matthew Todd. Similarly, Lee Coppock and his family showed superabundant hospitality in Charlottesville, Virginia. Finally, the Chamberlain family of Branford, Connecticut, surely went above and beyond what could be expected in hosting a ragged historian.

Beyond physical hospitality, I appreciate the intellectual hospitality that has welcomed me and my ideas into conversation. I specifically enjoyed academic conversations with Harry Stout, Herb Sloan, Steve Alter, and Thomas Kidd while on the road. David Gellman helped with conversation about the Jay family. Mark Noll has been not only a fellow researcher in nineteenth-century Princeton but a constant champion of this project and a great encourager of my work.

This project is also better because of the responses I received from commentators at conferences. I am grateful for responses received from Pauline Maier, John Fea, Jonathan Sassi, Chris Beneke, Joanne Barker, Kenneth Minkema, Randolph Scully, Dee Andrews, Yonatan Eyal, and Mark Hall. Others have read parts or all of the manuscript and given good guidance. I am grateful for the help and encouragement offered by John Fea, John Turner, Chris Beneke, and Johann Neem, as well as the three anonymous readers for the University of Virginia Press. The book is better for their advice. Where it falls short in fact or interpretation, the responsibility is, of course, mine.

At the University of Virginia Press, the project has been shepherded by Richard Holway. I appreciate his interest in the project. I am also thankful for the press staff who have helped to produce this volume and give it physical reality.

This work grew into a book at the University of Northwestern–St. Paul, Minnesota (formerly Northwestern College). There, in the history department, I appreciate the presence of colleagues Charles Aling, Clyde Billington, and Matthew Miller. The Berntsen Library staff has earned a great deal of credit for helping me to find obscure eighteenth-century materials. I am also glad for student interlocutors, and for those student workers who provided practical support: Amanda Cowden, Stephen MacFarland, Sarah Howell, Adina Johnson, Tomm Carlson, Ariel Johnson, Justin Myhra, and Jessica Johnson.

Finally, it is a great joy to recognize those personal debts that I have incurred along the way. I so appreciate the friendships I have shared, especially with people such as Raymond Erikson, Jerry Park, Michael Lee, and John Calvin Traver, who have heard about this project since its inception. In more recent years, I am grateful to have shared life experiences with the Bock, Caneday, and Howard families.

I have saved the best for last—I am extremely thankful for the family connections that bring me back to the twenty-first century while I am thinking about the eighteenth. Thanks go to my siblings, Joshua and Joy Den Hartog, for putting up with their academic brother. My parents, James and Martha Den Hartog, nurtured my love of learning and have encouraged me at every step of the way. I am grateful for the Caspers, who have welcomed me into their family, too.

I am unspeakably grateful for my own little platoon of a family. My children, Abigail, Hannah, Caleb, and Lydia, are joys worth the daily investment. I look forward to telling them more about the past—and so many other things. Perhaps one day they will see how the Federalists mattered for American history. Our home exists only because of the person who deserves the most thanks, my wife, Jacqueline. She has lived with this project almost as long as I have, and has listened to me, edited chapters, and been the best conversation partner imaginable. I am blessed beyond words that she is my spouse. So, to Jackie: you excel them all.

PATRIOTISM *&* PIETY

Timothy Dwight, president of Yale. John Trumbull. *Timothy Dwight (1752–1817), B.A. 1769, M.A. 1772*, 1817. Oil on canvas. (Yale University Art Gallery, gift of the class of 1817)

Introduction

FEDERALIST POLITICS AND RELIGIOUS STRUGGLE IN THE NEW AMERICAN NATION

ON JULY 4, 1798, THE TWENTY-SECOND ANNIVERSARY OF THE DEC-laration of Independence, President Timothy Dwight of Yale College stepped before his New Haven congregation to deliver the Independence Day sermon. His hearers would quickly grasp that Dwight did not believe things were going well in either the religious or political spheres. He had selected for his text an obscure apocalyptic prophecy from the book of Revelation, which he used to warn of the judgment about to fall on the American nation. Judgment would come as a result of too-close attachment to France and the religious errors ("infidelity") that the French promoted. Dwight's passion grew throughout the sermon until it peaked in a series of questions. "For what end shall we be connected with these men [infidels and French revolutionaries]?" he asked. "Is it, that our churches may become temples of reason, our Sabbath a decade, and our psalms of praise Marseillois hymns? Is it, that we may change our holy worship into a dance of Jacobin phrenzy? Is it that we may see the Bible cast into a bonfire? . . . Shall we, my brethren, become partakers of these sins? Shall we introduce them into our government, our schools, our families?"[1]

Dwight was addressing the immediate threat that he believed the French Revolution and French sympathizers in America posed to religion and government. Should their principles triumph in America, the republic would collapse, religion would be overturned, families would be destroyed, and the entire American way of life would be irretrievably lost. His only hope was that Americans—and especially Christians in America—would rally to defend the republic. He went on to call for political unity and separation from French ideas and alliances. In so doing, Dwight was directly attacking the Democratic-Republicans, whom he believed were either French dupes or the advance party of Jacobinism in America. The alternative was strong support of the national government and the Federalist party, which portrayed itself as the true "friends of government."[2]

Historians of the early republic have seen in Dwight's sermonizing a close alliance between New England's clergy and Federalist politics, and this sermon did indeed highlight a number of Dwight's concerns: his attacks on French religious ideas ("infidelity"), his linking the Democratic-Republicans to France, his appeal to support the government and Federalist party in order to defend the nation's Constitution, republic, and way of life. Yet, these observations leave additional questions unanswered. What had brought Dwight to the point of delivering such a sermon? What effect did he have, apart from igniting some oratorical fireworks? Did these ideas have any bearing on Federalist politicians? By treating this sermon in a vacuum, both Dwight's significance and the motivations and actions of his political allies become distorted.[3]

Dwight clearly believed that he and his compatriots were embattled, trapped in a struggle both religious and political. Although his language was overheated, Dwight was responding to real reports of the bloody results of the French Revolution's Terror. There, political fanaticism led to extreme bloodletting, often in pursuit of a Jacobin policy of dechristianization. In this campaign, church properties were seized, nonjuring clergy were executed as enemies of the state, and even nuns were torn from their cloisters to be executed. Further, Jacobins desacralized space through removing names of saints from the landscape and reoriented time, beginning the calendar with the French Revolution—instead of *Anno Domini*—and shifting the seven-day week to a "decade." This new religious outlook culminated in the celebration of the "Festival of Reason," in which, following a procession, an infamous opera singer was enthroned in the Cathedral of Notre Dame as the goddess of Reason. Drawing on these images, Dwight worried that they might be replicated in an America which hosted Jacobin clubs and Democratic-Republicans who celebrated the cultural liberation of France. With such a dramatic overturning of the moral and religious order, Dwight could respond with nothing less than apocalyptic language. Perhaps the world really was coming to an end.[4]

The newspaper responses to the sermon would only have reinforced Dwight's fears, since they directly challenged his account and authority. "Democraticus" wrote that Dwight's sermon failed to help the public. "[A] few may be amused with it," he wrote, "but they can be neither Christians or Republicans—for instead of the love and good will to mankind so strongly recommended in the Gospels, it breaths a spirit of enmity and distinction adverse to the principles of Christianity." For this writer, Dwight's sermon displayed both a shocking lack of Christian principles and an absence of sound, republican politics. Whereas Dwight had claimed to defend Christianity and republican government from French and American dangers, Democraticus believed the real danger came from the "persecuting spirit" of Dwight and his clerical fellows.[5]

Critical responses to Dwight point to an important characteristic of the early republic—it was a realm of intense religious struggle. Lacking an official church establishment, the nation's religious character was open to definition. Sensing the opportunities this presented, multiple groups rushed to fill the blank space, but they divided over both theology and the church's relation to the state. Religious Federalists operated as just one claimant to the public religious culture of the new nation. The divisiveness of the period reflected the intense competition for the prize of defining the nation's religious character.

This religious conflict was not just a matter for the clergy; laity also eagerly participated in it. Consider the treatment given to Massachusetts Governor Caleb Strong, an evangelical Federalist politician. He was honored by other Federalists for his attempts to bring religious beliefs to bear on political matters. Following his defeat at the polls in 1808, Strong was honored by a mounted procession of "Young Federal Republicans" who noted his "political integrity and moral worth." Citizens across Massachusetts would reiterate this commendation later in the year when they subscribed in support of a volume of Strong's speeches, entitled *Patriotism and Piety.* The introduction to the volume commended the "political, moral, and religious sentiments" that Strong had demonstrated.[6] The volume points to the significance that many Federalists invested in the dual concerns over support for the American republic (Patriotism) and their religious values (Piety). These Federalists were concerned about both the nation's political and religious character. This study explores their endeavors in both spheres, which they saw as connected. They sought to preserve their republic in multiple ways, including, but not limited to, politics. The result was a broad-based movement, composed of clergy and laity, for public involvement. The combination of patriotism and piety, though, was far from easy. No clear blueprint existed for how it might be done. As a result, Federalist leaders produced multiple solutions to the problem, but these answers changed over time and even clashed with other Federalists goals.

. . .

FEDERALISTS HAD FIRST BECOME FEDERALISTS IN THEIR SUPPORT OF the Constitution of 1787. They supported its creation of a national government that would provide order and stability. Having worked to put the Constitution in place, they labored to defend it over the coming decades. They were very ready to link their Democratic-Republican opponents— often unfairly—with the Anti-Federal opponents of the Constitution. A weak government, Federalists believed, could only be useful to empower demagogues to exploit democracy for their own ends.

While the Constitution put a government into place for the republic, it left much undefined—it produced "a roof without walls."[7] Federalists waded into the fray to define what type of character the nation would have. They hoped to create a Protestant, Christian nationalism in which citizens voluntarily worshipped properly and lived morally. From this Protestant morality would flow a republican virtue that would support the constitutional order. In such a society, citizens would acknowledge ministers, support the churches (whether established or not), and generally defer to the more learned members of the community. Federalists' activities in preaching, haranguing, voting, and organizing religious societies all reflected their desire to guarantee that the nation took on a character of which they approved.

Activity was necessary because the early republic was a scene not only of bitter partisan rivalry but of intense religious conflict. Federalists felt threatened precisely because the religious character of the nation was in flux. The religious landscape in the early republic fractured along lines of theological belief and attitudes to the political role of religion. On the theological spectrum, the major division was whether the groups attempted to defend traditional Christian orthodoxy, reinterpret Christianity, or reject it altogether.[8] The orthodox on both sides of the partisan divide defended traditional Christian beliefs related to the divinity of Christ, the reliability of the scriptures, and the need for human salvation. One group of orthodox believers was the evangelical party, marked by their emphasis on conversion and heartfelt religion. The term "evangelical" could be applied to many Congregationalists and Presbyterians, but it equally applied to Baptists and Methodists in the early republic.[9] Among those who wished to modify Christian beliefs, Unitarians—especially in Massachusetts—sought to redefine Christian understandings of Christ's divinity, removing him from an equally divine position with God the Father. This led to a rejection of the Trinity and the definition of God as singularly monotheist.[10] Finally, a group of writers, including Thomas Paine, Elihu Palmer, and Ethan Allen, sought to repudiate Christianity altogether. These thinkers, informed by European skepticism, argued for an outright deism.[11]

Religious disputes also fractured along how the religious group should relate to state and national political authority. Here the tension was between those who defended religious establishments (either formal or informal) and those who rejected them, or between those who took a custodial view of their place in society and those who adopted an individualist, libertarian outlook. Congregationalists in Massachusetts and Connecticut worked to defend their functioning establishments. Unitarians, however, also favored establishments for their social function—as levers of moral influence. Groups such as Presbyterians in the Mid-Atlantic states recognized the pluralism that was present in their region but also appreciated the religious tenor their denomination afforded to public culture. Similarly, in the South after the Anglican Church was disestablished, Episcopalians and Presbyterians could still work to defend an informal dominance of their denominations over society. In general, establishmentarian Christians viewed their role as a priestly function, endorsing the republic and the social order as it existed. This outlook proved amenable to many Federalists.

Others in the early republic favored a stance of disestablishment for a variety of theological reasons. Baptists remembered—and in some cases were still suffering under—the persecution and taxation encouraged by establishments in New England and the South.[12] Methodists, never having been part of an establishment, did not seek one. They rejected the close ties between religion and society promoted by establishments. Many of these Christians took a prophetic stance, arraigning the society as it existed for its injustices and inequities. As historian Nathan Hatch has demonstrated, the populist style of these evangelical groups made them natural allies for the emerging Democratic-Republicans.[13] Free thinkers also opposed religious establishments, which they viewed as tyrannical, unwarranted political control of human reason. To any of these groups, the Federalists appeared very differently than how the Federalists thought of themselves. Any attempt to continue practices of public religiosity was deemed oppressive, and the well-meaning custodial vision could look like the leading edge of tyranny from which the revolution had just liberated them.

The combination of religious concerns with Federalist politics explains the political energy of the Federalists in the 1790s and the first decade of the 1800s. Those who believed their politics had a religious meaning were apt to be more active in their support of a political party.

While governing, Federalist politicians—including national, state, and local officials—honored and defended traditional expressions of corporate religiosity, including proclaiming fast and thanksgiving days and nurturing ties with prominent denominations. Thus, religious concerns should be understood as an essential element of Federalist politics. On the other hand, the religious component of Federalist politics strongly contributed to the party's undoing in two ways. First, as the religious impulse had fueled party activism, the redirection of religious energies into voluntary societies lessened the party's momentum. Second, the religious differences within the party led to splintering and hampered coordinated partisan activity. These developments altered not only the Federalist party but the practice and perception of religion in America. Faith became more individualistic, voluntaristic, and issues-oriented as a result of the actions of religious Federalists.

Three religious streams coexisted within the Federalist party: evangelical, Unitarian, and Southern establishmentarian. Federalist evangelicals could be found in Congregationalist, Presbyterian, and Episcopalian churches. Unitarians tied religious belief to social stability. Differing from the evangelicals in theological matters, they largely shared views of the proper form of republican society. Finally, Southern establishmentarians—whether Episcopalian or Presbyterian—decried formal church establishments yet sought to preserve the close ties between religious institutions and established Southern society. Of these three groups, the evangelicals were the most innovative and transformative for Federalist politics. Indeed, much of this study focuses on the actions of evangelical Federalists and the responses these actions generated. These Federalists confronted a new American nation that, lacking an establishment, witnessed open religious competition. Federalists were forced to become creative in their appropriation and application of religion in political matters. Even so, the theological differences mattered, producing divergent emphases and strategies for the new nation. Ultimately, differences also caused ruptures among the various camps, contributing further to the Federalists' demise.

Although changes occurred unevenly, Federalists experienced three successive stages of religion's relation with politics: "Republican," "Combative," and "Voluntarist."[14] The first, a Republican attitude toward religion, emerged from the American Revolution and the first years under the new Constitution. It was an optimistic perspective that saw an easy relationship between religion and the American government. It posited Christianity as naturally supporting the government and creating the morals and virtue upon which a healthy republic would depend. Federalists in this early key believed they were carrying on the revolutionary legacy and establishing the conditions necessary for its continuance to successive generations. In so doing, they were drawing on prominent elements within the revolutionary tradition.[15]

Such a perspective could only endure so long as it was not challenged. In the 1790s, under the pressure of external threats and internal divisions, many believers in the Federalist camp came to a Combative perspective on religion and politics. They believed that energy was necessary to defend both their faith and their republican government. They expressed their faith in public activity and in zealous work for the Federalist party. They identified the party as the true representative of the healthy cooperation between religion and the republic they had earlier articulated. The difference lay in the stakes they perceived (for both Church and Nation) and the intensity with which they pursued their public objectives. Feeling besieged, they organized and acted much more publicly. Even their religious statements took on a more partisan cast. In this period, evangelical attitudes became more dominant in the movement.

Finally, in the first decades of the nineteenth century—and especially after the War of 1812—many Federalists adopted a Voluntarist strategy, increasingly turning to voluntary religious societies as a means of preserving the republic.[16] In this development, they experienced both push and pull. They were pushed out of politics in the face of Democratic electoral success, but they were also pulled in this direction by the successes they saw resulting from early voluntarist endeavors. As they invested their energy in these societies, they decoupled themselves from Federalist politics. In such societies, they were able to express an interdenominational piety, one much more typical of antebellum America. These societies proved very useful for dealing with evangelism or individual moral issues, and they functioned as democratic expressions, appealing to large numbers of people. These concerns subsequently fed into antebellum reform, shaping movements against slavery, Indian removal, and spirituous liquors.[17]

Faced with pluralism and disestablishment, religious Federalists pioneered new ways of living within the increasingly democratic republic. This development might appropriately be labeled a "Federalization of American Christianity." Ironically, this Voluntarist strategy was simultaneously democratizing and centralizing. While dispersing activity, these organizers maintained control through national organization. By providing structure, they channeled the populist religious impulses erupting in the new nation. By creating national organizations at a time when the federal government was weak, the Federalists contributed to the building of national identity, one with a decidedly Protestant cast. That it was Federalists, not their Democratic-Republican brethren, who developed these strategies should give pause: in this way, the Federalists better understood how to affect the tenor and trajectory of American culture. In constructing an approach that grew out of earlier ideals and concerns, Federalists revealed that their strategy had both losses—they had to shed a large part of the comprehensive vision of Federalism—and gains, as they preserved and advanced their moral and religious concerns. While a cultural triumph, Federalists also revealed their incapacity for pursuing success in the political realm.

In their wrestling with how to bring religion into the public realm, Federalists were shaped by their experiences of both the late colonial period and the American Revolution. Whether accurate or not, Federalists remembered the colonial period as one of social stability and hierarchy, and they sought to replicate those social arrangements in the early republic. Religion—by which they meant Protestant Christianity—was an important part of their vision of society and was necessary for social health. Further, Protestantism had been wrapped up in the British nationalism that they had largely celebrated.[18] Just as religion had helped to tie together colonial society, so they believed it could hold together the burgeoning American republic. They also remembered an ordered society, where ministers and the "better men" helped to set the tone for the entire community. They were deeply troubled by the leveling processes they observed in the new nation, as common folk spoke back to clergy and unknowns became prominent in politics.[19] Part of Federalism's social program was thus to use creative means to conservative ends, as they sought to carry the vision of religion and society they remembered from the colonial days into the new republic.

Federalists' actions were further shaped by their experiences in the American Revolution, when religion became more politicized. Ministers and laity during this period equated God's purposes with those of the newly independent nation, and for some the revolution was part of God's millennial designs. Rather than creating tension between itself and the new government, belief seemed to support the republic. Patriotism and piety could be one and the same thing. This outlook shaped those who had a role in the revolution, whether as legislators or members of the army. With such an outlook on the combination of religion and politics, it only made sense that they would seek to continue it in the new nation.[20]

Religious Federalists were advancing a positive social vision because they believed in Protestant Christianity's significant place in the American republic. They insisted that, if faith remained strong, society would naturally remain stable, and the republic would be well supported. Religion could produce republican virtue and the willingness to sacrifice self-interest for the common good. Moreover, the republic could provide added support to the churches by recognizing their importance, encouraging religious participation, and creating government-recognized sacred time through fast and thanksgiving proclamations. Pursuing constructive nation-building, they shared the hope for improvement with many others in the early republic. Working for improvement "through time," that is, commercially and culturally, the Federalists hoped to create a national culture and religious republic.[21] Although differing on the exact shape of that public religious culture, Federalists hoped for a republic that honored faith and relied on religion as the source of a republican morality. Through belief, they could produce spiritual development, moral refinement, and fully responsible republican citizens.

Given this vision, the Federalists reacted defensively when their ideals came under attack, both politically and religiously. When confronted with "friends of liberty" who organized into political societies, believing Federalists clearly sided with the "friends of government."[22] To them, the Jeffersonian Republicans were directly opposed to the Christian republic they hoped for. Moreover, they saw such Republicans aligned with an international enemy—revolutionary France. Federalists like Dwight viewed their opponents as American "Jacobins," intent on doing the same thing to America as the Jacobins had done to France. In opposing Frenchified Americans, Federalists formed part of a transatlantic anti-Jacobin movement. The French Revolution loomed over Federalist political activity, leading both to the use of violent language and the attempt to squelch popular cosmopolitanism.[23]

In addition to these efforts, Federalists worked to counter the problem of Jacobin irreligion. Federalists labeled the dangerous French belief "infidelity," a term that encapsulated to them the entire religious-political attack on the nation. Infidelity questioned the reliability of the scriptures and the truth of Christianity. If citizens no longer had faith and left the churches, they would quickly adopt immoral behavior, losing their republican virtue. Such a decayed republic would be an easy target for demagogues and tyrants. Federalists believed the Democratic-Republicans were pursuing this very strategy. Consequently, their enemies were not just politically wrong; they were morally and spiritually wicked. To defend a Christian republic, both clergy and politicians were ready to fight infidelity in whatever form it took. Federalists thus both participated in and encouraged the cultural and political polarization of the nation, as their religious beliefs added greater charge to separate the forces of pious, patriotic light from the forces of Franco-American unbelief, anarchy, and darkness.[24]

This work examines the individual Federalists who worked to preserve a religiously informed polity and believed they were thereby demonstrating "Patriotism and Piety." It begins with John Jay, whose qualifications as a Federalist were impeccable: patriot, contributor to the *Federalist Papers*, first chief justice of the U.S. Supreme Court, negotiator of the Jay Treaty, and governor of New York. Jay's experience connects the later Federalist movement to its roots in the American Revolution and the struggle for the Constitution. During his public life, Jay illustrated the first two stages of religious development. In the 1770s and 1780s, Jay was a preeminent example of a Republican orientation of religion and politics, finding an easy congruence between his own Anglicanism/Episcopalianism and the revolution, and later the Federalist push for a new Constitution. Only after his return from England in 1795 and under the stresses of partisan and religious divisions did he begin to demonstrate a particularly Combative approach to religion and politics. Religion took on a new salience for Jay's Federalist politics in the later 1790s, as it did for many other Federalists.

Chapter 2 examines two clergymen, Timothy Dwight—a grandson of Jonathan Edwards—and Jedidiah Morse, who played significant roles in inserting religion into Federalist politics and producing a Combative approach to religion and politics. The chapter begins by tracing the positive vision of a Christian republic that Dwight and Morse shared, but it shifts to a key negative concept for them: infidelity. To counter such a threat, both men not only preached against it but worked politically, spoke and published incessantly, and organized strategically. They did so within a larger network of Federalist ministers and politicians who picked up their language and attitudes, demonstrating their widespread impact. After 1800, Dwight and Morse began to turn to voluntary societies, thereby draining the energy away from a Combative Federalist politics.

The next two chapters consider active evangelical Federalist politicians to examine how evangelical belief affected their politics. Chapter 3 examines Caleb Strong of Massachusetts, who demonstrated a politics of personal piety, using personal religious beliefs to support his policies during a long career in both national and state politics. As governor of Massachusetts, he advocated an orderly, religious society and issued proclamations that reflected his evangelical Federalist vision. The chapter concludes that, ultimately, Strong's politics of personal piety were a dead-end, unable to secure a lasting political imprint. By contrast, Elias Boudinot, a New Jersey lawyer and politician, pioneered a different, Voluntarist approach that pointed beyond the Federalists. Serving in the Continental Congress and the first three Congresses as a representative, Boudinot demonstrated an evangelical Federalist approach by advocating "public righteousness"—a politics characterized by justice, morality, and religion. In his retirement, Boudinot combined his conversionist impulse with his Federalist outlook of national unity for greater effectiveness. The result was his work for national voluntary societies, primarily the American Bible Society. In so doing, Boudinot ironically contributed to the decline of both the Federalist party and the Combative religious outlook. In decoupling Combative religion from the Federalist party, Boudinot helped to sow the seeds of a Voluntarist approach, a nineteenth-century vision of religion and politics with a more democratic tone.

The study then turns to two chapters that consider alternatives to the evangelical camp. Chapter 5 discusses the Unitarian Federalists John Adams and Henry Ware. These figures were not only important for their political and theological leadership; they acted as significant figures in defining a Unitarian politics centered around rational morality and an orderly republican society. A religious rationalist, Adams defended a role for a public religiosity, and as president, he advocated a political use of public religion. Henry Ware, as Hollis Chair of Divinity at Harvard University, propagated a Unitarianism that clearly supported an orderly society with a rationalist, moralistic religion undergirding republican institutions. Despite sharing political concerns with evangelicals, their public cooperation was hindered by very real theological differences. If religious belief was to shape political involvement, religious differences would cut against larger goals of Federalist cooperation.

Chapter 6 directs attention not to theological differences but to sectional variations. Charles Cotesworth Pinckney and Henry William De Saussure, both South Carolinians, offer perspectives on how Northern Federalist approaches were altered in the South. Pinckney and De Saussure shared with the Northern evangelicals a concern for an ordered society, a strong government, and even theological orthodoxy. They differed in their appropriation of the Voluntarist tendencies from the North, refusing to embrace them wholeheartedly. The presence of slavery and their lack of concern for formal church establishments diminished the push for the forthright public religiosity favored in the North.

In the final chapters, John Jay's sons, Peter Augustus and William, inscribe the decline of the Federalist party and the transformation of a Combative Federalism into a diversified, full-throated Voluntarism. The sons' lives reflect alternate trajectories growing out of Federalism, as they witnessed the sustained collapse of the Federalist party. Peter Augustus began as an active Federalist, but he found his political opportunities repeatedly curtailed. Although personally religious, Peter Augustus did not stress religion in his public pronouncements but emphasized morality as the key component for public behavior and supported nonreligious voluntary societies. He thus limned a retreat from public religiosity in favor of a public morality. William, by contrast, showed the possibilities for a zealous religiosity connected to largely apolitical moral reform. Educated by Timothy Dwight, William embraced the vision of evangelical religion influencing society and poured his energy into a variety of reform movements, culminating in abolitionism. In advocating public morality and reform movements separated from a political party, John Jay's two sons illustrated how Combative Federalist religion had lost its political and social edge, taking on characteristics more suitable for a Voluntarist Jacksonian America.

FOCUSING ON INDIVIDUALS MAKES SENSE OF THE "PERSONAL POLItics" of the Federalists. They paid special attention to the persons acting. Valuing more than honor, they cared about personal integrity and the moral authority of the person acting.[25] They emphasized the decision-making of the person in the office, rather than the outcomes. In their politics, they downplayed the policy results; they largely lacked a politics of legislation. It mattered more to the Federalists *who* was acting than the results of their decisions. By understanding who was acting for the Federalists, we can better appreciate the interaction of religion and Federalist politics at multiple levels of government.

To describe Federalism's significant religious component, the study examines both politics and political culture. Although explicitly political actions are important to this work, it also describes attitudes, beliefs, and actions that, while impinging on politics, existed beyond politics. In a manner similar to the work of Daniel Walker Howe, the book addresses, "not only the explicit [political] analyses and proposals . . . but also the mood, metaphors, values, and style" of political attitudes and action. As an explicitly meaning-bearing system, religion in early America was ideologically, linguistically, and metaphorically intertwined with political issues.[26] In this period, beliefs, convictions, and organizations that at first might seem quite removed from politics significantly informed how individuals thought about and acted within formal politics.[27] Put another way, this approach presents a new perspective on the "cultural politics" of the period.[28] Religion as an aspect of culture was hotly contested in the early republic, and examining its usage by the Federalists returns it to the historical narrative as a significant arena of debate and a factor influencing political thought. Without grasping both the obvious and subtle influences of religious culture, an understanding of the political culture of the period is incomplete.

This book grounds such intersections of belief and behavior in the lives, faiths, and actions of individual Federalists. These individuals shared a similar cultural and political outlook, although they argued over religious belief and its social implications. They found themselves linked by family networks, political alignment, and religious cooperation, connections that reinforced perceptions and strategies. By examining a sample of Federalists, we understand the world through their eyes and grasp how they attempted to answer the challenges they perceived in the early republic. Through grounding their responses in a biographical form, we can trace how developments in culture both acted upon and were transformed by specific individuals who chose to respond in certain ways. It thus preserves the contingent decisions of individual actors, while setting them in larger contexts. Understanding these developments at the individual level best accounts for changes that occurred.[29]

Because the selection of characters matters a great deal for such a study, let me affirm that the choice of these individuals rests upon geographic dispersion and archival corroboration. The Federalist story is a national story and required individuals beyond the confines of Federalist New England. Although space prohibits a consideration of leaders from every state, this study gauges developments in all regions of the new nation. Further, I carried out this investigation by doing wide-ranging archival research, with broad reading in newspaper and pamphlet literature, as well as private correspondence. As the research mounted, it became apparent that I was discovering significant networks that connected the Federalists in this study in their pursuit of Federalist political and cultural success. Communicating with each other, they were each significant in the direction that Federalism as a movement took. Far from

being a tautology ("religion looks important only because the author selected religious individuals"), these figures point to wider developments
in religion and early national politics, as is confirmed by how the main
figures in this study interacted with other Federalists who, though only
mentioned here, also brought religion into their politics.

In choosing these male actors, I in no way intend to deny the activities of women in the period or to ignore the significant gendered element
of Federalist politics and ideology that recent scholarship has demonstrated. Women were granted roles in political activity and performance
as long as they did not challenge gendered assumptions. Ironically, the
Federalists had more place for women in their politics than did the Jeffersonians, whose sole political actor was the white male. Because of
Federalist belief in hierarchy, Federalists could envision political engagement on differentiated levels. Political involvement thus could occur in
a gender-specific way. Women were present at political gatherings and
could be invoked as symbols for moral and political ideals, as was Elias
Boudinot's wife, Hannah. Similarly, women could comment on elections,
as did Abigail Adams and the women of the Jay family. By the close of
the War of 1812, however, with the ascending power of the Democratic-
Republicans, all political options were foreclosed, as women were pushed
away from outright political involvement in a "backlash."[30]

At the same time that opportunities for political participation were
withdrawing, however, women found the voluntary societies founded by
Federalists to be amenable openings for participation. Through auxiliary
societies, women could gain a certain level of public involvement and
publicity. This participation included many women connected with the
Federalists in this study, such as when John Jay's daughter Maria attended
American Bible Society meetings or Elias Boudinot's daughter Susan
supported other reform organizations. These societies provided opportunities for nonelite women to participate as well.

Finally, gendered concerns about marriage and masculinity shaped
additional elements of the Federalist agenda. One component was a defense of traditional marriage ideals, which Federalists believed were under attack. Here, Mary Wollstonecraft became an easy target for ridicule.
She became a symbol for the havoc that democratic politics and infidel
religion would wreak on society. As Dwight suggested in his 1798 sermon
and subsequent essays, religious Federalists believed that the French Revolution and its sympathizers in America were working to undermine not
only politics but marriage and female virtue.[31] Another component was

the reassertion of a public masculinity for Federalist leaders. Especially for the rising generation of "Young Federalists," public participation, which included a defense of religious institutions, marked an opportunity to claim manhood in the new nation. In this study, Peter Augustus Jay best articulated these concerns, but they can also be traced in other figures of the period.[32] Put together, these concerns about women as limited political participants, their involvement in voluntary societies, the place of marriage in a larger social vision, and the possibility for defining masculinity demonstrate a gendered component for Federalist activity.

PATRIOTISM AND PIETY OFFERS IMPORTANT INSIGHTS FOR UNDER-standing both politics and religion in the early republic. Although the ideas and politics of the revolution, the ratification debates over the Constitution, and the early years of the republic remain of perennial concern, the past decade has been a particularly fruitful time in the study of the early republic. Whereas older studies focused on political organization or ideology, more recent studies have taken the insights of social and cultural historians into account.[33] Historians have grown attentive to a wide range of political practice in the early republic—from celebrations to clothing, toasts, marches, and even a mammoth cheese.[34] They have widened the definition of political actors in the early republic to include printers, African Americans, young men's groups, women, sailors, and apprentices.[35] These studies, with their interest in how cultural attitudes can interact with politics, have shed a great deal more light on the political contours of the early republic. While noting religious elements of this cultural politics, however, most have not investigated them as centrally important. A full reconsideration of the Federalists requires reassessing religion's role in their politics.[36]

Religion was essential to the identity and ideology of the Federalist party. Although Federalists have traditionally been portrayed as supporting commercial growth, the national bank, and a strong national government, this important religious dimension has been overlooked. Rather than paying attention simply to Alexander Hamilton and John Adams, a greater appreciation of Federalist activity on all levels of politics is required.[37] Since the states were more significant political entities in the early republic, how the Federalists behaved in the states dramatically mattered. Following the lead of political historians after the cultural turn, this book pays attention to the religious commitments of Federalists as a central, constitutive component for their cultural ideals. The individuals in this study highlight the important role religion had in party formation and party goals, as well as its subsequent decline. Historians misunderstand Federalism when they ignore the religious component of their language and activity.

This study further integrates religion into an explanation for the Federalists' demise. Older assumptions focused on problems of politics and political organization. In the standard narrative, the Hartford Convention—a protest against the War of 1812—marked the turning point when Federalists separated themselves from the nation's interest, receiving electoral opprobrium for their troubles. The problems afflicting the party, however, had begun well before 1815. From another perspective, in a classic historical work, David Hackett Fischer emphasized the split between the "Old Federalists," who did not want to participate in party activities and partisan campaigns, and the "Young Federalists," who did, albeit not fast enough to counter the Democratic-Republicans. But a simple political answer seems insufficient. The "Young Federalists" did an impressive job of organizing and publicizing their ideas that could have succeeded. The Federalists possessed many levers of influence that should have enabled them to continue competing with the Democratic-Republicans. Moreover, the pall that settled over the Federalists in the early nineteenth century seemed to go beyond mere electoral defeats.[38]

If the Federalists' failure was not only or even primarily a political one, then other factors must have contributed to their downfall. For a fuller understanding of this decline, historians need to take social, geographic, and cultural forces into account. Although beyond this study, the changing social composition of the nation undoubtedly weakened Federalist appeal. In its social vision of settled communities of uniform, British stock that had participated in the revolutionary experience, the Federalists demonstrated limited ability to reach beyond such groups. Further, Western expansion weakened community bonds and gave rise to new communities along an unevenly settled frontier. Whereas elites in established communities demonstrated great affinity for Federalists and could encourage citizens to support them, such elites had little sway in these new settlements to which old hierarchies could not be imported. Thus, not only did the Jeffersonian ideal of westward expansion serve an ideological goal of encouraging yeoman farmers; it also produced a political result of setting up communities in which the Jeffersonian Republican ideal made greater sense.[39]

For our purposes, the cultural and religious factors in Federalist decline loom large. The Federalists offered both a cultural and religious vision. In their religious account, self-government worked best when, organizationally, church and state cooperated, providing a significant public role for religion. For Americans increasingly likely to emphasize individual activity for both church and political involvement, this idea of corporate religiosity made less and less sense. Further, religious Federalists were not only pushed out of politics—they experienced the pull of other, voluntarist organizations. Their leaving or reducing their activity further weakened the party, as did intraparty theological sparring. Through complex cultural and religious changes, then, the Federalists could no longer find enough electoral support to continue in existence.

For Federalists, mixing religion and politics was an endeavor that went far beyond clerical figures. Clergy undoubtedly shaped religious Federalism, and several clergymen show up in this work as important figures.[40] Yet, religious concepts would not have gained the traction they did in Federalism without the willing support of lay leaders. The religious beliefs of Federalist laity, coupled with how those beliefs shaped their politics, to this point have not been explored. Clergy and laity together shaped religiously inspired models for political participation and together experienced how that participation shaped their religious outlook and how competing models clashed within Federalism.

As these religious individuals acted in the public sphere, their activity came as an outgrowth of their beliefs. Other historians of religion have pointed to the value of lived religion—the practices that shape and contain religious meaning for people.[41] Candy Gunther Brown has argued that evangelicalism be understood to include the activities following conversion, as well as the conversion experience itself, expanding the "picture of evangelicalism by bringing into fuller view some of the day-to-day relationships, concerns, and practices of lay and clerical individuals who identified themselves as evangelical."[42] This outlook on religious practice suggests that many activities can be seen as religious outgrowths of belief, and at least some of the figures studied here clearly demonstrated a use of politics as a type of lived religion. Piety motivated individuals to become involved in public matters, and they saw inherent connections between religious and political practice.

Finally, the encounter with Federalism strongly shaped American Christianity. In addition to a narrative that stresses democratization in this period, a concurrent "Federalization of American Christianity" also occurred.[43] Rather than being a footnote to a story in which Methodists and Baptists alone defined American Christianity after 1800, Federalist

Christians worked creatively to shape and order the energy of American evangelicalism. Without Federalists leading the way in creating the structures within which evangelism would take place in the nineteenth century, much of the zeal expressed in the early republic would have dissipated. In pioneering religious voluntarism, these individuals took Federalist concepts about national bodies directing dispersed local activity to form national organizations in the same way that the U.S. Constitution shaped the practice of political federalism. The end result was to give a voluntarist, reforming, socially engaged direction to expressions of American Christians throughout the union—an effect that would last long after the Federalist party had disintegrated.

EVANGELICALS & FEDERALISTS

1 John Jay and the Shift from Republican Religion to Evangelical Federalism

IN 1809, CONGREGATIONALIST MINISTER JEDIDIAH MORSE WROTE to the retired statesman John Jay to ask for advice about writing a history of the American Revolution. Jay responded that "a proper history of the United States . . . would be singular, or unlike all others." Jay believed such a history would be exceptional because "it would develop the great plan of Providence, for causing [America] to be gradually filled with civilized and *Christian* people and nations." The American republic was significant to Jay because God had willed both its existence and its character as a Christian nation. Clearly Jay saw a close tie between Christianity and the politics of the new nation. Before he closed his letter, he reiterated his opinion that "the historian, in the course of the work, is never to lose sight of that great plan."[1] Whether the historian grasped it or not, Jay believed that Providence had been overseeing the settlement of America, its independence, and its growth as a nation.

What should we make of such claims? One possible response is that they were mere window-dressing, part of the vocabulary of the day. Another might be that Jay in his later years was turning his thoughts to eternity and letting the expanded interest in spiritual matters cloud his memory of the past. A third could be that Jay was using religious language to justify his actions and those of political allies. Although all of these motives may have been present, Jay's claims still deserve historical attention because over thirty years of public life, he repeatedly cast political issues in terms of Providence.

The contexts of Jay's repeated references to Providence make clear that he meant it in an orthodox Christian sense—that the Christian God not only had intervened in the world in the person of Christ but continued to be active (often through secondary causes) to fulfill his own purposes.[2] Jay's belief in Providence also called him to active service as a response to the divine will. Jay's Providence was thus more than a personal belief;

it had important national consequences. A Protestant perspective shaped Jay's public activities by giving transcendent significance to temporal political affairs, and those activities influenced the development of the new nation.[3]

By understanding how and why Jay deployed ideas of Providence, this chapter traces an evolution of his thinking during his public Federalist career, as a Republican attitude gave way to a Combative one.[4] It uses Jay's life to understand how religion emerged as salient in his public behavior, as well as how that religious belief and its influence changed over time. In the period 1774–1800, Jay maintained a Christian providential nationalist interpretation of the American experiment, which led him to active political participation. Through an interaction with events and ideas of the period, however, the tenor of that providentialism transformed from a formal Republican vision of the revolutionary period to an activist and forthright Combative position in the 1790s, leading to more direct political results.[5]

Jay's piety was deeply rooted and long lasting. His father, Peter, raised his children in a context of piety that blended the Huguenot seriousness of his ancestors with the family's newly adopted Anglicanism. While attending King's College in New York City, John regularly participated in services at Trinity Church. His attachment to Trinity Church would last many years, and he would be active in both the church and the emerging Episcopal denomination.[6] As an adult, Jay publicly defended orthodox Christianity. Responding to a minister who had sent him a refutation of Tom Paine's Age of Reason, Jay confessed, "I have long been of opinion, that the evidence of the truth of Christianity, requires only to be carefully examined to produce conviction in candid minds." Jay believed there were good—even rational—reasons to defend Christian belief. When confronted with the unbelief of the era, he scornfully rejected it. The Age of Reason, he felt, "never appeared to me to have been written from a disinterested love of truth, or of mankind."[7] Similarly, during his peace mission in France, Jay was confronted by atheists who challenged his belief in Christ, which, according to Jay's later report, prompted him to respond "that I did [believe], and that I thanked God that I did."[8] Jay's public words and deeds suggested a strong attachment to a traditional, even evangelical, Protestantism that emphasized moderation, duty, and resignation to the will of God.

Jay saw Providence at work in specific ways in American political development, but those perceptions evolved during his career. At first, in the revolutionary moment, Jay saw Providence working for the establishment of political liberty. In the Confederation era, Jay saw Providence behind the defense of order and preservation of national unity, demonstrating a Republican view of religion. In the 1790s, Providence seemed to be threatening judgment because of the corporate failings of the new republic. The "political storms" and "moral epidemics" of the period pushed Jay to adopt a Combative approach to religion's place in defending the nation. In these ways, religion was structurally important to the nation. Thus Jay's religious beliefs helped to energize and actuate his assumptions about politics and the larger world.

Jay and the Providential American Revolution

New York sent twenty-nine-year-old Jay, because of his recent involvement in patriot activities in New York City, to the First Continental Congress. There, allied with his father-in-law, William Livingston, he fully participated in debates. Congress decided to direct an address to the British people, and Jay's proposed draft was quickly accepted.[9] In his address, Jay leveled the familiar charges that Britain was attempting to enslave the colonies, remove the right to trial by jury, and destroy American commerce. Jay also included a religious objection to the Quebec Act. He protested that "we think the Legislature of Great Britain is not authorized by the constitution to establish a religion fraught with sanguinary and impious tenets, or to erect an arbitrary form of government in any quarter of the globe."[10] Jay decried the fact "that a British parliament should ever consent to establish in that country a religion that has deluged your island in blood, and dispersed impiety, bigotry, persecution, murder, and rebellion, through every part of the world." Here Jay was drawing on the widespread assessment of Roman Catholicism that had done much to shape British nationalism, even in the colonies. Drawing on that theme, Jay warned that a successful policy of denying British rights to the colonists could easily be replicated in Britain itself. In this nefarious plan, the present ministry had enlisted the support of Roman Catholics in Canada. The peace ending the French and Indian War had been made by people "unfriendly to the Protestant cause, and inimical to liberty," and the current ministry was endeavoring to use those Catholic allies to bring the other American colonies into subjection.[11] Jay's thinking at this early stage drew on traditional anti-Catholicism. He was attempting to show that the colonists' complaint was intended as a defense of tradition and in line with the Protestant character of English nationalism.

Through rhetorical appeals drawing on shared religious language, Jay hoped for reconciliation between the colonies and Britain.[12] Instead of peace, circumstances moved toward greater conflict, leading to the outbreak of war. Even so, Jay continued to push for conciliatory measures, such as John Dickinson's Olive Branch Petition. When the final break with Britain came, Jay (by then in New York's Provincial Congress) directed the state's endorsement of the Declaration of Independence. He later asserted that "our country was prompted and impelled to independence by necessity and not by choice." Jay embraced independence and put his whole effort into making it succeed, motivated by a belief that Providence was at the center of events.[13]

Early in the revolution, Jay's view of religion's role in politics was decidedly particularist and Protestant. At the First Continental Congress in 1774, he was unsure of the legitimacy of a clergyman opening sessions in prayer because he might offend other denominations. At this stage, Jay valued denominational distinctions so much that he failed to see commonalities.[14] Even more dramatically, in the New York Provincial Congress he attempted to shape the state's constitution to exclude Roman Catholics from the political process. He proposed that members of "the church of Rome" be excluded from citizenship until they would forswear the authority of "pope, priest, or foreign authority," as well as "the dangerous and damnable doctrine, that the pope, or any other earthly authority, have power to absolve men from sins or their obligation to the state of New York."[15] Although this measure was rejected, Jay succeeded in requiring that for naturalization, immigrants would "renounce all subjection to all and every foreign king, prince, potentate and state, in all matters, ecclesiastical as well as civil."[16] Although illiberal, Jay's political strategy had a logic to it: if Catholics were opposed to liberty, were ruled authoritatively by foreign powers, and were hoping to enslave Protestant Americans, they could neither be good republicans nor participate in the Protestant republic Jay hoped would be formed. Although this Protestant nationalism was now disconnected from England, it still carried a great deal of weight in Jay's thinking. Ironically, the logic behind the New York Provincial Congress proposal calling for discrimination against Catholics enabled him to overcome his scruples against other Protestant denominations. In subsequent years, Jay would thus be much more cooperative with other Protestant groups than his 1774 objections suggest.

Because Providence favored the American cause, Jay could display a guarded optimism in his *An Address of the Convention of the Representatives of the State of New York to Their Constituents.* Jay used the pamphlet, published in December 1776 during the darkest days of the British Army's advance into New Jersey, to strengthen New Yorkers' flagging morale by highlighting his belief in the providential character of the contest. Jay pictured the Americans as having received their lands and their freedoms "under the auspices and direction of divine Providence." They were thus called to defend their "inheritance" against a king who had declared them out of his protection and waged war on them. The king's armies had "no regard for religion or virtue" and had even desecrated churches. Even more importantly, only a free people could advance God's kingdom on earth, since "the Almighty will not suffer slavery and the gospel to go hand in hand."[17] On both political and spiritual levels, Jay cast the struggle in monumental terms, with an impact to be felt for generations to come.

Given such stakes, Jay's recommendations are striking. Rather than focusing on tangible actions, Jay issued a call for a reformation of morals, since vices had always brought people into slavery. In that light, the war for independence might have a purifying effect, "to punish the guilt of this country, and bring us back to a sense of duty to our Creator." Jay envisioned a communal guilt and hence the possibility of communal repentance and blessing. Jay expanded on this thought when he exhorted, "The King of Heaven is not like the King of Britain, implacable. If his assistance be sincerely implored, it will surely be obtained. If we turn from our sins, he will turn from his anger. . . . Let us do our duty and victory will be our reward." Jay here viewed repentance on a state and even national level as both possible and necessary. A merciful God would surely help a nation that implored his favor—especially when their cause was just. In the face of an advancing British army, Jay demanded, "Let universal charity, public spirit and private virtue, be inculcated, encouraged, and practiced. Unite in preparing for a vigorous defence of your country, as if all depended on your own exertions. And when you have done these things, then rely upon the good providence of Almighty God for success; in full confidence that without his blessing, all our efforts will inevitably fail." In a pattern Jay would often repeat, human actions were decidedly required in the political realm. If people applied themselves, God's providence would bless those actions with success. Faced with such a clear formula, Jay offered his readers a choice: accept slavery or courageously "do your duty."[18]

As the war progressed, Jay continued to urge on American efforts with religious language. This strategy was evident in his charge to the first grand jury empanelled under the new state constitution. Having been given his choice of offices in the state government, Jay chose the post of state chief justice as a means of using the law to insure the proper ordering of society and functioning of government. In the charge, he encouraged the jury to active citizenship by pointing to the divine sanction of the revolution. He noted "so many marks of the Divine favour and interposition" that has made its success "miraculous." Divine sanction eased the way for Christians to support the government. Americans should ascribe the events to their *true cause*," and "instead of swelling our breasts, with arrogant ideas of our prowess and importance, kindle in them a flame of gratitude and piety, which may consume all remains of vice and irreligion." Again, Jay was suggesting that America's newly constituted citizens needed to embark on moral and religious reforms. As "the first people whom Heaven has favoured with an opportunity of deliberating upon, and choosing the forms of government under which they should live," Americans had a particularly strong obligation to support their new state constitutions.[19]

In the winter of 1778, the New York legislature called on Jay to leave his post as chief justice to represent them in Congress again, where Jay was shortly elected its president. That position enabled him to observe the actual operations of national politics, and what he saw was not to his liking.[20] Congress was riven with faction, preventing much work from being done. In addition to the weak currency, the young nation struggled in its diplomatic relations with potential allies France and Spain. In a letter to George Washington, Jay listed the problems confronting the nation, including "laws dictated by the spirit of the times, not the spirit of justice and liberal policy—latitude in principles as well as commerce—suspension of education—fluctuations in manners, and public counsels, and moral obligations—indifference to religion, &c." The problems were thus political, cultural, and religious. Both the rulers and the ruled needed improvement. Society was in flux, and in the upheaval, manners, morals, and religion itself were in danger. Several years into the revolution, then, Jay was sensing the need for reform and predicting "a long storm and difficult navigation." Still, Jay closed with the hope that, by Providence, "things will come right, and these States will be great and flourishing."[21] Jay thus held realism and a guarded optimism in tension, because of his trust in divine oversight.

Jay's work for independence reached its conclusion with his diplomatic mission to Europe. As president of Congress, Jay spent much of his time dealing with foreign affairs, and soon Congress sent Jay as minister to Spain, hoping for financial or military assistance. Leaving America, Jay believed the task worthwhile because "America exhibits a new spectacle to the political world, and is rising to empire and greatness in a manner so singular as to render her steps interesting to all mankind, and especially to the people of that country." Convinced of this, Jay hoped his mission would contribute to its success, but he was not sanguine. Jay's prognostication proved correct: the Spanish court paid him little attention and offered America little help.[22]

Jay's frustration in Spain eventually ended, as he was commissioned to go to Paris in 1782 as one of America's peace negotiators. There, he led the way in defending American interests against the encroachments of both France and Spain. Due to John Adams's absence and Benjamin Franklin's illness, he often worked alone. When Adams finally arrived from the Netherlands, Jay found that they agreed on the best course of American policy. They moved to negotiate with Britain without consulting the French—much to the surprise and displeasure of the Comte de Vergennes, the French foreign minister. In the end, Jay's shrewd, legal approach to the negotiations led to a treaty very favorable to American interests.[23]

With the arrival of peace, Jay asserted his belief that Providence had been active in obtaining it. Writing to his mother-in-law, Jay observed, "I sincerely join with you in ascribing [the peace] and every other of our blessings to the Supreme Author of all the good that ever was and ever will be in the world." Just as Providence had been inspiring the war from the beginning, so it had safely seen the nation to the conclusion of conflict. Jay wanted to make sure adequate recognition was given to God. At the same time, he realized that independence brought even greater responsibility to all Americans. Both divine and human action would have to be combined for the success of the newly recognized republic. Further, since divine help would not fail, only the citizenry could be held responsible for political failure. Such an attitude explains Jay's words to his friend the financier Robert Morris: "The Definitive Treaty is concluded, and we are now thank God in the full Possession of Peace & Independence. If we are not a happy People now it will be our own Fault."[24]

Providence and National Union

Immediately after the treaty was signed, Jay turned his attention to the necessary means of preserving the infant nation. He saw an immediate need to encourage national spirit, which he believed would grow commensurately with the strengthening of the national government. These concerns came together for Jay when he observed to his father-in-law that "A continental national spirit shd. therefore pervade our Country & Congress shd. be enabled by a grant of the necessary powers to regulate the Commerce & general Concerns of the Confederacy."[25] National spirit thus meant both seeing the United States as a single nation and the willingness to empower it to act like one.

In addition to a national spirit, Jay desired a well-ordered government, demonstrating the citizens' willingness to live under the laws they themselves had made. To Jay, "The People of America must either govern themselves according to their respective Constitutions & the Confederation or relinquish all Pretensions to the Respect of other Nations." The country's lack of such order seemed to Jay "as injurious to the peace & happiness of Society as war & Enemies from abroad." The lack of energy in governments on all levels weakened both the nation and the rule of law. To rectify this, Jay recommended "impressing by precept, influence, and example, the indispensable necessity of rendering the continental and State governments vigorous and orderly."[26] Although Jay was glad for the coming of the peace, at times even in 1783 he was not optimistic about American prospects. Instead, he focused on the problems confronting the nation. His interest in strengthening the government thus dated to the months immediately following peace, when he could actually look beyond merely ensuring the nation's survival.

No longer willing to be detained in Europe, Jay sailed for home in June 1784. Jay's initial optimism, however, would soon be tempered by the reality of governing the new republic, as he learned that he had been elected as a delegate to Congress from New York. Congress subsequently appointed him its secretary for foreign affairs. While in that position, Jay had to deal with a number of foreign problems involving the fulfillment of the peace treaty obligations, Indian tribes in the Northwest Territory, the intrigues of French consuls, and the demands of the Barbary pirates. In attempting to settle Spanish claims to control the lower Mississippi, Jay jousted with the Spanish chargé d'affaires Diego de Gardoqui. The Jay-Gardoqui talks did not produce a treaty, but they did poison attitudes in the South, as Southerners believed the national government was willing to sacrifice their interests. As secretary, Jay struggled with the difficulties imposed on him by a weak government. He could not always enforce the responsibilities imposed by the Treaty of Paris. In dealing with other nations, he often dealt from a position of weakness rather than strength. These circumstances confirmed Jay's earlier suspicions of the need for a stronger government and made him long for the reforms that would put the nation on a firmer foundation.[27]

Watching events unfold in 1786–1787, Jay sensed more and more the coming of a crisis that would produce change. Although Jay noted Shays's Rebellion—the farmers' revolt in western Massachusetts—in passing, he believed the greater challenge came from the overall disapproval that more and more Americans felt toward the national government, due to its weakness. He was himself losing confidence in the nation's course, as its public actions no longer seemed just.[28] Writing to Thomas Jefferson, Jay observed, "An uneasiness prevails through the country, and may produce eventually the desired reformations, and it may also produce untoward events." The public disquietude threatened danger but it also offered a chance for reform, if done quickly and wisely—a task for active, informed leaders.[29]

To contribute to such reform, Jay wrote a number of letters diagnosing the problem. In contrast to the revolutionary period, Jay observed, "The case is now altered; we are going and doing wrong, and therefore I look forward to evils and calamities, but without being able to guess at the instrument, nature, or measure of them." An expectation of punishments following injustice comported well with Jay's providential vision of the nation. Jay believed that part of the reason the national government was doing wrong was because of its inability to do right. "When government," Jay wrote, "either from defects in its construction or administration, ceases to assert its rights, or is too feeble to afford security, inspire confidence, and overawe the ambitious and licentious, the best citizens naturally grow uneasy and look to other systems."[30]

Mentioning the "best citizens" points to Jay's political elitism, which caused him to worry about the opening a weak government gave to the "ambitious and licentious." Elsewhere, Jay denounced "political mountebanks" who would act as demagogues to sway popular opinion. Because "the mass of men are neither wise nor good," Jay worried that ambitious individuals would prey on the public and deplete the store of public virtue. Meanwhile, this condition would separate "the better kind of people" from their government.[31] Desiring stability, they would long for a government less friendly to liberty.

Jay was also strongly concerned about the fate of liberty and republican self-government. Both were endangered by a poorly administered national government. Citizens might be tempted "to consider the charms of liberty as imaginary and delusive."[32] In one of his more emotional outbursts, Jay complained, "I feel for the cause of liberty, and for the honour of my countrymen who have so nobly asserted it, and who, at present, so abuse its blessings. If it should not take root in this soil, little pains will be taken to cultivate it in any other."[33] A poorly run government caused the citizens to question both the liberty embodied in the American Revolution and its belief that a country could govern itself. For someone like Jay who had sacrificed much for it, squandering liberty caused pain. Further, a failure of self-government in America would lead to its discrediting throughout the world. Jay thus saw the constitutional movement as growing out of the principles of the revolution. He hoped to guarantee liberty and self-government, making sure the revolution had not been in vain.

To that end, Jay suggested practical reforms. To several correspondents he recommended a division of powers and checks and balances among branches of government. Jay did not believe that Congress was able to perform the functions of a legislative, executive, and judicial body simultaneously and so needed to be restructured. Jay hoped that the Constitutional Convention would be effective in producing reform, believing "a national government, as strong as may be compatible with liberty, is necessary to give us national security and responsibility." The convention offered the best hope for the continuance of the union. To preserve it, though, required skill, wisdom, and properly established means for reform. Significantly, Jay did not want government imposed on people from above. He believed popular government, channeled properly, to be necessary in a constitutive role.[34]

In the midst of his decrying the weakness of government, during the very time when his letters sound despairing, Jay held on to the hope that the same Providence which helped to create the American republic would also sustain it.[35] Jay's religious view thus offered him compelling reasons to carry on, such as in a letter to Washington, where Jay concluded America's independence had happened "almost miraculously" and so the nation could hope for future divine aid.[36] Jay echoed these ideas to an English correspondent, writing, "I cannot persuade myself that Providence has created such a nation, in such a country, to remain like dust in the balance of others."[37] Stressing American exceptionalism, Jay believed that the nation's purposes would soon appear, and hoped that political reform would strengthen the nation to perform whatever tasks God might have for it. With such a providential interpretation of even the Confederation period, Jay had reason enough for working for the national good.

Jay was not sent to the Constitutional Convention, apparently because the New York legislature wanted a small, moderate delegation able to keep Alexander Hamilton's strong nationalist views in check. Yet, on reading the proposed Constitution, Jay approved. He informed John Adams, "For my part I think it much better than the one we have, and therefore that we shall be gainers by the Exchange; especially as there is Reason to hope that Experience and the good Sense of the People, will correct what may prove to be unexpedient in it."[38] The Constitution embodied Jay's concerns for three branches of government, with checks and balances among them. It also provided a great deal more energy in the government, allowing it to tax and fulfill its assigned duties.

Once the Philadelphia convention had produced the Constitution, Jay used his influence to secure ratification in the important state of New York—a particularly difficult job given the Anti-Federalist sentiment in the state outside of New York City. Jay combined his efforts with Hamilton and James Madison in the production of the *Federalist Papers*—although illness prevented his more active involvement—and also argued for ratification in his *Address to the People of the State of New-York, on the Subject of the Constitution*.[39] In several places Jay coupled an argument from Providence with a prudential argument to support ratification.

Particularly in Federalist 2, Jay employed Providence as an argument for ratification. There, Jay began by pointing to the preexisting, divinely ordained unity of the nation. Providence had created a geographic unity, "one fertile, connected, widespreading country," ideal for trade and communication. He further noted America's shared culture, that "Providence has been pleased to give this one connected country to one united people—a people descended from the same ancestors, speaking the same language, professing the same religion, attached to the same principles of government, very similar in their manners and customs." The primary unity lay in a prepolitical state, defined by religion, culture, and mores—one that had been the will of God. Jay went on to observe that this unity had been forged into political reality through the sacrifice of the War for Independence—a sacrifice that could be secured through the new Constitution. "This country and this people seem to have been made for each other, and it appears as if it was the design of Providence that an inheritance so proper and convenient for a band of brethren, united to each other by the strongest ties, should never be split into a number of unsocial, jealous, and alien sovereignties." For Jay, Providence itself argued for strengthening the union through adopting the Constitution.[40]

Similarly, in his widely read *Address to the Citizens of New York*, Jay urged practical reasons for ratification, couched in biblical allusions. In this longer pamphlet, Jay used deliberative rhetoric to gain his readers' support and to point to the possibility of positive reform with the adoption of the Constitution. Jay described the Constitution's ability to advance commerce and preserve peace among the states. By failing to institute good constitutional government, Americans would deal the "cause of freedom" a great blow, and "the minds of men every where, will insensibly become alienated from republican forms." On the other hand, by showing that republican self-government was possible, Americans could have a worldwide impact in favor of liberty and self-government.[41]

Jay's persuasive abilities also proved important at the New York Ratification Convention, where he was instrumental in winning over moderate Anti-Federalists. In contrast to Hamilton's oratorical fireworks, Jay's steady argumentation helped the Constitution's cause. He was conciliatory while using strong logic. To one sympathetic observer, "Mr. J—y's reasoning is weighty as gold, polished as silver, and strong as steel."[42] Also, Jay helped to lead the threefold Federalist strategy of delaying a vote until enough support could be raised, threatening to lead New York City into secession if the Constitution was not adopted, and insuring passage once news arrived that both New Hampshire and Virginia (the ninth and tenth states) had ratified, leaving New York with little choice but to follow suit. At the last moment, Jay headed off an attempt to force a conditional ratification, which would have based acceptance on future amendments. In the end, Jay significantly aided the victory of Federalism in New York and the cause of union for the nation.[43] Through his activities at New York's ratifying convention, Jay could be satisfied that he had contributed to the creation of a beneficial, just government which could further the aims of Providence.

Providence, "Political Storms," and the Rise of a Combative Federalist Use of Religion

Jay believed that the Constitution would provide for a stable, orderly government, but his most sanguine hopes were not realized. Instead, during the 1790s, political conflict divided the country, as parties developed over disagreements regarding the interpretation of the Constitution and the proper response to the French Revolution. Jay himself was at the center of these storms in the mid-1790s. In Jay's analysis, the nation's political differences came from unscrupulous demagogues, immorality on the part of the citizenry, and the influence of infidel (maliciously unorthodox) religious beliefs. Under these pressures, Jay's Republican schema for relating religion and politics broke down, forcing Jay to adjust how he dealt with religion's place in politics. As a result, he articulated a Combative perspective—one that highlighted religion's place in political and public life. It was much more active, impassioned, and attuned to religious differences than his earlier stance had been. The "moral epidemic" of the 1790s thus allied Jay much more closely with evangelical Federalists such as Jedidiah Morse and Timothy Dwight.[44]

With the new Constitution ratified, Jay grew more optimistic. Because of his long-term work in the government and his support for the Constitution, Washington allowed Jay his choice of offices, and Jay chose the position of chief justice of the Supreme Court. Just as Jay had chosen to be the chief justice of New York, so he again elected to lead the judicial branch of the new government. His reasoning was similar: law was central to government and so in that position, he could effectually strengthen the nation. Jay saw his post as a means of shaping national law and policy, as well as supporting the nation against foreign powers.[45]

Jay also took advantage of his position, using it as a bully pulpit. Forced to ride circuit every year, traveling to multiple locations to hear cases, Jay deployed his grand jury charges, delivered at each stop of the circuit, as a means of educating the citizenry in republican principles. In his first charge, delivered throughout New England, Jay opened with his belief in the providential origins of the national government and the responsibilities incumbent on his hearers to preserve it. "Providence has been pleased to bless the people of this country with more perfect opportunities of choosing and more effectual means of establishing their own government, than any other nation has hitherto enjoyed," he told his hearers. Hence, "for the use we may make of these opportunities and these means, we shall be highly responsible to that Providence, as well as to mankind in general, and to our own posterity in particular." Providential help implied a duty to that Providence, to posterity, and to the whole world, which would be watching the practice of republican government. Such a challenge laid the groundwork for Jay's description of the jury's duties as an expression of republican service. In Jay's words, "We are now a nation—and it equally becomes us to perform our duties as to assert our rights." Jay was calling for personal sacrifice and not just demands of rights, thereby challenging his Anti-Federalist opponents. To Jay, "our individual prosperity depends on our national prosperity; and how greatly our national prosperity depends on a well organized, vigorous government, ruling by wise and equal laws, faithfully executed."[46] Syllogistically, Jay linked serving as a jury with the defense of the national government, with the well-being of the government, and ultimately with his hearer's prosperity. Jay was hoping his juries would think nationally, act locally.

While riding circuit, Jay also had opportunities to make connections with Federalists in other states, especially New Englanders and clergy. This process had begun even before he joined the Supreme Court. While secretary for foreign affairs, the Jays had hosted a number of guests, including clergymen such as John Witherspoon, John Mitchell Mason, John Rodgers, and William Linn. Jay's travels allowed him to broaden such connections. To give one example, Jay's correspondence with Jedidiah Morse followed Jay's work in Massachusetts. Such connections would prove important in the coming years, as Jay would work with New

John Jay as chief justice of the Supreme Court. Gilbert Stuart. *John Jay,* 1794. Oil on canvas. (Gift [partial and promised] of the Jay Family. Courtesy National Gallery of Art, 2009.132.1)

England's Federalists, both evangelical and otherwise, in political and religious causes.[47]

Jay's tenure on the Supreme Court also corresponded with rising tensions over the nation's relations with France and Great Britain. Determined that a course of neutrality was best, Jay took steps to insure it.
Support for neutrality formed a strong part of his addresses to the grand
juries in 1793. "Strict Impartiality," he told the jury in Richmond, Virginia, "is our Duty in all Cases where former Treaties do not stipulate for
Favors. And it is no less our Interest than our Duty to act accordingly."
Both duty and prudence favored neutrality. Jay hoped to mobilize the
country to support the administration in this strategy, as a means of insuring national strength. "The Nation must either move together, or lose
its Force," he asserted.[48] To further bolster that neutrality, Jay aided the
Federalist offensive against Citizen Edmond-Charles Genet, the French
Jacobin minister. Genet sought U.S. approval for equipping French priva-
teers in American ports, for the purpose of attacking British ships. Genet
hoped to use popular pressure to get Washington to step away from his
announced position of neutrality. When the Federalists charged Genet
with threatening to "appeal from the President to the People," Jay was at
the center of the attack. Jay and Federalist senator Rufus King certified
that Genet had made the claim and bore much of the weight of attack in
the newspapers. Jay's involvement makes sense as a political move into
the public arena designed to unify the nation in support of Washington's
policy of neutrality.[49]

Jay's support of the government's policy led to another opening for
service, as a special minister to Great Britain. Returning to Philadelphia
in 1794, Jay dined with Washington, where they discussed the rising tensions with Britain. Within the week, Washington had asked Jay to serve
as an envoy to England to negotiate a treaty, and after encouragement
from New England Federalists Caleb Strong and Oliver Ellsworth, Jay accepted.[50] When Jay attempted to explain his mission to his wife, Sarah,
he fell back on familiar concepts. "I feel the impulse of duty strongly," he
wrote. "I ought to follow its dictates, and commit myself to the care and
kindness of that Providence in which we have both the highest reason
to repose the most absolute confidence." In going, Jay believed he would
be doing God's work in the political realm by saving the nation from the
hardships and horrors of war. He would be God's providential instrument for helping America to steer a Federalist course. Within two weeks
of arriving in Philadelphia, Jay—with his son Peter Augustus—was on a
ship to England.[51]

In England, Jay avidly pursued a treaty with Britain. Jay's experience with British negotiators in 1782–1783 encouraged him to seek compromise. At the same time, he fought for American interests—contra later critics. From his time as secretary for foreign affairs, he knew the dangers the British could cause for the new republic. The end result was a treaty that, as others have noted, was likely the best possible given the circumstances. Even when the treaty was signed in November 1794, Jay was realistic about its chances of acceptance while already resigned to the outcome, observing, "If I entirely escape censure, I shall be agreeably disappointed. Should the treaty prove, as I believe it will, beneficial to our country, Justice will finally be done. . . . my mind is at ease."[52]

While waiting to return to America, Jay spent much of the winter visiting a number of important Britons, including the Archbishop of Canterbury and the Scottish philosopher Dugald Stewart. More importantly, other visits contributed to Jay's outlook on politics and religion. He met with Edmund Burke—already known for his attack on the French Revolution. Such contact sensitized Jay to the dangers of Jacobinism, which he would see expressed in Republican opposition, and strengthened his support for an orderly society. Similarly, John and Peter Augustus had the opportunity to spend a day with the parliamentarian and reformer William Wilberforce, which led to an ongoing correspondence.[53] Wilberforce, in working to refine the morals of England and end slavery, was a proponent of evangelical Christianity resulting in moral political reforms. Such attitudes would color Jay's later thinking about religion's place in public life. Just as his trips to New England helped him to form important connections, so too did Jay's mission to England allow him to make transatlantic connections that would influence his outlook on the world.

When Jay returned to America, his expectations that the treaty would meet with opposition were not disappointed. The Republicans had opposed Jay from the time he was nominated, and once the treaty became public knowledge, he received even more abuse—especially being burned in effigy. Invective filled the partisan press, including an extended poem imagining Jay requesting to kiss the king of England's posterior. An anonymous Republican in Boston expressed the outrage felt by many: "Damn John Jay! Damn every one that won't damn John Jay!! Damn every one that won't put lights in his windows and sit up all night damning John Jay!!!"[54] Jay was denounced as a Tory, a traitor, and the servant of the devil. In the face of such abuse, Jay's response was notable: he remained largely silent, a reflection of both his continued belief in the need for a deferential politics and his religious resignation to the vicissitudes of life.[55] Trust in Providence allowed Jay to view political happenings with a certain amount of detachment. As he had earlier told his wife, "He who governs all makes no mistakes."[56]

The conflicts engendered by the treaty, however, crystallized Jay's understanding of the political dynamics in the country. Although not opposed to differences in politics, Jay feared factions that would use political differences merely to increase their own power, without regard for the public good. Such, he thought, characterized much of the opposition to the treaty. Jay grew increasingly worried about the influence of the Democratic-Republicans. Concerned with order in society, Jay fretted about the makeup of such groups: "With these parties would naturally be associated the Jacobin philosophers, the disorganizing politicians, and the malcontents of various descriptions; together with the many who have little to lose and much to covet." Here, Jay clearly linked the Republicans with the French—especially the utopian revolutionaries who brought about the Terror. Foreign influence would harm America, as Frenchified idealists would be happy to work with "malcontents" and others who hoped to use the unsettled period for their own gain. They would then take advantage of a mass of men who could easily be led. Once demagogues were allowed to operate, Jay was sure they would do exactly as they had done in France: bloodily destroy all of society. "If . . . the clubs and their associates should acquire a decided ascendancy, there will be reason to apprehend that our country may become the theatre of scenes resembling those which have been exhibited by their brethren in France."[57] Given such dangers, every means of opposition would be justified.

In the face of such analysis, Jay came to support three responses, as possible checks to the Republican "faction": emphasizing American nationalism, resisting political change for its own sake, and increasing public religious practice. This combination formed the core of Jay's adoption of a Combative outlook to religion and politics. Jay meant his first strategy, of stressing American nationalism, to check the foreign (French) influence he saw among Republicans. Until Americans were more united, Jay told Timothy Pickering, "Our Jacobins will not cease to perplex the measures of our government, however wise and salutary."[58] To counter "our Jacobins," Americans needed to see themselves as an independent nation, not tied to any other power. Given Jay's earlier connection of the Republicans with the French, he was arguing the need to remove the energy of the Republican opposition.

Jay's second strategy was to resist unnecessary reform strenuously. He

believed that calls for change (in administration, in policy, in form of
government) were typical of his opponents. The best strategy was not to
give them an inch. "Liberty and reformation may run mad, and madness
of any kind is no blessing," Jay asserted. "I nevertheless think," he continued, "that there may be a time for reformation, and a time for change, as
well as for other things; all that I contend for is, that they be done soberly,
by sober and discreet men, and in due manner, measure, and proportion. . . . We must take men and things as they are, and act accordingly;
that is, circumspectly."⁵⁹ Jay's realistic anti-utopianism had taken on a
stridency. He wanted to defend the constitutional order he had worked
to create. Jay was objecting to reform disconnected from realities in the
American political environment. While not denying the possibility of reform, he was denying that the current conditions were right for reform
and that those who were calling for reform were the right men to do it.

Jay would implement his third strategy, increased public religiosity, as
governor of New York. Jay found out about his election to the governorship upon arriving back in America from England in 1795. In addition to
dealing with the treaty's aftermath, Jay had to wrestle immediately with
executive duties, such as coping with an epidemic of yellow fever. In the
wake of the fever, Jay issued an official thanksgiving day proclamation,
a clear indication of his intent to use his office to make religious statements. Although common in the New England states, such an act was
much more unusual in New York. Jay's proclamation represented a creative attempt to advance religion's place in New York public life by mir-
roring New England's godly commonwealths. In the proclamation, Jay
stated he was "perfectly convinced that national prosperity depends, and
ought to depend, on national gratitude and obedience to the supreme
ruler of all nations." This reference to the dependence of the state on its
attitude toward God occurred several times in the proclamation. Similarly, he asserted, "The great Creator and Preserver of the Universe is the
Supreme Sovereign of Nations, and does . . . reward or punish them by
temporal blessings or calamities, according as their national conduct rec-
ommends them to his favour and beneficence, or excites his displeasure
and indignation." Jay was urging his countrymen to note the significance
of his proclamation: divine pleasure or displeasure was hanging in the
balance, and the actions of New Yorkers mattered desperately.⁶⁰

Jay then asserted that public actions were necessary to guarantee continued divine favor. The proclamation insisted on "the *public* duty of the
people of this state collectively considered, to render unto him their sincere and humble thanks for all these his great and unmerited mercies and

blessings." Duty was not only a personal category; it could be applied to the citizenry corporately. Jay was attempting to obligate the entire community to give thanks and join in prayers. In the proclamation, Jay mixed religious and political themes. He gave thanks that America had been blessed with "the civilizing light and influence of his holy gospel," with God's leading during the revolution, and with "wisdom and opportunity to establish governments and institutions auspicious to order, security, and rational liberty." Looking backward, Jay was repeating his belief in the significance of Providence in both the revolution and the establishment of the Constitution. Looking forward, he encouraged the citizens of the state to pray for God's blessing "to promote the extension of true religion, virtue, and learning—to give us all grace to cultivate national union, concord, and good will; and generally to bless our nation." Jay believed that only an acknowledgment of God would produce such benefits. Such calls for union, however, could just as easily read as opposition to the partisanship emerging in the nation—especially a rejection of the surging Republicans.[61]

Jay's opponents received his proclamation as an attack against them and were less than impressed. The Republican *Aurora* claimed, "Governor Jay's proclamation for a day of Thanksgiving is considered as a party production and as such has disgusted multitudes of people." Another newspaper item suggested, "His late proclamation possesses such genuine ingredients of the whining cant of religious hypocrisy as tender him worthy of a cardinal's hat." Jay's opponents rejected the idea that the proclamation possessed any genuine sentiment. Their opposition to Jay's proclamation was mixed together with their ongoing critique of the Jay Treaty and criticism of the president. Despite such attacks, Jay also met with encouragement and support from others, and he remained content for having enacted a strong statement of the place of religion in public life.[62]

Jay's desire for a public religiosity also colored several of his other official acts. He often opened sessions of the legislature with prayers, such as his request in 1796, "May the same benevolent, wise and over-ruling providence which has so constantly and remarkably sustained and protected us, preside over the public deliberations and suffrages." He introduced into the legislature a measure for Sabbath observation in the state, claiming, "If the Sabbath be, as I am convinced it is, of divine appointment, this subject ought not to be regarded with indifference." To Jay's disappointment, this measure failed. He directed the legislature to create legislation for the incorporation of religious societies, which did pass.[63]

Finally, he pressed for the abolition of slavery in the state, which he saw as a moral issue. After years of trying, Jay was able to sign a gradual emancipation bill into law in 1799.[64]

Apart from the ravages of political attacks and the scourge of yellow fever, Jay also had to deal with threats of war with France. With war possible in 1798, a number of towns sent Jay petitions expressing their support of the government. To an address from Washington County, Jay replied, "It is worthy of consideration that we have no liberty to acquire, but much to preserve; we already possess all the liberty that men can have—the entire and perfect liberty of governing ourselves."[65] Jay not only perceived a threat from the French, but he was coordinating with President Adams's Federalist administration to defend the country in case of attack. Jay intended to defend liberty, which to him implied the liberty of self-government. Although the war fever would abate, the mobilization provided Jay with one more opportunity for rallying the populace to support his vision of liberty and the nation.

While worried about political dangers and military threats, Jay became alerted to an even more insidious one—the danger of religious infidelity, specifically the Bavarian Illuminati. The Illuminati were a shadowy organization supposedly behind the French Revolution and committed to atheism, immorality, and the overthrow of all governments around the world. Jay not only read Jedidiah Morse's fast day sermon, which purported to uncover the Illuminati plot; he also corresponded with Morse (see chapter 2). By the summer of 1798, Jay was convinced of the basic argument Morse had laid out, observing, "It is also remarkable that the most decided and active Enemies are to be found among the admirers & advocates of the new Philosophy, and the abettors of sedition and Licentiousness both in Europe and America." Jay quickly drew out the political implications of Morse's attack. He immediately connected "the new Philosophy"—the dangerous infidelity of which Morse had spoken—with "sedition and Licentiousness"—the Democratic-Republicans. Jay remained concerned about such connections into 1799, by which time he thought he discerned negative fruit developing. He wrote Morse, "The seeds of trouble are sowing & germinating in our Country, as well as in many others. Infidelity has become a political engine, alarming both by the force & the extent of its operations."[66] Infidelity as a political engine gave a more dangerous tint to political opponents, who were operating in "secret societies"—the Democratic-Republicans, again. If infidelity was the political engine motivating the Republicans, then they threatened to bring on all the harm that had befallen religion and society in France.

A year later, Jay remained dissatisfied with public attitudes. Writing to Lindley Murray, he commented, "As yet there appears but little reason to believe that Philosophicalism is losing ground in our country." Despite evangelical warnings, the public had not repudiated Illuminism to the extent that Jay had hoped. Instead, "Indications of Immorality are neither less frequent, nor more odious & disgraceful in common estimation than were before time. A moral epidemic seems to prevail in the world."[67] In the moral world, matters remained as bad off as they had been previously. Americans continued to fail the test. For Jay, Morse's concern over the Illuminati and their attendant infidelity had now transformed from merely a single event to an ongoing concern that could continuously threaten the public. Its threat to public morals (its immorality) and political sense (its utopian philosophies) remained constant dangers. As governor, Jay had been won over to seeing the danger of a politics of infidelity. He had adopted a Combative approach to religion's place in defending the nation, and had been prepared for a greater participation in the evangelical campaign against it.

Jay's describing to Morse the "moral epidemic" that he thought was overwhelming the world points to his growing tendency to give a moral analysis of current events. Jay increasingly believed that the lack of moral character explained a great deal of the political problems of the decade. Although Jay's concern for a religiously informed morality had been present in the 1770s, it grew increasingly significant in the 1790s, as cultural tumults made him worry about Christianity's place in the republic. As early as 1794, he had written, "I think we are just entering on the age of revolutions, and that the impurities of our moral *atmosphere* . . . are about to be purified by a succession of political storms."[68] Several years later, Jay observed to Rufus King, "The political world appears to be in a strange state every where; nor is the moral world in a much more eligible condition."[69] Unsettled morality and an unsettled political situation went together, and Jay remained concerned—and prepared to influence the nation in ways other than political.

Tied to his concern for the morals of the nation, Jay expressed a growing dissatisfaction with much of the citizenry. He trusted their character less and less. As a result, his earlier realism took on an edge as he grew more stridently anti-utopian. He increasingly asserted that real reform would only come with the rule of Christ in the millennium. Before that, too rosy hopes would quickly fail. Writing to his friend Benjamin Vaughan, Jay stated, "I do not expect that mankind will, before the millennium, be what they ought to be; and therefore, in my opinion, every political theory which does not regard them as being what *they are,* will probably prove delusive."[70] To Benjamin Vaughan's brother William, Jay expressed similar sentiments, claiming he was just being realistic. "Human knowledge and experience will doubtless continue to do good, in proportion to their extent and influence," he wrote. "But that they will ever be able to reduce the passions and prejudices of mankind to such a state of subordination to right reason as modern philosophers would persuade us, I do not believe one word of it."[71] Jay thus expressed skepticism about claims over human reason, especially as laid out by Tom Paine. Reason would never be able to advance far enough to control human passions. Governmental systems that suggested reason could do so would prove disastrous. Belief in the millennium, coupled with an immediate realism, biased Jay against most political reforms, which he judged too optimistic.[72]

At his retirement from public life, Jay was still advocating continued support of the constitutional mechanism of government, resistance to too-quick reform, and the encouragement of religion—all Federalist elements. Responding to the election of Thomas Jefferson in 1800, Jay urged continued support of the government chosen legitimately by constitutional means.[73] Although Federalists should accept the selection of the people, Jay believed they should continue to defend the Constitution itself from too much change. Informing New York's Federalists that he did not intend to run again for governor, Jay told them, "I declare to you explicitly that in my opinion we ought to resist innovation, to adhere to our constitutions and governments, to give them a fair trial, and to amend them from time to time according to the dictates of experience, and not according to the views of demagogues or the visions of theorists."[74] Here again, Jay was attacking the influence of popular leaders and idealistic utopian philosophers. Instead, he called upon his allies to "resist innovation." Amendment could happen, but it should be done wisely. Just as Jay had fought for the Constitution's ratification, so he was now urging continued striving for its defense. Similarly, to Benjamin Vaughan, Jay delineated his political principles and included among his goals, "to promote religion, industry, tranquility, and useful knowledge, and to secure to all the quiet enjoyment of their rights, by wise and equal laws irresistibly executed."[75] Government's actively promoting religion would have the value of strengthening the morals of the populace, which would further promote "tranquility," since people would be more willing to be governed by their chosen rulers. Given the uncertainty still present in 1801, Jay retired from public life. In the years to come, his efforts would be connected to his attempt to head off the "many evils" he saw as threatening the country, but he would do so in nonpolitical ways. In that, he would be joined by other Federalists—including his two sons.

Providence and Federalism in the Early Republic

Jay's use of Providence reveals much about the place of religion in the early republic. First, as a central figure in political developments for three decades, Jay was instrumental in contributing to the new nation. His use of Providence suggests that a providential discourse could sit easily alongside the other languages of politics in the early republic, even for elite leaders.[76] Second, Jay's thinking evolved over time. In the 1770s and 1780s, Jay was articulating a Republican notion of religion, one popular in the revolution and with the first generation of revolutionaries. By the 1790s, though, it was showing signs of strain, as a possibly unworkable approach.

This Republican approach was characterized by its formality—perhaps part of its appeal to Jay's rather formal personality. It was formal in its concern for the form of government and society, addressing the structural relation of religion to government. Religion (or Jay's use of Providence) had the ability to inculcate morality and duty, necessary props for republican government. Meanwhile, it seemed to bless and inspire the formation of an American nation. Government, then, could reciprocate by endorsing religion's usefulness and encouraging its practice.

Such an approach was not without problems. One might ask whether Jay was employing Providence to justify what he already wanted to do. If that was the case, was perhaps Jay using the idea of Providence, rather than Providence using Jay? Similarly, with its stress on duty and morality, Jay likely was guilty of too easily conflating religion and morality. As other divines were pointing out even in the eighteenth century, the two were not identical. Such a conflation would weaken the ability of full religious belief to gain public expression. Next, by tying Providence to the growth of the American nation, Jay sacrificed his ability to maintain a critical distance from the nation. If God really wanted the revolution to succeed, really wanted America to have the Constitution of 1787, how could it be otherwise? The danger of hubris and blind patriotism were extremely high.

The Republican notion of religion in the republic, then, was flawed. It cracked under the pressure of political conflict in the 1790s. Jay was shaken from his earlier complacency by events, personal alliances, and political conflict. New Combative approaches, which demanded a greater place for religion in the public sphere, would be pioneered both by clergy such as Timothy Dwight and Jedidiah Morse and politicians, Federalists in and increasingly out of power. Jay, too, participated in the process. His thanksgiving day proclamation clearly was meant to use governmental authority to encourage religious faith. Similarly, his resistance to Democratic-Republicans that he connected with the French Revolution, his concern over the moral problems of the early republic, and his alarm over the Illuminati show that he increasingly believed that a forthright public Christianity was necessary to preserve the republic.

2 Timothy Dwight and Jedidiah Morse

THE POLITICS OF INFIDELITY

ALARMED BY FRENCH ATTACKS ON AMERICAN SHIPPING AND French threats made to American diplomats in Paris, President John Adams called for a national fast on May 9, 1798. Ministers across the country complied, holding public services. On that day, Rev. Jedidiah Morse stepped before his congregation in Charlestown, Massachusetts. He posed a question to his audience: "Have we not reason to suspect there is some secret plan in operation, hostile to true liberty and religion?" This "secret plan," Morse continued, was "deep-laid and extensive" and had "for many years been in operation in Europe." At the heart of this extensive plan was a shadowy group of Bavarian Illuminati. These irreligious men, followers of atheistic philosophy, had concocted a plan for global domination that had already worked successfully in Europe and was now threatening the United States. From that plan came "that torrent of irreligion, and abuse of every thing good and praise-worthy, which, at the present time, threatens to overwhelm the world."[1] Troubles in religious matters, in morality, and in politics could be traced back to the machinations of these Illuminati. They were behind the Jacobins in France, and the Jacobins were behind destabilizing elements in the United States, by which Morse meant the Democratic-Republicans. The peace and even existence of the American republic were at stake, and Morse urged his hearers to respond to preserve both their religion and their republic.

Morse's sermonizing would seem to support common perceptions of the New England clergy in the early republic as willing accomplices of the Federalist order, united to keep social and political control in the hands of the elites. In this telling, Federalist clergy were reactionaries, unable to cope with changing circumstances. They were, however, willing to use their public influence to support a struggling Federalist party and savage their opponents. In this portrayal, Morse is but the most egregious example.[2] More recent historians, by contrast, have shown how this popular understanding is wrong. They have described the Federalist clergy as devout in their faith and sincere in their actions. They were wrestling with the intellectual and practical challenges of their day, and attempting to continue communal moral and religious ideals in the early republic.[3] This chapter carries that argument further by describing Federalist ministers as innovative contributors to the public culture of the early republic who were seeking their own ends, not dupes of Federalist politicians.

Two ministers, Timothy Dwight and Jedidiah Morse, played central roles in developments among evangelical Federalists, especially clergy.[4] This chapter explains their motivations—and consequently the motivations of those they influenced—by focusing on a central religio-political category: infidelity. Dwight, Morse, and other Federalists began with a positive vision of a Christian republic, where Christianity harmoniously cooperated with the government. Their energetic increase in political activity in the second half of the 1790s and the early 1800s reflected a Combative stance growing out of the sense that their hoped-for Christian republic was under attack. Their main enemy was "infidelity," which they believed combined a rejection of Christian orthodoxy with political views that threatened the very existence of the republic. Theirs was a politics defined by opposition to infidelity. Dwight's and Morse's active opposition to infidelity also makes sense of the new Voluntarist strategies that they pioneered after 1800.

Dwight and Morse typify clerical support for the Federalists, support growing out of distinctly religious sources. In their early careers, they held two parallel concerns—a Christian republicanism and an evangelical theological orthodoxy. In the mid-1790s, these two concerns fused, creating an impassioned desire to suppress infidelity. The result was a wide-scale clerical movement against infidelity and the Jeffersonian Democrats that embodied it—a Combative view of religion in the republic. Their concern about infidelity energized the call to religious and moral reform, a strategy which proved so successful that their attention to politics would ultimately wane.

Two Streams: Republicanism and Orthodoxy in the Early 1790s

Timothy Dwight's attachment to America as a Protestant Christian republic began during the revolution, when he strongly supported the patriot cause despite his family's splintering over the issue. After studying divinity with Rev. Jonathan Edwards, Jr., Dwight was ordained in 1777 and joined the Continental Army as a chaplain. In this post, he encouraged the troops while finishing *The Conquest of Canaan,* an optimistic, patriotic allegory implicitly comparing the Israelite cause and the American. After the war, he became the minister at Greenfield, Connecticut, in 1783. While there, he composed *Greenfield Hill,* his poetic idealization of the American nation as a Protestant, New England village writ large. The angelic "Genius of the Sound," which at the end of the poem prophesies national blessings, stands in for the divine blessing that Dwight believed would be on the new republic.[5] By 1790, Dwight had spent over a decade advancing the cause of the American republic and hoping that its Christian character would lead to national blessing.

In 1791, Dwight preached the Connecticut Election Day sermon and enlarged upon his positive religious republicanism. In *Virtuous Rulers a National Blessing,* Dwight stressed the need for rulers who would not be governed by avarice, ambition, or selfish honor, but would instead practice "real or scriptural virtue." From a religious motive, a godly magistrate would undertake "a faithful, uniform pursuit of the public interest, in preference to any private one." According to Dwight, any ruler would influence the religion of the state or nation, and so the virtuous ruler's first concern should be to support religion. Dwight charged the ruler to fulfill his duty through a "general train of virtuous measures," which would "in a gloomy waste of vice and impiety, [call] up a new creation of beauty, virtue, and happiness."[6] Dwight believed that moral concerns fell within the purview of the governor, and by laws and actions, the ruler could promote righteous living in his citizens. Dwight took this a step further by pointing to the personal example of the ruler, which could be an added incentive to the populace, especially the young. Thus the republic was inherently religious, with its religious and political spheres commingled. Dwight was here advancing a Republican religious perspective that viewed an easy cooperation between faith and the American republic. Within such a framework, Dwight could contentedly preach the gospel while Federalists governed Connecticut and held the reins of the federal government.

In June 1795, following the death of Yale's moderate Congregationalist president Ezra Stiles, Dwight was elected the college's next president.[7] He was positioned to lead a significant educational institution that not only trained the next generation of Congregational ministers but served as an institutional locus for Reformed Christians in America. The next month, he had the opportunity to address the Connecticut Society of the Cincinnati, and in the address, Dwight continued to advance his vision of republican happiness sustained by Christianity. Dwight declared that the primary means of insuring national success came from inculcating virtue in all citizens, which would produce a society whose happiness would be "great, stable, and secure." Instead of merely restating republican platitudes, Dwight defined virtue as "that enlarged and Evangelical sense, which embraces Piety to God, Good-will to mankind, and the effectual Government of ourselves." True republicans would first be devoutly religious. Only the recognition of the divine would make citizens observe their duties to others and aim for the public good. He concluded that piety "is to be deemed the real, the natural, and the universal foundation of social good."[8] From religious belief flowed a commitment to republican principles and the involvement of citizens to support public institutions and steady habits.

Dwight's positive Republican vision would soon be threatened by political upheavals abroad and at home. By 1795, he had begun to sense that the republic, which he believed was built on the cooperative insights of "Experience" and "Revelation," was under attack from political theorists. Dwight mocked this theory, which went under the title "Philosophy," believing it would soon go "down the stream of contempt into the ocean of oblivion . . . being of no use." Sounding like Edmund Burke, Dwight asserted the only effect of such speculative philosophizing would be to ruin the sound government of the American republic. Indeed, Dwight believed the attacks had already begun, as evidenced by "intrigue, calumny, and insurrection." Sensing trouble in the resistance to the federal government by the "Friends of Liberty" (Democrats), Dwight called on his hearers to act corporately to defend true liberty.[9] Dwight had begun to look beyond just the magistrates to the entire citizenry to support the republic. In the coming years, Dwight would grow increasingly sharp in his critique of his adversaries and increasingly active in his political stances—especially as he felt threatened by infidelity.

Morse, nine years Dwight's junior, followed a different political trajectory. Whereas Dwight had served in the Continental Army, Morse's father had gotten him released from the draft due to his poor health.[10] Instead, Morse continued his education at Ezra Stiles's Yale. After graduating, he stayed on as a tutor. Morse's political concerns developed during the Confederation period, and his first political comments came regarding the movement for the Constitution. He observed to his father in 1786, "The common opinion is here that our public affairs are in a very critical situation."[11] Because Morse believed that God was ultimately the source of social and political peace, he hoped that Providence would provide it through human governance, which made Morse ready to accept Federalist ideas for a stronger national government.[12] After the Constitution was ratified, Morse could praise it as "a grand machine constructed by wise men, & I hope & trust that by the blessing of heaven it will diffuse peace, harmony, prosperity, & happiness throughout our land."[13] Pleased with the Constitution and confident it carried divine approval, Morse would work to continue the healthy functioning of the republic in the years to come.

In the same years, Dwight and Morse grew increasingly concerned about unorthodox religious belief. Before approximately 1796, infidelity to them meant merely theological beliefs that deviated from the Calvinism in which they had been instructed—primarily doctrines positing universal salvation or Christ as less than fully divine. From the 1780s, Dwight had been on the offensive against these heresies. As early as 1783, the Boston minister John Eliot had written that Dwight "thunders out his anathemas" against any who held Charles Chauncy's idea of universal salvation. "He hath said . . . that he hath supposed himself raised up in Providence to overset this system of errors." Chauncy, a long-lived, rationalist Congregational minister in Boston, had developed a theology of universalism that deviated from orthodox teaching about hell.[14] From early in his ministry, Dwight was on the watch for theological deviation, ready to pounce.

In one of his earliest attacks on infidelity, *The Triumph of Infidelity* (1788), Dwight used rhyming couplets and satire to scorn his opponents. Dwight hoped to turn the weapon of mockery on those who had used it against Christianity. By showing their folly, he hoped they would turn back to the truth of Christianity.[15] In the poem, Dwight connected the contemporary infidelity to unbelief throughout the ages and to Deist authors of the eighteenth century. Although Jonathan Edwards—"That moral Newton, and that second Paul" (who was also Dwight's grandfather)—had dealt Satan a mighty blow, Dwight's Satan had launched a new offensive with Chauncy's Universalism.[16]

Dwight attacked Chauncy on two levels: his method and the results of his ideas. In challenging Chauncy's rationalist theology, Dwight was defending the Augustinian notion of a fallen human intellect and will. Chauncy and other universalists had argued that human notions of benevolence enabled them to judge traditional doctrines by their own reason. Trusting human reason for Dwight led to pride, not truth. Dwight also questioned the results of such infidelity. The universalists believed that their teachings would lead to greater virtue and more zealous activity. Instead, Dwight suggested that taking away the fear of judgment made men worse, not better.[17] Without giving a political analysis yet, Dwight was arguing that faulty individual ethics could have disastrous societal effects. Dwight had begun to sense infidelity in many aspects of American intellectual life in the 1780s—Ethan Allen and Joseph Priestley each received their own sections in the poem—and consequently the need for theological watchfulness.[18]

Similarly, Morse found his early pastorate enmeshed in theological debates. After studying with Jonathan Edwards, Jr.—just as Dwight had—Morse became the minister of the Congregational Church in Charlestown, Massachusetts, in 1789.[19] He soon found himself preaching on contested issues. In his first sermon to his congregation, Morse defended a traditional Christology and called the Trinity "the very foundation of the Christian System."[20] When his turn came to preach the well-attended, communitywide Thursday Lecture series in Boston, he took the opportunity to defend the Trinity and the divinity of Christ. After preaching these lectures, he commented that "I shall be called on to publish in defence of the Divinity of Christ. It is about to be publickly attacked. If it is, it *must* be publickly defended." Morse saw himself as the champion of orthodoxy in the midst of liberal Boston. If no one else was going to defend trinitarianism, he would take on the responsibility himself. The sharpness of the young minister's doctrinal position ignited debate throughout the region, teaching Morse that he was surrounded by heterodox opinions—"a mental epidemic"—and would have to take a combative stance in defending orthodox evangelical beliefs.[21]

The Confluence of Streams: Infidelity as a Religious and Political Danger

Whereas up to the early 1790s, both Dwight and Morse had defined infidelity in primarily theological terms, in the mid-1790s, their concerns for doctrinal orthodoxy and a Protestant, Christian republic merged. They came to see infidelity as an engine of religious, political, and social upheaval. The political intensity, defensiveness, and Combative-ness of evangelical Federalism for these clergy started in this period, not before. Only when religious and political concerns fused could they devote such intensity to combating infidelity wherever it appeared. Within such a setting, the Bavarian Illuminati crisis makes sense if understood as simultaneously an indication of the sincere concerns of the period and as an over-the-top burst of fear of conspiracy.

This fusion of religious and political concerns arose under the pressure of the French Revolution and its echoes in the growing partisan conflict of the early republic. The Federalist clergy as a whole welcomed the initial stages of the French Revolution as a continuation of the American Revolution. In 1789, Morse had hailed the revolution in his thanksgiving day sermon. A few clergy, like Yale's Ezra Stiles, never gave up this optimism.[22] As reports of the violence in France reached America, clergy turned increasingly against the revolution. Even more disturbing to them was the irreligion demonstrated by the Jacobins in their rejection of Roman Catholicism as part of the *ancien regime*. Clerical opposition to the French Revolution also grew through contact with like-minded evangelicals in Britain, who were strong anti-Jacobins.

Simultaneously, concern among Federalist clergy grew over the increasingly strident actions of the Democratic-Republican coalition. In the midst of political arguments, clergy were much more likely to unite with the Federalists in support of the Standing Order, the cooperative arrangement of ministers under the state church establishment and political leadership designed to promulgate social stability. Influenced by Federalist polemics, clergy increasingly identified the Democratic-Republicans with the Jacobins of the French Revolution. The fact that so often the Democratic-Republicans were open about their own identification with France only reinforced Federalist attitudes.[23] The political passions of the mid-1790s fired clerical imaginations as much as they did other citizens. This turmoil helped them to create a picture of the political landscape that was inherently tied to religious concerns and led to their development of a particularly Combative Federalist defense of religious belief and the constitutional republic.

These connections also crystallized for Dwight and Morse. Morse by 1794 had come to oppose Citizen Genet's efforts, as well as those of James Madison's supporters in Congress. Much of his news came from the High Federalist Secretary of the Treasury Oliver Wolcott, Jr., guaranteeing that he would receive pro-Federalist, pro-British information.[24] Through his publishing activities, Morse had close contact with Noah Webster, one of the first Federalists to attack the French Revolution strongly.[25] By 1796, Morse was convinced that he had seen the "true character of the French nation. . . . Very few of the Clergy in the circle of my acquaintance seem disposed to pray for the success of the French since they have so insidiously & wickedly interfered in the management of our political affairs."[26] The interference Morse supposed was the French support of the Democratic-Republicans. Given these assumptions, Morse's concern for the stability of the government was extremely high in the mid-1790s.

Meanwhile at Yale, Dwight cooperated with the interlocking networks of elites that comprised the Standing Order—the "Speaking Aristocracy" of Connecticut. As a result, his influence was usually private and personal, rather than public and forthright, although Dwight was a strong advocate of the Connecticut establishment.[27] Dwight also revealed his growing political concerns in 1795 about Democratic parties, writing, "The reign of democratic clubs, and the prevalence of democratic measures, as contradistinguished from our own governmental character, is the reign and prevalence of anarchy, of all despotism the most to be dreaded. Of this evil, I have had the most painful apprehension." Dwight had begun to draw distinctions between the republican functioning of the government and the activities of the Democrats. To his mind, greater activity on the part of "steady and well disposed inhabitants" was necessary.[28] From 1797 onward, Dwight would work to rally those steady citizens and become more involved in political questions—changes reflected in the sermons he preached.

A year before the Illuminati furor, Dwight preached a pair of sermons to his students at Yale on *The Nature, and Danger, of Infidel Philosophy*. These sermons—expanded for print—clearly set out Dwight's growing concerns over infidelity and his initial thoughts about what should be done. Dwight made clear his desire to rescue true philosophy, opposing only that which was wrongly used to attack Christianity.[29] Dwight was arguing against the polemical rationalism that characterized the "skeptical enlightenment" in America.[30] Tracing a lineage that included ancient philosophers, English Deists, skeptics like David Hume, and French *philosophes*, Dwight pointed out that in religious matters, they relied on human reason rather than on divine revelation—their primary error. As a result, these philosophers disagreed among themselves, faced constant changes in their religious systems, and tended downward toward atheism. Consequently—and for Dwight, this was the clinching argument—infidels produced immoral ideas and immoral lives. The lives of the philosophers were unacceptable, and if anyone attempted to live by the doctrines they proposed, the results would be likewise immoral. To Dwight's mind, the logic was simple: "That faith therefore, which is best supported, is the most rational, and ought to confer the superiority of character."[31] Christianity was better supported historically, was more "rational," and produced better humans.

If infidel doctrines produced immoral individuals, they would have even greater consequences for society. Dwight portrayed these results as the moral reversal of society. "How soon would man, ceasing to reverence

his God, cease to regard his neighbour?" he asked. The moral ties of society could not endure without divine backing. Dwight believed human
nature was such that the passions could easily overrun the best intentions
of a person or a society. Infidelity would produce the loss of any moral
virtue and consequently the stability and happiness of a society. This process had already occurred in the French Revolution. The Christian responsibility was to make sure such dangers did not occur elsewhere.[32]

Lest his hearers miss his point, Dwight noted that in America,
"the effects of this convulsion [the French Revolution] . . . are less perceived. . . . But even here the evil in a degree exists." Although the situation was not yet a crisis, Dwight warned his listeners to prevent the same
process from happening in America.[33] To avoid this evil, Dwight re-
asserted the connection between Christianity and republicanism:

> Rational Freedom cannot be preserved without the aid of Christianity.
> Not a proof is found in the experience, not a probability is presented to
> the judgment, of man, that Infidelity can support a free, and at the same
> time, an efficient, government. In this country, the freest, and the happiest,
> which the world has hitherto seen, the whole system of policy originated,
> has continued, and stands on the single basis of Christianity. Would you
> preserve these blessings during your own lives, would you hand them
> down to posterity, increasing multitudes of those who are not Christians,
> and all those who are, with one voice tell you "Embrace Christianity."[34]

The American republic, with its practice of "Rational Freedom," was impossible without the influence of Christianity. By contrast, infidelity, the
producer of immorality and vice, had never shown itself capable of producing good government and was directly opposed to the republic. In
a way he had not done previously, Dwight had connected his Christian
republicanism with his concern for the spread of infidelity. The support
of the nation and the warning against its main enemy would energize
Dwight in the coming two decades. In the process, he would grow more
invested in Federalist politics as a means to preserve a Christian republic.

Meanwhile, American relations with France deteriorated. Naval conflict produced the undeclared state of hostilities known as the Quasi-War,
and French demands for bribes to their diplomats in the XYZ Affair en-
flamed American patriotism. Against such a background, President Adams called for a national fast day on May 9, 1798, and Morse rose to warn
about the Illuminati. Much of his sermon was devoted to the themes that
he and Dwight had been developing regarding the political and religious
spheres. Morse linked "the unhappy divisions that have existed among

us, which have so greatly disturbed our peace, and threatened to overthrow our government" to the influence of France in American politics.
Thus political divisions, including partisans who would question Adams's
calling for a fast, were unhealthy and unwelcome. They opposed the federal government, which Morse still believed "the most perfect, the best
administered, the least burdensome, and most happyfying to the people
of any on earth." On the religious side, Morse pointed to "the astonish-
ing increase of *irreligion*."[35] For Morse, this irreligion (synonymous
with infidelity) threatened to undermine all of society. So far, much of
Morse's sermon was standard fare for evangelical Federalists. What set
the sermon apart was Morse's taking his analysis a step further to posit a
cause for the increase in irreligion and political intrigue: the "deep-laid
and extensive plan" of the Bavarian Illuminati. Morse reached this conclusion through reading two European works, one by the reactionary
French cleric Abbé Augustin Barruel and the other by the Scottish academic John Robison. Barruel and Robison had described a secret society
of linked lodges dedicated to Enlightenment reason, hostility to Christianity, and the overthrow of established governments. Although some
Illuminati lodges existed in Europe as a variety of Free Masons, they were
not operative in the United States, nor were they promulgating a deep
conspiracy.[36] Nonetheless, perceiving and believing in just such a danger,
Morse called for a rallying around both the institutions of government
and the American churches. He left his hearers with a sobering question:
"If . . . infidelity and atheism prevail, what will the righteous do?"[37]

Dwight was not surprised at Morse's claims, as he had even suggested
some of the resources to Morse. Still, Dwight himself grew increasingly agitated over the danger of the Illuminati as a type of corporate
infidelity during 1798.[38] By July, Dwight would tie Voltaire, Jean le Rond
d'Alembert, and Denis Diderot together in an organization cooperating
with the Illuminati through Masonic lodges.[39] Dwight next connected
these groups to the French Revolution and finally to the Democratic-
Republicans in America. He saw them cooperating in a design to destroy
American liberties. In such a dangerous circumstance, these ministers
believed their public protests were entirely justified.

Dwight and Morse corresponded throughout 1798–99, strategizing
about how to present their evidence and deal with challenges.[40] Dwight
also took advantage of his next opportunity to present a political argument, his July 4 sermon, to warn Americans of their danger because of
malicious infidel influence. In *The Duty of Americans, at the Present Crisis*, Dwight placed events within a prophetic framework and offered an

interpretation of Revelation 16 about the "deceiving spirits" that would be present in the end times—and infidel Illuminatism was at the top of his list.[41]

To counter such evils, Dwight proposed a multilayered response. First, he called for religious reform on both personal and corporate levels. Religious reform was necessary because, "where religion prevails, Illuminatism cannot make disciples, a French directory cannot govern, a nation cannot be made slaves, nor villains, nor atheists, nor beasts."[42] Christianity in the hearts of the citizens promised the best remedy for the irreligious forces conspiring against the nation. Second, Dwight called for a complete separation from France. He asserted, "All connection with them [infidels/Illuminists] has been pestilential. Among ourselves it has generated nothing but infidelity, irreligion, faction, rebellion, the ruin of peace, and the loss of property." Contact with the infidel nation of France had produced greater infidelity, as well as political factions. Thus the onus lay on the Democratic-Republicans to justify themselves, as if their allegiance to France alone had produced partisanship. The Democrats were foolish to hope that an American alliance with France would produce anything beneficial. More likely, the result would be harm and possibly ruin.[43]

Once the nation had separated from evil and regained its unity, it could finally offer a firm resistance. "Religion and Liberty are the two great objects of defensive war. Conjoined, they unite all the feelings, and call forth all the energies of man," he believed. If war with France was to come—Dwight thought it likely—he believed it should be a religious war, combining patriotism and piety in support of a Christian republic. If such a struggle were lost, Dwight did not believe that even external peace would be tolerable. "Without religion we may possibly retain the freedom of savages, bears, and wolves; but not the freedom of New England. If our religion were gone, our state of society would perish with it; and nothing would be left, which would be worth defending."[44] Dwight's vision of liberty had positive content—the evangelical republican attitudes of New England. To preserve that, all struggle was justified. Although the conflict would not escalate to war, Dwight would struggle for the next two decades to preserve his religious ideals.

Meanwhile, Morse would preach two more sermons related to the Illuminati. Although he would reference the Illuminati in the sermons, most of his description of them, as well as his replies to his critics, were contained in extended appendices. Rather, Morse continued to use the majority of the sermons to inculcate his Christian Federalist message.

In his November 1798 thanksgiving sermon, Morse continued to show his Federalism in praising the Constitution, while warning that it was now endangered "by the spread of *infidel* and *atheistical* principles, in all parts of our country." To preserve the Constitution, Morse called for his hearers to reject such principles and amend their ways: "If, as a nation, we progress in impiety, demoralization, and licentiousness . . . this circumstance alone will be sufficient, without the aid of any other cause, to subvert our present form of government." Even apart from Illuminati interference, the nation was facing a moral challenge to its existence. Only a virtuous citizenry could continue to support the free government of America. Morse believed the Illuminati were engaged in promoting "demoralization," and such temptations were finding willing hearers among Americans. If people did not listen to his warning, he predicted dire outcomes, including "revolution, anarchy, and military despotism."[45]

Morse's next public utterance was on the national fast day of 1799, a year after he made his first allegations. In that intervening year, the public war fever had cooled, while critics of his claims about the Illuminati had increased. With this sermon, Morse made his most dramatic claim yet, announcing, "I have now in my possession complete and indubitable proof that such [Illuminati] societies do exist, and have for many years existed, in the United States."[46] Morse included his "proof" in his appendix, involving correspondence from Virginia and abroad. He included lists of purported Illuminati societies and members. This flimsy evidence was soon refuted, as much of it actually referred to legitimate organizations of Free Masons. Morse's proof was quickly shown to prove nothing of the sort, but he continued in his belief in secret Illuminati conspiracies.

More long-lasting than Morse's nonfactual claims was the role he staked out for himself and other ministers as watchmen in both the spiritual and political realms. He saw these as inseparably linked. "Our dangers are of two kinds," Morse wrote, "those which affect our religion, and those which affect our government. They are, however, so closely allied that these cannot, with propriety, be separated." Confronted with such dangers, Morse believed it was his duty—along with other Christian ministers—to raise alarms. "The faithful Christian Clergy in every age and every country," he insisted, have "exerted their talents and influence to support the religion and lawful government of their country." Of course, Morse shaped the types of political preaching he mentioned to be particularly appropriate for what he was addressing in the late 1790s, thus ignoring the historical character of his defense of "preaching politics." Still, he believed that this position was his duty, and that the attacks against him came because he and other ministers were "opposed to those atheistical, demoralizing, and detestable principles, which their emissaries are endeavouring to disseminate in *our* country, as in others, to prepare the way for our overthrow."[47] To Morse's mind, opposition was more evidence that he was on the right track. Even after the Illuminati "proofs" had been debunked, this aggressive, Combative attitude remained.

The alarm that Morse and Dwight raised produced echoes among both clergy and laity. Morse's colleague David Osgood warned his hearers that the French intended to "strip you of your virtue and of your religion"—a disaster that could only be averted by a return to public Christianity.[48] Similarly, theologian David Tappan addressed the graduates of Harvard College, warning them about the dangers they would confront, especially French philosophy and the Illuminati. Only through resistance could they make their country "the destined barrier against the threatened universal inundation of irreligious and political fanaticism."[49] Other correspondents also wrote of their belief in the Illuminati. The prominent Presbyterian John Rodgers reported that Morse's claims had been well received, although they were opposed by "Infidels & warm democrats."[50] Morse likewise received the attention of Federalist politicians. George Washington and Timothy Pickering sent polite notices, and John Jay wrote several encouraging notes endorsing Morse's claims. Much of Morse's "evidence" apparently came from Oliver Wolcott, Jr., who continued to correspond with him.[51] Finally, a number of ordinary citizens voiced their support. John Abeel wrote in the summer of 1798 to thank Morse for exposing "the development of a plan which must have originated in hell," which "attempted the total disorganization of civil society," while others wrote to lend further "evidence" to Morse's case. Letters even arrived from William Wilberforce in England and correspondents in the Caribbean.[52] The sermonizing and publishing of Dwight and Morse received a national and transatlantic hearing. A national audience was thereby exposed not only to the Illuminati but also to the larger concerns that Dwight and Morse had for religion in the new republic.

At the same time, critical voices responded. One deft attack came from the contrarian Episcopalian opponent of church establishments John Cosens Ogden. Ogden penned several attacks on Dwight and his colleagues. In one, Ogden charged that "President Dwight is making great strides, after universal control in Connecticut, New-England, and the United States, over religious opinions and politics." In addition to misleading students, Dwight was pushing for ever-greater support of denominational institutions, such as Congregational Yale. If he and his clerical brethren had their way, they would produce "a revolution in church and state in America, which would reduce this nation to a Calvinistic Popery." Rather than protectors of republican liberty, these ministers were threats to it.[53] In a second pamphlet, Ogden warned that the danger came not from the Bavarian Illuminati but from the "New England Illuminati." He worried that the truly dangerous secret societies were ministerial associations and those who would use public monies for sectarian purposes. Ogden cleverly turned the rhetorical tables on Dwight and Morse, ironically charging that they posed the real threat. Further, the "strong propensity to deism and skepticism" arose from these very ministers' meddling in public affairs. The only way to reestablish "public tranquility" was to guarantee true religious toleration and remove all vestiges of church establishments, including state support of Yale College.[54]

Challenges to Dwight and Morse also came through anonymous newspaper writers, especially those in the Democratic-Republican New London *Bee*. In multiple articles, these authors singled out Dwight and Morse as leaders to be attacked. They accused them of letting their imaginations run wild, as when Dwight's "overheated imagination adopts chimeras for realities . . . not corrected by cool reflection or mature deliberation." Writers criticized them for stepping out of their proper role to address political issues, becoming "mere political declaimers." If they were to act as politicians, they should expect to be treated as other political figures—and exposed to the same critique. As "An Old Friend" claimed, "You have employed clamours concerning infidelity, illuminatism and Jacobinism, in a manner which degraded your situation and dignity."[55] For these Democratic-Republicans, these ministers were bringing religious belief into disregard even as they attempted to defend it. Similarly, "A Sincere Christian" suggested, "The causes of infidelity are very generally and very *absurdly* attributed to French politics and principles, while they exist in the practices of Christians themselves. . . . Political fasts and sermons—clamors about Thomas Paine . . . —and federal politics—create deism." Infidelity as a political weapon could be used in multiple ways, and Democratic-Republicans found they could also wield it against the ministers. Having entered the arena of print and politics, Dwight and Morse found themselves in heated exchanges that questioned the very presuppositions of their claims and demonstrated the ongoing religious conflict in the 1790s.[56]

The Illuminati conflict was significant for the Federalist clergy, then, but for reasons other than normally assumed. Basing their evidence on two European works of dubious reliability, clergy ignored contrary facts or failed to investigate American realities. Believing they saw a conspiracy against both Christianity and the republic, the ministers ratcheted up their rhetoric to a level previously unknown. In the process, they overplayed their hand. Much like John Adams with the Alien and Sedition Acts, their moderation failed them at a critical moment, and they had to live with the damage that resulted.[57] Such claims opened them to very valid attacks from Democratic-Republicans, called their standing as societal authorities into question, and ultimately weakened their position.[58] Still, the incident had energized the clergy and their supporters for an ongoing defense of Christian republicanism. Further, the criticisms directed against them only reinforced their view of themselves as embattled heroes standing against malicious forces. Although Morse continued to push his Illuminati claims past 1801, the matter soon came to an end. When the public agitation over the Illuminati dropped away, the larger religio-political agenda remained. Thus, for the clergy and other Federalists, the Illuminati incident was the apex of the moment when religious and political concerns fused in the late 1790s, forging a Combative outlook in the white heat of fear and controversy. Grasping that concern for Dwight, Morse, and others is critical for understanding their actions in the first decades of the nineteenth century.

Other ministers certainly agreed, demonstrating how Dwight and Morse had organized a ministerial phalanx against infidelity. Thus in 1798, Rev. Nathan Strong could fulminate against "'Infidelity!'—This is of various degrees, from such as begin to doubt or deny a part of God's word, to those who deny the whole, and throw human nature back for instruction, to its own weak reason and wicked lusts." By the next year, the New England Association in Hampshire County could agree, "We believe the growth of infidelity & impiety to be very rapid, feel ourselves impressed with the same ideas . . . with regard to 'the critical & very alarming state of our country & of our holy religion.'"[59] That a wide range of ministers came to view infidelity as a serious danger—and themselves charged to be active against it—demonstrates that the work done by Morse and Dwight had a galvanizing effect. Energized, these evangelical Federalists were ready to join the battle in the nineteenth century.

Challenging Infidelity in the Nineteenth Century

As the nineteenth century dawned, Dwight kept up his attack against infidelity. Reflecting on all that had occurred over the past hundred years, Dwight singled out infidelity as "the most interesting and prominent characteristic of the past Century." Dwight asserted that its appeal was not that it was more intellectually rigorous, but "Infidelity has been assumed because it was *loved . . . to quiet the mind in sin,* and *to indulge the pride of talents* and *speculation.*"[60] Identifying a moral character to intellectual debate, Dwight argued that infidel claims against Christianity were covers to justify moral misdeeds and inflate pride. Such tendencies continued to threaten the moral and spiritual health of the state. In this regard, Dwight warned, "Infidelity has been formed into a regular school," an organization to "demoralize" humanity and destabilize societies. Because of the continuing danger of infidelity, Dwight called on his hearers (and readers) to declare their opinions openly and "take your side."[61] To defend society, Dwight, Morse, and their allies engaged in three significant endeavors in the next two decades: political involvement, religious publication, and advancing religious renewal through revivals and voluntarist societies dedicated to missions and moral reform.

Dwight and Morse both followed the elections of 1800 closely. Early in 1800, Dwight urged Connecticut's Federalist Senator James Hillhouse to political activity, claiming, "Unless you make some exertions . . . you will lose perhaps the only and certainly best, opportunity of securing the public safety. The introduction of Mr. Jefferson will ruin the Republic; the postponement of his introduction will . . . save it."[62] Dwight, Morse, and others believed that Jefferson's election really would make the difference between the ruin and salvation of the republic. Whereas in the past years they had taken comfort in the fact that Adams appeared to support religion, they now worried that an infidel as chief executive would have the power to overthrow the religion, and hence happiness, of the whole country. In 1799, Morse had warned that, should America ever elect a magistrate who had embraced infidel principles, the nation would face God's judgment.[63] Now, that very possibility loomed before Federalists, and they found it terrifying.

Not only did Dwight and Morse privately urge Federalists to organize to reelect Adams, but they encouraged public efforts to do so. Both William Linn and John Mitchell Mason, ministers in New York City, had corresponded with Morse, and they offered some of the strongest attacks against Jefferson. In so doing, they articulated sentiments very close to what Dwight and Morse had previously argued.[64] In their first barrage, *Serious Considerations on the Election of a President,* Linn and Mason argued that Jefferson should not be elected president due to "his rejection of the Christian Religion and open profession of Deism."[65] They mustered several selections from Jefferson's own writings to show this was the case.

For instance, Jefferson's musings in *Notes on the State of Virginia* called into question the biblical record of Adam and Eve and of a worldwide flood. Also, Jefferson's claim that "It does me no injury for my neighbor to say there are twenty gods, or no gods" undermined the connection between religion and morality necessary for good government. Electing an infidel would dishonor God by preferring one in rebellion against him to one friendly to Christianity.[66]

In an era of polarized politics, such claims elicited a predictably strong response. In the South, the decidedly evangelical Baptist John Leland rallied support for Jefferson.[67] In New York, the Republican lawyer Tunis Wortman defended Jefferson from the attacks on his character and beliefs. Wortman asserted that the ministers had missed their duty to "preserve that religion, pure, holy & unadulterated, unmixed with temporal pride and worldly ambition." By "mixing" with politics, the ministers had made religion "an engine of politics." Rather than protecting its purity, they had corrupted it, endangering the state. In a comment directly addressed to Dwight, Linn, and Mason, Wortman proclaimed, "I have ever been convinced, that a political divine is a dangerous character." By keeping the religion and government "separate and distinct," Wortman believed the purity of the church and the integrity of government would be preserved. His claim—which turned the Federalists' ministers argument on its head—was that the liberty of the republic was best preserved by their not being involved in political matters. Of course, these appeals by Wortman to high principles also had a political purpose: removing the voices of clerical opposition to Jefferson and the Republicans.[68]

Mason responded to such criticism with a second pamphlet, setting forth a more theoretical reasoning for his opposition to Jefferson. To the question of "Why mingle religion with questions of policy?" Mason answered, "Because Christians are deeply engaged already: Because the principles of the gospel are to regulate their political, as well as their other, conduct: Because their Christian character, profession and prosperity are involved in the issue." Christian character, Mason claimed, should affect political engagement, and failure to do so would reveal an impoverished faith. After mustering further evidence, Mason challenged his readers to face the truth: "Christians! Lay these things together: compare them; examine them separately, and collectively: ponder; pause; lay your hands upon your hearts; lift up your hearts to heaven, and pronounce on Mr. Jefferson's Christianity. You cannot stifle the emotions; nor forebear uttering your indignant sentence—*infidel!!*"[69] Mason believed that Jefferson's infidelity was incontrovertible and threatened the government by undermining the necessary connection of religion, morality, and government. If Christians were to vote for Jefferson, they would tacitly acknowledge that infidels were acceptable in society and could fill the highest offices of the land. Convinced of Jefferson's infidelity, Mason urged Christians to defeat him.[70]

As 1800 progressed, Dwight and Morse grew more and more concerned over the direction established by each succeeding state vote. As the votes were tallied, a decided pall settled over the Federalists. The election of Jefferson and Aaron Burr "will be an awful calamity to our country," Morse wrote to his father. "Neither of them are Believers in the Chn. Religion, & neither are accustomed to attend public Worship. For a Chn. people to be governed by *their own choice,* by professed Infidels, is indeed shocking."[71] Morse could not imagine what had convinced Christian Americans to elect "professed Infidels." The American people were either seriously deceived or much worse off than supposed.

Amid such discouragement, Dwight and Morse took comfort in the sovereignty of God and the good sense of the citizens of New England. Dwight admitted that for many, "the heart is alarmed; anxiety is on the wing," but he continued to rely on divine help.[72] He also believed some hope lay in the virtue of New England's citizens, as a political remnant. As Dwight told Morse, "I think every thing will be well here. Our people appear to be more spirited, & if possible more firm than before the late election. I think N. England will be saved from ruin." Similarly, after a few months, Morse could take comfort that "I have hope that Jacobinism is not on the whole increasing in New England," and that instead the people would "be vigilant & active in opposing their nefarious designs against our happy & wise Institutions both civil & religious."[73] The ministers believed they would not have to worry about divine help. They could, however, rally the citizens to their cause.

In the context of Jefferson's election and Federalist weakness, Morse especially worked to find a way to rally Federalists and stay on the offensive. One idea germinated into the creation of a Federalist newspaper, and Morse was able to purchase an existing Boston paper, *The Mercury and New-England Palladium.* In organizing the paper, Morse consulted with Federalist printer Theodore Dwight (brother of Timothy), and his first editor was Warren Dutton, a recent Yale graduate who came with Dwight's full support. Morse declared in his prospectus for the paper that he hoped it would preserve "the government, morals, religion, & state of Society in New England. To defend these on the one hand, & on the other to expose *Jacobinism* in every form both of *principle & practice,* both of *philosophism & licentiousness.*"[74] Morse hoped to preserve New England and the republic by opposing infidelity and its political practice in Jacobinism (i.e., the Democratic-Republicans). As the motive force behind the *Palladium,* Morse worked to use print as a weapon to rescue the republic.

Dwight, besides encouraging Morse, contributed several series to the new paper. In these, he labored to defend New England's traditional society, its religious character, the necessary role of ministers in it, and Christian marriage. To do so, he cast his argument in a populist form, directly addressing the nonelites whose support the Federalists would need to continue to govern. In the first series, "Farmer Johnson's Political Catechism," Dwight expressed his argument in the question-and-answer format familiar to New England's Calvinists, and appealed for commoners to participate in a Federalist New England. He presented his approach not as mere politics but as a desire to conserve the habits and way of life that had made New England successful. He defended such practices as a limited franchise, a traditional militia, the value of small holdings of property, and a sense of social contentment.[75] Dwight believed that the established habits of New England life were essentially good, and "innovation" would risk destroying them. In subsequent letters, Dwight expanded his defense of New England institutions to the region's support of schools and colleges and to its church establishments.[76] Echoing points he had made earlier, Dwight argued that public worship created religious citizens who benefited the community by bringing God's direct blessings on a people and by creating individuals who would fully perform their social duties.[77] Dwight hoped to create the type of citizens who could support the republic and who would do so consistently and from a sense of internal obligation. To that end, he sought to inculcate an understanding of New England's institutions. No other "pillars of happiness" could be quickly invented to take the place of current institutions, since "innovations" would be "the offspring of passion, or accident, and not of wisdom; therefore no good can be hoped from them."[78]

In his subsequent "Morpheus" essays, Dwight addressed the issue of women and marriage in society, through imagined dream sequences. In these pieces, Dwight deployed satire to mock the British advocates of rationalist philosophy and free love Mary Wollstonecraft and William Godwin for suggesting the dissolution of marriage and the removal of children from parental oversight. Dwight suggested that such "philosophers" were so impractical that if their ideas were ever implemented, they would lead to the total overthrow of society. Dwight's attack was redou-

bled by his Yale colleague Benjamin Silliman, who in essays treated Wollstonecraft as both a Jacobin and a female Illuminati. Together, Dwight
and Silliman made clear the connections they perceived between the disorder of the French Revolution and the disorder of families. Women, the
marriages they contracted, and the religious sanction of those marriages
thus worked together to provide another basis for social stability in the
early republic.[79]

As Jefferson's administration continued, Dwight, Morse, and their
clerical colleagues remained nervously on their guard. Morse vacillated
in his opinions. At points he thought Jefferson was merely a poor politician who was weakening the nation. At others he expressed his fears
that if Jefferson brought Jacobinism to the United States, New England
would be "drawn into a vortex, in whh our religious, political, and literary Institutions, & all the principles & habits, whh are their fruits, & whh
are our glory & happiness, will be ingulphed and lost."[80] Dwight, from
his post at Yale, continued to instruct his charges about the dangers of
infidelity. Commenting on Jefferson's second inaugural address, he wrote
a minister in England, "We hear much in the President's late speech . . . I
know almost everything contained in the speech to be grossly erroneous." Dwight had begun to oppose Jefferson, not only for his erroneous
beliefs but for his malfeasance in office. Dwight believed Jefferson's administration was proving that idealistic philosophers, cut off from reality,
could not govern. As a result, Dwight could paint no more than "a melan-
choly picture of this country." Jefferson's poor governing was all the more
damaging because it was occurring in an increasingly dangerous world,
the horrors of Jacobinism having yielded to the violence of Napoleon.
Dwight's assessment of the situation was dire. "The moral and political
world is violently agitated. . . . A general unhinging of the minds of men
has taken place."[81] Because Dwight had always perceived the moral and
political worlds intertwined, he now saw them in mutual upheaval. For
one trying to conserve a Christian republic, its existence seemed to be
slipping away.

Others agreed with Dwight and Morse, as is evident in the sermons
of one of their clerical Federalist allies, Elijah Parish, the minister at Byfield, Massachusetts. Parish demonstrated the ongoing concerns over
infidelity during the Jefferson administration. In an 1804 thanksgiving
sermon, Parish traced why the people mourn when the wicked rule. He
listed a number of reasons, including that a wicked ruler is evidence that
the people themselves are wicked; that a wicked ruler confirms and in-
creases the nation's depravity; that the people lose the positive influence

of a good ruler; and that the wicked will persecute the best members of the community (like Federalist judges and clergy). Parish suggested that the nation had reason to mourn over its leaders, and he then directed the rest of his address against Jefferson. He repeated many of the charges made by Mason and argued that such beliefs would undermine all morality and social order.[82] In 1808, Parish was still warning his hearers about the dangers of infidelity. He noted the hazards of having any connection with Napoleonic France, the "impious, infidel power." Only by continued separation would America escape the political tyranny and subsequent divine judgments that French connections promised. The proper response was self-examination and then political opposition to infidelity.[83]

In 1808, however, Americans elected James Madison as president over Federalist Charles Cotesworth Pinckney. In the face of continued disputes on the seas and frontier, Madison led the nation into war with Great Britain in 1812. "Mr. Madison's War" brought the next clerical protest about the danger of infidelity.[84] Responses among Federalist clergy varied, with some offering moderate support while others saw the war as unjust and unjustifiable—even to the point of urging people not to fight.[85] Ministers opposed the war for four reasons. First, they saw it as an offensive, rather than defensive, war. Because the United States initiated the war, it could not be justified.[86] Dwight, although not declaring the war unjust outright, did bemoan the fact that "a great part of our countrymen believe the war . . . to be unnecessary and unjust."[87] Second, clergy worried that the war was not prudent, because the United States was unprepared.[88] Third, the war would bring great moral evils to the land, which would then do great damage to the state. It was therefore incumbent on all "to check the corruptions, and prevent, as far as possible, those moral evils to which the American people are now more particularly exposed." Fourth, the ministers worried about the connections with France such a war would produce. To make such an alliance would be to side with God's enemies against Britain, the defender of Protestantism. According to Dwight, "To ally *America* to *France*, is to chain living health and beauty to a corpse dissolving with the plague." Elijah Parish similarly opposed the war as a means to protect the nation from infidelity.[89] Religious concerns thus significantly undergirded the clergy's questioning of the war.

Revivals, Missions, and the Voluntarist Turn among
Federalist Clergy

To confront infidelity, Dwight and Morse also developed an aggressive religious response in the nineteenth century, promoting revivals and missions. Through their experiences and the political battles of the 1790s, Dwight, Morse, and their allies came to see the internal logic of their descriptions of society: if a republic was based on virtue and virtue on religion, the means to defend a republic would be through the religious faith and moral behavior of its citizenry. In the process, they arrived at a new Voluntarist strategy. Although their political roles may have been important, greater influence could be had through encouraging true religion and individual morality. To this end, Dwight and Morse dedicated much of their energy after 1800. They thereby began a disengagement from Federalist politics and a turn away from Combative religion.

One direction their return to piety took was their encouragement of revival. Both Dwight and Morse were key figures in the early stages of the Second Great Awakening. Dwight, following the lead of Jonathan Edwards, encouraged revival at Yale and throughout Connecticut. This was not, however, a duplicitous strategy as was suggested by skeptics.[90] Instead, his was a much more orderly, persistent revivalist approach.[91]

Morse, meanwhile, served as a clearinghouse for information on the revival. His role as a nexus for information began with his work with his magazine, the *Panoplist*. As its editor, he printed stories of the revival and thereby encouraged its spread. Because of his role, many individuals wrote to him giving their own reports of revivals. Richard Hall wrote from New Hampshire to report, "There is in this place, a very powerful & general rivival [sic] of religion." Prominent Presbyterian Ashbel Green wrote to inform him that the revival at Princeton "has been truly glorious." Green conveyed the belief that "If any thing short of the power of God could convince infidels of the excellence of evangelical principles I should suppose it would be a view of the change on the tempers and in the lives of those on whose hearts their principals have made a practical impression." Green's comment points to the way that those in correspondence with Dwight and Morse saw revival as an antidote to infidelity and unbelief.[92]

Fuelled in part by the energy of the revivals, Dwight and Morse were both active in the formation of a number of voluntary societies designed for spreading the gospel. As early as 1800, Morse was corresponding with ministers like John Mitchell Mason about the formation of local societies to support outreach and about connecting scattered societies into larger cooperative groups. Using Federalist language, Morse reflected, "I cannot but hope our correspondence will form a bond of indissoluble Union between the two Societies, & operate as a powerful stimulus to joint exertion in spreading the precious Gospel of our Lord."[93] The strategy in these groups would follow Federalist principles: local organizations connected into national bodies to create energy for accomplishing a greater purpose. This strategy was increasingly adopted in the first two decades of the nineteenth century. Other societies were designed to spread the scriptures and other religious literature. Dwight became the president of the Connecticut Religious Tract Society, and Morse headed up the New England Bible Society and served as secretary for the Society for Promoting Christian Knowledge.[94] These local societies contributed to the formation of national organizations: the American Bible Society (ABS) and the American Tract Society. Morse was involved with both. He attended the convention that created the ABS in 1816. At the same meeting, Dwight was named a vice president for Connecticut.[95] These organizations allowed the vision of evangelical religion to be presented to a wider audience. To Dwight, "The exertions, made by these missionary and Bible societies, form a new aera in the history of Christianity."[96] Coupled with these societies were moral reform societies, to transform not only hearts but lives and societies as well. For men like Dwight and Morse, this strategy of evangelical religion tied to moral reform represented the best hope for the republic after the War of 1812.

Other societies supported mission endeavors at home and abroad, and both Dwight and Morse worked to encourage missions. Dwight, by promoting evangelical orthodoxy at Yale, created an environment conducive to missions.[97] Both Dwight and Morse were active with the American Board of Commissioners for Foreign Missions (ABCFM), addressing its convention at various times.[98] Morse, meanwhile, encouraged missions in a variety of ways. He actually went on several, traveling in one instance to the Isle of Shoals in Maine and at other times to visit Indian settlements.[99] He directed the *Panoplist* as a missions magazine, receiving missionary reports from locations ranging from Georgia and New Orleans to Canada, China, India, and Africa.[100] Morse was thus part of a spreading, international network of Anglo-American evangelicals committed to missions. His actions allowed him to spread his influence, ideas, and interpretation of Christianity beyond the bounds of New England.[101] Before such global designs, the interest in Federalist politics would perforce decline. Morse, especially, was learning that even bigger possibilities were open to him and his fellow ministers.

By the end of his career, Morse had grown more optimistic. Addressing the ABCFM in 1821, Morse gladly announced the spread of the kingdom of God. He described the coming of this kingdom as gradual, "that is, in the use of means, by the agency of men, raised up in succession, and qualified to be coworkers together with God, in preparing this inheritance for his Son." The means Morse referred to were the numerous societies that he and Dwight had been encouraging, particularly (in this case) the ABCFM. To Morse, all the exertions had been worthwhile, and the situation was much brighter than it had been. If Morse thought about the Illuminati, it would have been to rejoice that their schemes had been defeated by Christian action. Given this optimism, Morse could call on his hearers to go forth and finish the task of evangelizing the world. "Here is a wide field for the operations of benevolence. Much is to be done," he urged.[102] By his last years, Morse could believe that the high hopes he had earlier entertained for the republic might at last be fulfilled through extensive Christian labor.

Historians need not accept Morse's optimistic tone to note that the actions of Morse and Dwight over several decades had produced significant results that would reverberate into the nineteenth century.[103] They had supported the establishment of the American republic as a government in which Christian principles could be established and practiced. Politically, they actively supported the Federalists, the party that they believed could best preserve the stability of society, the republic, and the Christianity which sustained both. Their actions took on even greater energy in the 1790s, when the specter of infidelity threatened to undermine both Christianity and the republic. The resulting Combative religious approach was a fusion of concerns and a charged political outlook, which motivated impassioned activity in both religious and political realms for the next two decades. Using print culture and correspondence, they helped to create a network of evangelical Federalists, composed of both clergy and laity, that would prove a significant part of Federalist activity from the mid-1790s into the nineteenth century.

Beginning after 1800, Morse and Dwight turned their attention increasingly to evangelism, moral reform, and voluntarism. Politically, the success of their religious labors ironically helped to cool their political interests in the 1810s and contributed to a disengagement from politics. This turning away from political alliances reduced the amount of energy the Federalists as a party could make use of, hastening the party's decline and disintegration. In this final act, the evangelical Federalist clergy revealed that they had only been co-combatants with the Federalists in their efforts to make a godly republic. Their allegiances were to the ideal, not to the party. Although the Federalist party ultimately failed, the ministers' social endeavors had great effect. Voluntary societies refashioned not just religion but all of antebellum American society. Moralistic politics found greater expression because of the language used by Dwight, Morse, and others. The clergy they trained fanned out to the West, carrying the gospel as well as a vision of a Christian republican society. They formed churches, schools, and colleges dedicated to this end. The political, social, and religious activity of the Federalist clergy thus laid the groundwork for a Voluntarist view of religion and politics and much of antebellum culture too.

Before these developments played out, however, other Federalist politicians attempted to advance the political vision that Dwight and Morse had articulated. Laymen such as Caleb Strong and Elias Boudinot would use innovative approaches to bring a religiously inflected politics to the new republic. Their social and political outlooks make little sense apart from the efforts of Dwight and Morse. In their language and their proposals, they echoed concerns articulated by Dwight and Morse. Even if the political attempts also fell short of their hopes, they advanced a vision of a republic informed by and relying on religious belief.

3 Caleb Strong and the Politics of Personal Piety

IN THE SUMMER OF 1812, WITH WAR AGAINST GREAT BRITAIN RE-cently declared, Caleb Strong, governor of Massachusetts, proclaimed a public fast. Such was a traditional duty for Massachusetts's governors, and Strong had a great deal of experience issuing such calls. Strong's proclamation was anything but neutral, though. He decried having to fight Great Britain, "the nation from which we are descended, and which for many generations has been the bulwark of the religion we profess." Strong hoped that God "would preserve us from entangling and fatal alliances with those governments which are hostile to the safety and happiness of mankind"—that is, France—and prayed that "Peace may be speedily restored to us."[1] Strong was not merely carrying out an antiquated duty; he was using the religious forum to state his misgivings about the war with Britain. The war threatened to set two Protestant nations against each other and drive the United States into an alliance with infidel, Napoleonic France. In this document, clearly, Strong's political and religious concerns were fused.

Although Strong also prayed that God would "save us from the baleful influence of party spirit," the proclamation contributed little to political unity. Instead, it polarized citizens both inside and outside the state. Federalists celebrated it. The *Columbian Centinel* quickly recopied it, as did Jedidiah Morse's *New-England Palladium* and the evangelical missions magazine *The Panoplist*.[2] At the same time, Democratic-Republicans vehemently denounced Strong.[3] The public sphere in the early republic would not allow Strong's assertions to go unchallenged. In addition to newspaper attacks, Strong was addressed directly in a number of Republican toasts. Philadelphians showed little love for him or Britain when they declared, "Eternal infamy and execration to the foul hypocrite who could be base enough to pronounce the most savage, unprincipled and blood thirsty nation on the face of the earth the '*bulwark of our religion*.'"

Britain did not qualify as a moral defender of any religion. Passyunk, Pennsylvania's orators were even more direct: "Execration to the hoary head traitorous vindicator of the barbarities of the monstrous government of England: His treason is only equal to his cowardice."[4] Public performances expressed a decided Republican rejection of Strong's complaint. Britain, in their eyes, was the last country to deem religiously superior.

Strong's religiously inflected political statement set off a serious debate. More than just an argument over the origins of the War of 1812, the exchanges often returned to the character of Caleb Strong and his uniting of religious and political concerns. The debate thus points again to the place of religion in the public sphere—and the person who articulated it, Governor Strong. His political career limns one strategy available to evangelical Federalists for uniting religious and political concerns, the politics of personal piety. Although many Federalists urged a politics of personal character, in which character was the most important consideration for electing officials, a politics of personal piety went a step further. This strategy urged voters to support a candidate because his character would be guaranteed by his religious beliefs. Voters were expected to vote for the man, rather than for his policies. In such personal politics, policy questions could be left to the side.[5]

Strong's career involved him in national, Federalist, and evangelical circles. Strong was not just a Massachusetts figure; he was tied into the larger networks of the Federalist party. To describe this context, the next section examines Strong's politics before 1800, a period when the religious component was less explicit than in later years, a quite typical Republican approach to religion's public role and one that stressed personal character. This description also provides a clear contrast to Strong's more religiously inflected attitudes and actions after 1800, when a Combative approach came to dominate his politics and when a politics of personal piety shone much stronger.

Religious faith played a creative role in Strong's life and political career. Strong was a traditional New England Congregationalist, while his family and religious ties connected him to broader trends within Reformed evangelical circles. As his early biographer Alden Bradford commented, "He was a religious man, not in name and profession merely, but in *deed and in truth*. No one was less ostentatious, or made less *shew* of his religion. But it was an active, all pervading principle, by which his whole deportment was regulated and sanctified."[6] Even if Strong did not at all points highlight his religious concerns, they were still present. Influenced by religious belief and tied into evangelical networks, Strong's politics (including his reference to England as a "bulwark of the religion we profess") were an attempt to take Northampton's model combination of society, religion, and politics and make it normative on a broader political plane. Four themes thus occur throughout Strong's life: a religiously sanctioned polity, a well-ordered society, a concern for educating the young in morality and a respect for ancestors, and a localism that was suspicious of outside threats. His religious language, coupled with a personally religious demeanor, helped to guarantee his election to office but revealed its weakness by its inability to suggest distinctive courses of action on specific issues. Although Strong was employing a possible strategy for combining religion with politics, his experiences highlighted its limitations for a positive governing strategy or for long-term success.

From Northampton to the National Stage

From birth, Caleb Strong was tied into the established patterns of the Connecticut River Valley. Born in 1745, he was likely baptized by Jonathan Edwards, then pastor of the Northampton church where his parents were members. Growing up, Strong witnessed a particular, Northampton-style blend of rigorous Calvinism and enforced social stability, a style begun earlier in the eighteenth century and continued by Edwards. Even after Edwards's ouster from the church, the ethos lingered in Northampton. Strong witnessed remnants of the old Puritan ideal of communities structured and supported by religious belief—an ideal he would attempt to carry over into republican America.[7]

Because he was the only son in the family, Strong received an excellent education. After studying with a private tutor, he enrolled at Harvard in 1760. Future patriots Timothy Pickering (subsequently a Federalist secretary of state) and Elbridge Gerry (subsequently a Democratic-Republican politician) were at Harvard at the same time, allowing Strong to form connections that would result in political alliances (and rivalries) later in life.[8] At Harvard, Strong was exposed to the rationalism of his day. Still, after examining the issues, he reaffirmed his commitment to orthodox Christianity and held to that for the rest of his life. Harvard also inculcated the judicious tolerance he would long display. Strong graduated in 1764 with honors. On his journey home to Northampton, however, he contracted smallpox, which severely weakened his eyesight.[9]

This misfortune hampered Strong's career, and much of the next decade was an uneventful time of slow labor, since Strong was determined to study law despite the hardships. Strong's father and sisters read law books to him, and in time, he was able to study in the office of Major Joseph Hawley.[10] In selecting Hawley, Strong demonstrated his propensity for forging connections with the leaders of western Massachusetts. Hawley was a prominent member of the Northampton church who had been at the forefront of those working for Edwards's dismissal. After Edwards removed to Stockbridge, Hawley had repented of his actions and reconciled with Edwards. Hawley's piety meant forcefully rejecting Arminianism and working to ensure that Edwards's memory was respected.[11] Significantly, Strong apprenticed under someone of a decidedly Edwardsean cast of mind. Hawley would serve as Strong's mentor for the next decade, and his influence would be significant.

By his twenty-seventh year (1772), Strong was ready to enter full personal independence. Two events marked this transition and defined two central poles for his life: faith and the law. First, he made his profession of faith and entered full church membership. One of his earliest biographers remembered that ever since Strong had "united himself to the communion of the church of Christ in Northampton," he had "uniformly adorned the doctrine of God our Saviour by his exemplary life, and his soundness in the faith."[12] Thus, even when Strong did not articulate his religious commitments, they were still decidedly present. Second, Strong was finally admitted to the Northampton bar. Despite periods of public service, Strong would practice law for the rest of his life. After Strong's death, another lawyer, remembering Strong's legal abilities, commented, "He was a very successful advocate to a jury. His address was pleasing and insinuating. . . . Not unfrequently, before those he addressed, or any one else suspected it, he had gained his point."[13] These legal practices reveal some of Strong's central strategies for operating in public life. His speeches did not have flowery eloquence, but they were extremely persuasive. Next, his appeal was personal in nature. Because people trusted him, they trusted what he said. Finally, although slight in stature and quiet of voice, Strong could be devastatingly effective—as opposing counsel and political opponents would find out. Strong had thus developed the character that he would take into public affairs for the next forty years.

Although not a revolutionary by nature, Strong was swept up in the tumult of the revolution, where his concern for localism (in this case, American self-rule) ultimately triumphed. Strong's early political steps inclined him to support the British. As a member of the bench, he signed addresses to the unpopular Governor Thomas Hutchinson and to the arriving British General Thomas Gage. These addresses would be used by political opponents throughout his career to cast doubt on Strong's character and true loyalties.[14] Such gestures, however, were customary for lawyers and did not disqualify Strong from political service at the time. By late 1774, he was actively engaged in the patriot cause, joining his mentor Hawley on both the Northampton Committee of Correspondence and the Northampton Committee of Safety. He was also selected to attend the General Court for the commonwealth.[15] In the personal realm, Strong in 1777 married Sarah Hooker, the daughter of Rev. John Hooker, the minister who had replaced Edwards in Northampton. The marriage brought Strong into a very pious family and further confirmed his social status, connecting him to the elite kinship networks of Massachusetts. These networks linked him to leading figures—Fisher Ames was a cousin by marriage—and contributed to his political outlook.[16]

Strong's service expanded farther when he was chosen by Northampton as a delegate to the Massachusetts Constitutional Convention in 1779. In the convention, Strong stood for political order and religious society, and played an important role on the committee that drew up the initial draft of the constitution, including the bill of rights.[17] Working with John Adams, he was specifically involved in the third article of the bill of rights, which continued the Massachusetts establishment of the Congregational churches. As the article declared, this support was premised on the idea that "the happiness of a people, and the good order and preservation of civil government, essentially depend upon piety, religion and morality; and as these cannot be generally diffused through a community, but by the institution of the public worship of GOD, and of public instructions in piety, religion and morality."[18] This notion of uniting piety, virtue, public order, and good government would appear often in Strong's political actions—especially during his terms as governor. Strong's later career, then, might be seen as an attempt to maintain religious affairs as they had been defined during the revolution.

Northampton disapproved of the constitution, but Strong remained well-respected by the town. He worked as the county attorney and continued to practice law. He was soon elected to the Massachusetts senate from Northampton. His service at the state level led to an appointment to the Governor's Council in 1786.[19]

Alert to dangers to society, Strong was shocked by the threat to public order that emerged in his own neighborhood. The outbreak of Shays's Rebellion in western Massachusetts severely upset the routine functioning of state government late in 1786. Centered around Springfield (just south of Northampton), the rebels closed down the courts to protest the high taxes forced on them from the Massachusetts General Court, to object to the requirement that taxes be paid in (scarce) specie, and to prevent loss of their homes due to nonpayment. The state militia was finally called out to restore order. Strong had been at home in Northampton during the rebellion, so he was well aware of events, which he viewed as a threat to public order—and which he had protested in the *Hampshire Gazette*.[20] Then, he was called to serve as one of the lawyers charged with resolving the legal aftermath of the rebellion. Throughout the winter of 1786–87, Strong worked with Elbridge Gerry and other lawyers to determine punishments for those involved in the rebellion and to offer certificates of loyalty for those not involved.[21] Whereas Henry Knox used Shays's Rebellion to rouse support for the Constitutional Convention, Strong did not need any convincing. He had seen firsthand the danger entailed by the breakdown of government. In the absence of a strong government, demagogues could emerge. He would long remember the threat posed by Daniel Shays, who Strong viewed as a demagogue who used the public upheaval to gain personal advancement. The moral he took from the event was that "the People will always have Charity for a Man who pretends to love them better than he loves himself."[22] Strong thus went to the Constitutional Convention predisposed to favor a stronger national government as a means of preserving order.

Strong attended the Constitutional Convention from late May to mid-August, when sickness forced him home. While there, he worked well with the other Massachusetts delegates, Nathaniel Gorham, Rufus King, and Elbridge Gerry. He was highly respected among his colleagues, and delegate William Pierce of Georgia described him as "a Lawyer of some eminence [with] a liberal education."[23] Strong's work at the convention is notable for his beliefs, allies, and agenda. First, Strong was memorable for his religious credentials. Already a member of the church he would support throughout his life, Strong's was a definite evangelical presence at the convention. As a supporter of the Constitution, Strong saw it as compatible with New England Congregationalism. Strong's presence in Philadelphia is a reminder that evangelical individuals were involved in drafting the Constitution. Second, Strong often worked together with Oliver Ellsworth to advance proposals. A key example of this support came in the debate over representation in the Senate. In backing Ellsworth's small-state plan, with its proposal for an equal number of senators, Strong asserted the danger from failing to compromise: "It is agreed on all hands that Congress are nearly at an end. If no Accommodation takes place, the Union itself must soon be dissolved." To support the Connecti-

cut plan, he asserted, "the small States had made a considerable conces-
sion in the article of money bills, and that [they] might naturally expect
some concessions on the other side."[24] Strong's demand of concessions
from the larger states was rather ironic—Massachusetts at this time was
one of the largest by population. In so doing, Strong argued that the need
for union was greater than any local or state concern. Strong shuddered
to think what might happen if the large states attempted to force their
system on all the states. As it was, Strong's vote on the issue two days later
proved critical. The votes of Strong and Gerry against the Virginia plan of
proportional representation in the Senate split the Massachusetts delegation and led to the defeat of the proposal.[25]

Finally, although Strong supported a strong, national government, the
proposals he supported were often designed to keep it decentralized and
democratic. For instance, he supported the annual election of representatives (although he accepted biennial elections), a small compensation for
representatives, and giving the House sole ability to originate money bills.
He opposed giving the executive a seven-year term, as well as setting up
a potentially undemocratic electoral college.[26] Strong observed, "It was
of great importance not to make the Govt. too complex which would be
the case if a new sett of men like Electors should be introduced into it."[27]
These democratic concerns reflected Strong's Northampton background.
The town meeting could be contentious, but it allowed a wide range of
men to participate. Making the government more complex would only
insure that fewer people could easily participate. Even with its imperfec-
tions, Strong ultimately approved of the final version of the Constitution
and would have signed the document had he remained until the end of
the convention.[28]

Strong quickly became an important figure in the ratification debate
in Massachusetts. He corresponded with Federalists from Massachusetts
and other states in planning strategy. Then, he was selected by Northampton to be one of its two delegates to the state convention. Although the
town counseled open-mindedness and prudence, Strong was unwaver-
ing in urging ratification.[29] As it was, Strong, Gorham, and King played
leading roles in defending the Constitution from Anti-Federalist challenges.[30] Strong was very important in explaining the various provisions
of the Constitution. For instance, he defended biennial elections of representatives, the need for a national capital, and apportionment of representatives. When John Hancock introduced amendments to recommend
along with ratification, Strong turned them to Federalist advantage, con-
futing the Anti-Federalist move to use them to thwart ratification. The

convention observer George Benson reported that "Mr. Strong . . . made a very Long & excellent speech on the articles propos'd as amendments—he was very Persuasive."[31]

More than just persuasive speeches or parliamentary tactics, Strong's arguments were decidedly personal. The ratification convention served Strong as an early forum in which to practice his politics of personal character—a forerunner of his politics of personal piety. During the convention, Strong's Federalist ally Theophilus Parsons commented, "Strong, you can do more with that honest face of yours than I can with all my legal knowledge."[32] Strong was trusted for his character, and his personal support of the Constitution went a long way in generating acceptance for it. This personal argument would occur often in Strong's life and would soon carry greater overtones of piety. In this case, Strong was known and trusted as an honest man, and he did not shy away from using that to political advantage. He offered up the Constitution as a document from honest men, claiming, "For my part I think the whole of it is expressed in the plain, common language of mankind. If any parts are not so explicit as they could be, it cannot be attributed to any design; for I believe a great majority of the men who formed it were sincere and honest men."[33] Strong was denying that anything in the Constitution was meant to deceive or hide a grab for power—thereby attacking one of the main arguments of the Anti-Federalists and offering his word as to the intentions of the entire group of drafters. When Massachusetts finally ratified, it was a personal victory for Strong.[34]

Strong's public involvement with and support of the Constitution led to his selection as one of Massachusetts's first two U.S. senators, and Strong went to New York City to make sure the new federal government would function as the Constitution-makers had intended. Strong built on the contacts and alliances he had made during the Constitutional Convention. He again found himself allied with Oliver Ellsworth of Connecticut, as well as other New Englanders, including Vice President John Adams. In his first term, Strong was quite involved in setting up the judiciary system—a personal concern for him as a lawyer and a significant bulwark to maintaining law and order.[35] He also served on a committee for establishing conference committees with the House and for selecting chaplains for Congress.[36] Being in the Senate proved an excellent setting for Strong to make connections with an even larger circle of allies. Elias Boudinot was at that time serving in the House, and John Jay was the chief justice of the Supreme Court. Strong's friendships were largely with men who shared his views of government. As the party divisions began to emerge, Strong aligned himself with the Federalist friends of order and government. He supported Alexander Hamilton's measures and Hamilton himself when he was attacked.[37] Strong saw the parties emerging firsthand and contributed to the process.

In foreign affairs, Strong moved from a moderate to an increasingly strong pro-British, anti-French stand. From the first session of Congress, Strong worked for positive trade measures with Great Britain.[38] By late 1794, Strong had also grown wary of the French Revolution. Whereas earlier he had joined others in Congress in sending the revolutionaries letters of friendship, by then he objected to Congress's answering friendly French correspondence. Here, his sense of diplomatic decorum—he argued that no reply was necessary—masked a desire not to move too close to France.[39] At the same time, Strong, along with other Federalists, was working to influence the government's stance toward Great Britain. Faced with threats as well as provocations, Federalists encouraged Washington to take a defensive stance while appointing a special minister to Britain. Strong met with Oliver Ellsworth, Rufus King, and Senator George Cabot of Massachusetts to convince Washington to send Hamilton. When Washington rejected that suggestion, the group urged John Jay—to whom Washington subsequently offered the position—to accept. They did so knowing that Jay was amenable to British demands.[40] When Jay returned with his treaty, Strong supported it in the Senate and voted the funding necessary to implement it.[41] Strong's support of the treaty accorded with both his sympathies and those of his constituents. Strong reported to Timothy Pickering that despite some opposition, most people in Northampton accepted the treaty, believing "that it is the best that could be obtained & thus for that they are satisfied."[42] Attentive to local opinion, Strong could take comfort in the belief that his neighbors supported him and the "friends of order."

Strong watched partisan divisions grow and complained about how the "Spirit of Party has hitherto delayed the publick Business."[43] That party spirit only increased, so that he would later object to those demagogues who "claim the Merit of superior Patriotism and a more ardent Love for the People than others boast of, and . . . excite a little opposition to the Government."[44] In short, demagogues would produce opposition to order and government by pandering to the people. Such shows sickened Strong and eventually led him to retire from the Senate in 1796. He retired believing, "We are at Peace with all other Nations and it must be owing to our extreme Folly if we fall out among ourselves—A majority of the Senate . . . are Friends to good Government."[45]

In retirement, he did his best to remain informed. In correspondence with former colleagues, he constantly requested news.[46] He watched the growing partisan struggle and the growing friction with France, kept informed by Federalists Theodore Sedgwick, James Hillhouse, Benjamin Goodhue, and Oliver Ellsworth. Strong warned his correspondents that the French were "hurried on by a boundless Ambition sustained by no Considerations of Decency or Justice."[47] While concerned for the good of his country, Strong left the actual political affairs to others.

In the first half of his career, then, Strong demonstrated Federalist politics and a Republican attitude to religion and politics. He stressed localism, social stability, and a strengthened federal government. Personal character, aided by his religious commitments, was an important element of his politics. Although personally pious, Strong's religious concerns only obliquely made their way into politics during this period. Amid the political conflicts of the later 1790s, Strong grew increasingly concerned about the state of the nation. With greater influence after 1800, Strong would change his stance and demonstrate a public, Combative religiosity not present beforehand.

Governor of Massachusetts

After the death of Governor Increase Sumner in 1799, Massachusetts Federalists confronted a lack of leadership. The Federalist legislative caucus nominated Strong as their candidate for governor in 1800. His selection helped to bridge the sectional divisions between eastern and western Massachusetts, and he emerged the victor in a close race.[48] In this new position, Strong would pioneer a politics of personal piety, basing his fitness for governing on his individual religion. With this approach, he moved into a Combative Federalist mode of advancing public religion. Beyond encouraging this religiosity and the continuance of a stable religious society, though, Strong's politics of personal piety left him without a long-term political agenda.

As governor until 1807, Strong presided over a number of ordinary administrative duties. For instance, he reported that the 1806 legislative session had been "tranquil and good humored." He observed that "few important laws of a publick nature have been passed, but if they have done but little good I think they have not done any great mischief, and this in a Legislative body seems to be a character of considerable merit."[49] Strong was content to preside over the regular functioning of a legislature, hoping it would, like a physician, first do no harm. In such a role, he expressed repeatedly his desire to cooperate with the legislature. He promised to "cheerfully concur with you in every prudent and salutary measure for the preservation of their [citizens'] rights, the advancement of their interests, and the improvement of their minds in wisdom and virtue." He firmly appreciated those times when he could work with minimal party spirit.[50]

If matters of regular administration did not allow openings for explanations of religious motivations, Strong found other outlets. Primarily, Strong's spiritual motivations emerged in his addresses to the state legislature. These addresses received broader exposure through their publication in newspapers and subsequent collection into a book. Strong used his position to make public declarations about the place of religion in society generally and its particular role in Massachusetts, envisioning Northampton writ large. These speeches reveal most clearly Strong's religiously inflected political ideals, in a decidedly Combative Federalist tenor.

In these speeches, Strong described religion as central to and necessary for society. Institutionally, he believed religion was best practiced in public, communitywide worship services; hence, he supported Massachusetts's religious establishment. To Strong, religion's public function (as opposed to its private purpose of salvation) was to inculcate both manners and morals. In this mode, religion was tied to education, which could also shape the manners of the citizenry. Both manners and morals were necessary for the success of the American republic. Strong hoped for the preservation of an ordered republican society that would insure liberty, equality, and justice. Such a society would also show great respect for its ancestors, as those who had established the order. Although some of Strong's sentiments might be found in the statements of a number of other Federalists, religion was more salient in Strong's speeches, and he stated his opinions coherently and repeatedly throughout his years as governor.

In one of his early addresses, Strong made a particularly powerful case for the necessity of religious beliefs in all governments, but especially for republics. He told the legislature, "There is perhaps no opinion, which has more generally prevailed among civilized nations, than that religious principles in the people are essential to morality, and a principal support of lawful government; and that the obligation to piety is imposed on man by his nature." Strong affirmed this sentiment and used it as a basis for his view of government. He went on to situate this belief in the contested nature of religion. In the midst of the concern for infidelity and the continued debate over the French Revolution, he believed Christians needed to work harder to prove their detractors wrong. "If, lately," Strong observed, "revealed religion, in particular, is represented as unfriendly to individual or social happiness, it becomes those who believe the truth of christianity, to endeavour to prevent the progress of these doctrines of unbelief by every mild and prudent method." In this statement, Strong alluded to the disputes over Christianity in previous years. Clearly he had in mind the such skeptical anti-Christian writings as Tom Paine's *Age of Reason* and Ethan Allen's deist tract *Reason the Only Oracle of Man,* as well as the Illuminati conflict just a few years previous. Strong undoubtedly shared the concerns of many other evangelical Federalists.[51]

To Strong, religious belief was the bedrock of society, and it could be promoted through the practices of public worship and education. Public worship meant that the state had an interest in ensuring religious observance. "As religion is the only sure foundation of human virtue, the prosperity of the State must be essentially promoted," Strong insisted, "by a due observance of the Sabbath, and by the meeting together of the citizens to learn the duties of moral obligation, and contemplate the wisdom and goodness with which the Almighty governs the world."[52] In this way, Strong tied together public worship with public assembly, as a school "to learn the duties of moral obligation." Morality and an appreciation of duty were the result of religion rightly taught. Revolutionary France served as the negative example of a case when the attempt was made to remove religion from society. Strong's use of educational language is important, since he believed that education would teach self-restraint, virtue, and submitting personal desires to the public good.[53] Education would reinforce religious instruction and produce virtuous citizens to continue the republic.

Strong offered a definite idea of the political order that should be preserved, a rightly understood regime of liberty, justice, and equality. Strong defined liberty as a legal and political state, "when the government under which they are placed, is of their own choice; when they conform to laws which are enacted by themselves or their representatives; and when no duties are enjoined, and no restrictions imposed by those laws, which are not conducive to the general happiness."[54] Liberty was truly in place when people acted under laws made by themselves or their representatives. It was not an anarchic, libertarian freedom, but one hemmed in by law and custom. Liberty understood this way accorded well with a Calvinist or Reformed notion of liberty as ordered and restrained, and Strong believed that such an interpretation should suffice for the entire nation. Tied to his notion of liberty was an equally firm understanding of equality, which he described as "an equality of rights, which ensures the same protection to each individual." Strong wanted citizens to enjoy equality before the law and equality of opportunity. Strong labored to define these ideas, lest, "if on these points [citizens] should entertain mistaken ideas, they might be in danger of losing substantial benefits, by aiming at those which are imaginary." In this reference, Strong implicated both the French revolutionaries and American demagogues who would promise seemingly "better" visions of individualistic liberty or economic leveling. Only a true establishment of political liberty and equality would be lasting and productive of "publick happiness."[55]

All of these ideas may seem similar to other New England Federalists of Strong's generation. It is possible to posit that these ideas could have been uttered with equal ease by Strong's Unitarian neighbor Theodore Sedgwick or by any free-thinking Federalist. The proclamations Strong issued for the state's annual fast and thanksgiving days, however, belie such an assessment. Strong wrote these proclamations himself, and they represent his decided opinions.[56] The content of what he wrote is striking in its evangelical specificity. Although these proclamations were in many ways customary, each governor managed to provide a distinctive emphasis in his proclamations, thus allowing for comparisons among them. Some of the proclamations from the 1790s retained a decidedly Christian element, as demonstrated by Samuel Adams's productions. John Hancock's, by contrast, were very formal proclamations, addressed to a distant God, and Increase Sumner's entirely omitted reference to Jesus.[57]

Strong's proclamations offer a sharp contrast by resisting the trend of making the religious references less distinct. His proclamations are filled with allusions to God the Father, Jesus Christ the Son, and the Holy Spirit.[58] He frequently ended his proclamations with a desire that the kingdom of God might be established in the earth, such as when in his 1807 proclamation he prayed "that he [God] would remove out of the way every thing that opposes the Redeemer's kingdom, and interest, and that all the children of men may become holiness to the Lord, and the whole earth be filled with His glory."[59] These proclamations reflect a familiarity and conscious engagement with a vibrant Christianity. As the 1807 quote suggests, with its references to Exodus 28:36, Isaiah 23:18, Psalm 72:19, and Isaiah 6:3, Strong made extensive use of biblical language. In other places, he called on the citizens of the state to join together, "that we may offer up our sacrifice of thanksgiving to the Father of Mercies, in whom we live, and move, and have our being, and ascribe the praise of all our peace and prosperity to His care and favour," in the process referencing Psalm 116:17, II Corinthians 1:3, and Acts 17:28.[60] The superabundance of these references throughout Strong's proclamations show this is neither a stylistic flourish nor an offhanded reference, but an intentional usage of scriptural language in transacting the religious business entrusted to the governor.

At the same time, Strong used the proclamations as political documents to address issues of public concern and, if possible, persuade those who disagreed with him. A prominent example of this approach is Strong's multiple references to infidelity. In comments showing the influence of both Timothy Dwight and Jedidiah Morse, Strong warned against the moral dangers of infidelity and prayed that "we may all cultivate the benevolent dispositions and offices enjoined by religion, and prove, by our conversation and conduct, that we are uncorrupted with vice and infidelity." Infidelity would undermine the moral character on which the health of the state depended. Such a charge, though, was barbed, since it was usually directed against Francophile Democrats. Speaking of France, Strong often prayed for peace in Europe, although it was clear that the French were the ones who "sacrifice the peace of nations to their ambition." Strong's tendency to address matters of peace and war would reappear in his second stint as governor. Finally, Strong was not above warning against party strife. In one proclamation, he hoped "that the people of this State may be of one mind and live in peace." Using the language of antipartisanship, Strong was opposing the pretensions of Democrats in the state—a strategy of partisan antipartisanship.[61] Political and religious concerns thus united in Strong's public proclamations—a tendency cheered by his allies and decried by his opponents.

Party competition increased in Massachusetts during Strong's governorship, and Republicans cut into his electoral majorities. Federalists, though, rallied to support Strong. In campaign literature, Strong's piety continued to feature prominently. Leading up to the election in 1806, for instance, an anonymous pamphleteer addressed *An Appeal to the Old Whigs of Massachusetts* and praised Strong's faith, his public pronouncements, and his administration. One reason to support Strong was that he "has ever been deeply devoted to the interests of Christianity, and has been long an avowed professor of its divine truths and doctrines." For this politico, personal piety *did* justify reelecting Strong. Not only that but Strong had "frequently described religion as the only sure basis of national happiness, and urged upon us the solemn observance of those holy

institutions." Some citizens had clearly been listening to Strong's statements. Again, religious language could strengthen the state by encouraging its citizens to upright lives. The pamphleteer also praised Strong's
"mild and conciliatory system of conduct" meant to lessen party animos-
ity. The irony that the author was making partisan attacks while praising
Strong's conciliatory approach was lost on the writer. Still, the writer very
clearly reflected Strong's style of governing. He mentions no particular
measures to support Strong but assumes that, since the state is happy and
flourishing, Strong's administration must be commendable. The pamphlet concluded with an attack on the character of Strong's opponent,
James Sullivan, whom it accused of having no fixed principles.[62]

At the same time, Strong's partisan antipartisanship was growing
more pronounced. He had earlier observed, "There is no evil, to which
free governments are more exposed, than the prevalence of party spirit.
The extreme violence of this spirit degrades the character of a nation, and
vitiates the morals of the people." Although men might have differing political ideas, they could be expressed without parties. The party organizer,
though, "who unnecessarily excites public alarm or resentment, is a dis-
turber of the peace—and, whatever his pretences may be, he is actuated
by improper motives, and has no regard to the interest of his country."
Partisanship disrupted the public order, threatened the unity necessary
for the survival of the republic, and caused legislators to lose sight of the
public interest.[63] Such denunciations apparently had limited effect. Republicans captured the General Court in 1806, the same year Strong nar-
rowly retained the governorship in a close vote that had to be adjudicated
by the legislature.[64] The following year, Strong was defeated.

Strong's loss demonstrated that, although Massachusetts was still a
Federalist state, Democratic-Republicans could gain traction even there
in the early republic. During this period, which demonstrated what historian Ronald Formisano characterizes as "the politics of the Revolutionary Center," those with a revolutionary heritage in either party could
find support. Thus Samuel Adams in the mid-1790s was popular, despite
his suspicion of the Constitution. After Strong's first stint as governor
(1800–1807), three Democrats held the office—James Sullivan, Levi Lincoln, and Elbridge Gerry. Democrats also occasionally gained control of
the state legislature. Thus the first decade and a half of the nineteenth
century saw party organization and party competition increase. Elections
became more competitive, and Democrats made inroads, proving especially strong in western Massachusetts.[65]

As Strong prepared to retire, he attended his final legislative session in Boston. As he was entering the town, he was honored by a group of "Young Federal Republicans" who accompanied him into Boston.[66] They also presented an address that honored Strong for his "political integrity and moral worth." This public spectacle was then reproduced when the address was printed in the *Columbian Centinel*.[67] Strong was subsequently honored by the Federalists when his addresses and proclamations were gathered together into the volume *Patriotism and Piety*. Hundreds of Strong's political supporters throughout the state subscribed for the book. The book's introduction praised Strong in observing, "His political, moral, and religious sentiments . . . are so many evidences of the goodness of his heart and the soundness of his understanding, and so many tacit pledges that the confidence of an honest people in SUCH A MAN can never be betrayed."[68] That observation, connected with the address of the Young Federal Republicans, suggest how Strong was seen by his supporters. He was honored for his character and piety; indeed, Strong was the embodiment of both patriotism and piety. Strong's political standing, influence, and success were predicated on his perceived religious character—a perception bolstered by his public addresses. The public trust was in the individual, only secondarily in his policies. Indeed, although Strong had a vision of religion's role in society, that had rarely translated into a concrete political agenda.

Strong's retirement saw his ties to evangelical Federalists grow even stronger through personal alliances, as his daughter Clarissa married Timothy Dwight's son Timothy Dwight, Jr., in 1810. After visiting Clarissa, Strong informed her, "Your Mama was much gratified to find how agreeable your connections and acquaintance are at New Haven. We had long known the excellence of Doctor Dwight & Mrs. Dwight." Strong closed the letter by instructing Clarissa to "give our Love to Mrs. Dwight, and our Regards to Doctor Dwight & Mr. [James] Hillhouse's Family."[69] Apart from the emotional ties between Clarissa and Timothy, the marriage reinforced the ties among Strong, the Dwights (who had originally been from Northampton), and the likeminded Federalist Hillhouses. Strong's retirement marked a strengthening of his Federalist ties.

Strong's connection to Dwight and other evangelical Federalists went beyond family ties. After leaving the governorship, Strong became involved in several religious voluntary societies. He joined his local Hampshire Missionary Society in 1809 and would serve as its president until his death.[70] He also became one of several "Visitors" for Andover Seminary—the institution that Morse had worked to found in response to Harvard's drift to Unitarianism. As a Visitor, Strong was expected to make sure the school remained orthodox—another vote in favor of his piety.[71] Through participation in such interdenominational Voluntarist endeavors, Strong's outlook would grow even more in line with the decidedly evangelical Federalism of men like Dwight.

Although Strong had believed his retirement to be permanent, events would prove otherwise. With the Federalists without a candidate and the threat of war with England looming in 1812, the Federalist caucus asked Strong if he would again stand for governor. He agreed, and the Federalists launched an energetic campaign against then-governor Elbridge Gerry. As one campaign piece pointed out, comment on Strong's character was "superfluous" since he had "for the several years sustained the office of Chief Magistrate with dignity, ability, moderation, and firmness."[72] If the campaign was again about character, Strong's shone brightly in contrast to Gerry's, whose scheme of drawing oddly shaped districts for political advantage brought scorn from the Federalists, who compared the shape to a salamander that they named the "Gerry-mander." Strong was returned to the governorship. With his election, he received congratulations from another Federalist in retirement, John Jay. Jay wrote, "Permit me to express the satisfaction which I derive from [your election]; and from the general confidence so justly reposed in your public and private character."[73] That Strong's character was held in high regard by such an eminent Federalist as Jay was praise indeed. The letter also showed the still-existing networks that Federalists had formed over the past decades. Strong had little time to enjoy the congratulations, though, as the nation soon plunged into war with Great Britain.[74]

With this political and religious background, Strong's 1812 "bulwark of the religion" proclamation becomes more intelligible. Confronted with a war against another Protestant nation, Strong reached for religious language to make sense of the circumstances. Since Strong's regular practice was to make religious declarations with biblical themes, he expressed his disapproval of the war in a familiar idiom. His opposition to the war reflected the Federalists' longstanding opposition to the French and the French Revolution. That opposition grew stronger under the impulse of evangelical Protestantism. Here, the French were not only politically dangerous but heretical and religiously threatening. In expressing his opposition, Strong was echoing the concerns of many Federalist clergy, including his in-law Timothy Dwight. Strong used public speech as a means of resistance to the national government's measures.

Apart from the political toasts mentioned earlier, several broadsides responded to Strong at greater length, and they revealed the distance between Strong's vision of religious and social continuity and the Democratic-Republicanism emerging even in New England. In *The Strong Fast; or, Hypocrisy in the Suds,* an anonymous wit attacked Strong's notion with doggerel verse, which opened:

> Conven'd on this appointed day,
> We thank the Lord of glory
> That STRONG we meet to fast, and play
> The hypocrite and tory.

The author was attacking Strong's religious interpretation, believing that Strong was using religion to cover over his own misguided political opinions. The author linked this abuse of religion to the faults of the Puritans, who with the same zeal, burnt Quakers and hung witches, suggesting a strong dissatisfaction with the state's Congregational establishment. The author further tarred Strong with the "tory" label, harking back to Strong's loyalty addresses before the revolution. The poet suggested that Strong's British loyalties continued and were undermining his patriotism. More important to the author was the fact that the British "have impress'd our tars, / And robb'd us on the ocean."[75] Both a demand for less political religiosity and a surging sense of nationalism propelled this attack on Strong.

Strong also received a rebuke from a clearly devout Republican source in a broadside entitled *The Bulwarks of Religion.* That anonymous author rejected Strong's claim that Britain had been or could be a bulwark to religion. With an attitude that would contribute to disestablishment in the future, he declared, "We acknowledge no human *bulwark.*—Christ is the head of his Church, and to him alone we look for its protection." Because the Church was a spiritual entity, it did not need human defenses. Strong was mistaken in thinking any were necessary. Indeed, looking to earthly powers was a mark of the Devil. As the author stated, "The religion of tories and traitors being from the Devil, it must of course depend on his servants as its *bulwark,* but the religion which we profess being from above, has Heaven for its *bulwark.*" Accusing Strong of being a traitor, this polemicist linked him to the satanic activity of Great Britain, which included persecuting Baptists, Quakers, and Puritans—in addition to waging an unjust war against America. The author warned that religion was being "prostituted for the vilest purposes" and had become "a stalking horse for ambition and treason."[76] Where Strong intended a religious argument, this disputant saw low politics and flawed theology, with a likely hellish origin.

Despite such responses, Strong continued in his anomalous role as wartime governor and opponent of the war. While not supporting the war effort, he still had to guarantee the defense of Massachusetts. In 1812, Strong refused to place the state militia under the command of the federal army and General Henry Dearborn. When Strong received orders to raise the militia for Dearborn, he consulted the Supreme Judicial Court of Massachusetts. Using a narrow interpretation of the Constitution, its justices decided that President Madison's order did not meet the strict requirements for placing militia under federal command (a direct order plus notification of immediate danger). Relying on that ruling, Strong resisted the federal orders, declaring that his refusal was meant to protect the state's rights and uphold the federal Constitution.[77] Strong then commenced months of wrangling with Dearborn. This decision was never seriously challenged, but Strong and the other Massachusetts Federalists were clearly making the interpretation that suited their resistance to the war. When in 1814 the federal government denied muskets and military supplies to Massachusetts, the response was likely payback for political noncompliance.

Strong's political resistance to the war is evident in a speech he delivered to the Massachusetts legislature in 1813. On the opening of the legislative session, Strong addressed the stated causes of the war—the British embargo, impressment—and dismissed them in turn. Strong also declared that neither national honor nor the possibility of territorial conquest justified endangering the life and health of the republic. He concluded by comparing the moral states of Britain and France, thereby enlarging on the point he had made in his "Bulwark of Religion" address. "In the present moral state of the world it would seem that our political friendships should be informed with some regard to that state. But are we encouraged by the moral qualities of the French government to take part in its wars?" he asked. "Or should we cultivate the friendship of France . . . because her manners, religion or policy are more congenial to ours?" This statement reveals how much Strong interpreted the war through a moral and religious lens. War with England would incline the United States to side with Napoleonic France. To Strong, such a move would be disastrous. French manners, religion, and morals were disturbing indeed, and Strong wanted no part with them.[78]

The year 1814 brought even greater trouble to Massachusetts, as British forces invaded, occupied several towns in Maine, and threatened the coast.[79] The war's coming to New England, coupled with the federal government's seeming inability or unwillingness to defend New England, contributed to the calling of the Hartford Convention—the final act of resistance to the war. As governor of Massachusetts, Strong was well-positioned to direct New England's response to the war. He encouraged the convention and assented in the naming of delegates. According to state senator Daniel Appleton White, Strong was "the father of the Hartford Convention." Appleton reported that Strong "said it was perfectly constitutional, and familiar to the people during our Revolutionary struggle; that it would serve to quiet the minds of the people, and prevent any illegal outbreak, while it afforded time for consideration of the best means of relief to the people from the intolerable burdens of which they so bitterly complained."[80] If Appleton remembered correctly, then Strong's support for the convention was rooted in his conciliatory temper. In the end, the "Resolves of the Convention" were moderate calls for constitutional reform—a fact overlooked by Republican attacks in the flush of victory in 1815.[81] Strong did not participate in the convention but remained in Boston, corresponding with members of the convention and circulating the "Resolves" to other Federalists, including Timothy Pickering.[82] In encouraging the Hartford Convention, Strong ironically contributed to the Federalists' demise.

Such events, though, would be in the future. With the coming of peace, Strong no longer felt obligated to hold the governor's chair, which he gladly relinquished in 1816. Strong left believing conditions were largely as they should be. With his final address, he returned to the concerns that he had stressed repeatedly during his years as governor. "Let us cherish those principles of government, and those systems of education, which have been derived to us from our ancestors," he exhorted, "especially the institutions which have a tendency to preserve in the minds of the people that reverence for the Deity, without which, neither public nor private virtue can subsist, nor the welfare of a community be secure."[83] Here again are those themes of reverence for ancestors, respect for the institutions of the state, respect for God, and the close tie of religion with virtue and happiness. He was reiterating his commitment to a Christian Federalism and its necessity for public happiness and security. Although Strong could restate this message, his overall effect was ambivalent. He did solidify Federalist standing in Massachusetts and turn the governorship over to another Federalist, John Brooks, but he was not able to set the state on a course of "Strongian" politics. If his particular religious contribution to politics was tied up with who he was, that same influence would leave office with him, leaving minimal imprint on the politics of the state.

This pro-Federalist election broadside from 1814 portrays Caleb Strong as leading the defense of American rights for all groups in Massachusetts, for "Commerce *and* Agriculture," for "Sailors *and* Landsmen." It also makes a pointed comment about what Strong and the Federalists opposed: "Direct Taxes! Conscription! Embargo! War!" *Ships of the Line!—No Shaving Mills.* Broadside. [Boston?: N.p., 1814]. (Courtesy of the Massachusetts Historical Society)

If the institutional questions of religion in politics disturbed Strong, he left no record of it. Instead, in his retirement he worked to maintain the presence of religion in society in a different way, by turning his attention to greater benevolent activities, thereby contributing to the shift from a Combative religious outlook to a Voluntarist one. The man ridiculed as the "Hampshire Deacon" now devoted himself exclusively to those concerns. He was an incorporating member of the Massachusetts Congregationalist Charitable Society.[84] He presided over both the Hampshire Bible Society and the Hampshire Missionary Society.[85] Soon after the American Bible Society formed in New York City, Strong's Hampshire Bible Society affiliated with it, thereby affirming the evangelizing mission the ABS pursued. Samuel Bayard reported to Elias Boudinot that Strong "thinks [the Hampshire Bible Society] will be supported with zeal & that it will contribute handsomely to the National Institution."[86] In working with the ABS, Strong joined other evangelical Federalist leaders such as Boudinot, John and William Jay, and Jedidiah Morse. Strong was even named a vice president for the ABS from Massachusetts. He supported it and lent it credibility.[87] Through Voluntarist activity, he sought to better the nation and the rest of the world through conversion. With these activities, Strong continued to influence the course of the nation and strengthen the cause of evangelical reform. Strong pursued such objectives until his death in 1819.[88]

Strong's life provides insights into the possibilities and perils of Combative combinations of religion and politics—especially the overreliance on a politics of either personal character or piety. As an individual, Strong was undoubtedly pious. As Alden Bradford observed, "He was a sincere and conscientious Christian . . . [characterized by] deep humility, and ardent piety."[89] Personal piety, though, had to be channeled into political directions. As such, it served as one more argument in favor of Strong whenever he was up for election. It was an assurance of his probity, simplicity, and honesty. In office, it gave his decisions credibility. For Strong, piety was a language through which to understand and describe society. It energized his pursuit of a religiously based, orderly society that corporately inculcated religion, morality, and education in its citizens. Strong attempted to continue the republican ideal of Northampton on a larger scale. The model, he believed, applied equally well to Massachusetts and the rest of the union. In making such a stretch, though, Strong ran up against very real differences, an increasingly pluralist society, and citizens who in no way wanted to replicate Northampton. As such, his religious approach energized his supporters while adding *frisson* to the opposition. His opponents rightly saw that he *was* using religion as a political tool.

Still, Strong's vision of politics proved inadequate. Strong's continued electoral support was somewhat anomalous for the nation as a whole. Even in Massachusetts, the Federalists had to work strenuously to maintain their political standing. Ultimately, Strong's approach failed through its inability to make programmatic suggestions. This pointed to the weakness of Federalism's personal politics generally. Not only did it carry little content, but it was increasingly difficult to sell to newly empowered voters, who would be required to trust the judgment of the official.

As a result, the influence of religion that Strong attempted to bring into politics was as transient as his time in office. Since the influence was personal, it could not be replicated and thus left office with him. A politics of personal piety was not enough. Other approaches would be necessary if religion were to manifest itself in Federalist politics. In his retirement, Strong's voluntarism pointed in the direction that evangelical Federalists might go.

4 Advocating "Public Righteousness"

ELIAS BOUDINOT AND THE TRANSFORMATION OF FEDERALIST RELIGION

IN THE FALL OF 1782, AS "WARM DEBATE" SWIRLED AROUND HIM IN the Continental Congress, New Jersey delegate Elias Boudinot penned a letter to his daughter Susan. Boudinot allowed himself to be distracted for only the most pressing concern—the condition of her immortal soul. He opened with a direct inquiry: "How stands it as to your preparation and hope in the prospects of a joyfull Immortality[?]" This would clearly not be a light letter with news from Congress. Instead, Boudinot proceeded to review the essentials of evangelical theology. "You are well acquainted," he reminded her, "that the most perfect & consummate doctrinal Knowledge, is of no avail, without it operates on & sincerely affects the Heart, Changes the Practice, and totally influences the Will." For Boudinot, even the essentials of theology were not sufficient. He was demanding conversion, a new birth. Further, he emphasized God's initiative in this conversion process. "Without the almighty Power of the Spirit of God, enlightening your Mind, subduing your Will, and continually drawing you to himself, you can do nothing." At the same time, humans were not to wait passively but could prepare themselves to receive this new birth. "Your own Constant unwearied Endeavours after Holiness and perpetual Applications to a merciful Saviour for this Aid, are as necessary as if you could accomplish your own Salvation, by your own Works." Using the means of prayer, studying the scriptures, and engaging in godly conversation with other Christians, a person could ready the soul to receive grace. After this review, Boudinot again challenged his daughter, "What have *you* done[?]"[1]

For an evangelical Presbyterian like Boudinot, true Christianity began with a conversion experience and emphasized the heart and the affections over intellectual knowledge alone. Boudinot was concerned about the state of Susan's soul, but as the setting suggested, he was also concerned about the soul of the state. Conversion and the health of the

Elias Boudinot, after the reception of the Paris Peace Treaty. Charles Willson Peale. *Elias Boudinot IV,* 1784. Oil on canvas. (Princeton University Art Museum, gift of Mr. and Mrs. Landon K. Thorne for the Boudinot Collection, y1954–266. Photo: Bruce M. White)

state were tied together in Boudinot's thinking. Susan's conversion would contribute to the preservation of the republic for which he was simultaneously working.

The image of Boudinot penning an impassioned letter to his daughter while congressional debate raged around him suggests how personal, religious, and political concerns intertwined for evangelical Federalists in the early republic. In Boudinot's life, religious belief influenced political involvement by inspiring a desire for "public righteousness," a religiously inflected government that pursued public justice. In his pursuit of "public righteousness," Boudinot was a "friend of government" who enacted a Combative Federalist religious outlook in opposing the rising strength of the Democratic-Republicans. Simultaneously, politics influenced his religious beliefs structurally by offering a vision for the potentialities of a national, centralized organization, thereby setting an agenda for a national array of voluntary societies. Boudinot worked to preserve republican government during his lifetime and insure its continuance for posterity. In this scheme, conversion played a central role, because Boudinot believed that Christianity was necessary to produce the morality and virtue required for the preservation of republican government.

As a Presbyterian, Boudinot shared these attitudes with others in the Reformed tradition, such as New England's Congregationalists, and together they could be characterized as Edwardsean and evangelical. Shared beliefs allowed for cross-denominational cooperation. Furthermore, as a Presbyterian, Boudinot participated in the dominant Reformed expression in the Mid-Atlantic states. He was thus positioned as a leader in a significant region of the new nation, among a strong body of active individuals. Boudinot's involvement in Reformed churches both shaped his individual religiosity and positioned him to influence how Reformed Christians dealt with the new nation.[2]

With this religious background, Boudinot supported the patriot cause, served in the Confederation Congress, and was later part of the first three sessions of the U.S. House of Representatives. In the process, he articulated a Republican belief in the interdependence of religion and good government. In the early republic, Boudinot quickly came to support the "friends of order." As a Federalist, his Combative linking of active public faith with politics led to his resisting the Democratic-Republicans, because he feared that they stood for both bad (even dangerous) government and anti-Christian religious principles. In his retirement, Boudinot used a Voluntarist strategy to promote Christianity, hoping that an improvement in belief would also preserve the nation.

In these endeavors, Boudinot worked for what he perceived to be the good of his nation—a political arrangement in which church and state, by doing their own tasks well, could informally support the other. A strong national government would promote peace and safety for its citizens, which would allow the Church to advance its mission of caring for the spiritual well-being of everyone in the nation and engender the virtues necessary for a republican government. Initially confident about the republic, Boudinot came to worry about its continuance in the 1790s. As Federalists and evangelical Christians lost influence in national politics, Boudinot reassessed his public involvement and decided to invest himself in explicitly religious activities. A reinvigorated Christianity seemed to Boudinot to be the only means of producing the virtue necessary for the survival of the republic. In the process, he contributed to the weakening of the Federalist party and the separation of his religious and moral concerns from a partisan identification. The evangelical Boudinot thus accelerated the transformation of religion and politics for Federalists in the early republic.

The American Revolution and a Republican Religious Outlook

From his earliest life, Elias Boudinot was connected to the evangelical networks in British North America. When he was born in Philadelphia on May 2, 1740, he was baptized by George Whitefield. Three years later, when the debates over the Great Awakening caused a church split, Boudinot's father led his family into the New Side Second Presbyterian Church. There he grew up under the preaching of the revivalist Gilbert Tennent.[3] After the family moved to Princeton, they were closely connected with the college and its circle. From Aaron Burr, Sr., Elias would have heard much millennial preaching. The Boudinots were also in town when Jonathan Edwards assumed his short-lived presidency of the college in 1757.[4] Boudinot thus grew up around key figures in the Great Awakening, and he seems to have listened attentively to their messages, even adopting their warm, hortatory style in his earliest correspondence, where he called on friends to be converted.[5] This warm evangelicalism was no mere youthful enthusiasm; Boudinot would make similar exhortations for the rest of his life.

Boudinot was admitted to the New Jersey bar in 1760 and established an office in Elizabethtown. His practice was successful, and he married Hannah Stockton in 1762. William Tennent, the evangelist about whom Boudinot would later write a popular biographical sketch, performed the ceremony. Boudinot's standing in the community increased, and his dedication to the Presbyterian church in Elizabethtown was recognized when the church elected him president of the church's board of trustees in 1765.[6]

In the face of increasing conflict with Great Britain, Boudinot defended American rights, advocating for the patriot position. His moderate approach to politics, however, precluded his advocating any rash political moves. For instance, he actively opposed John Witherspoon's attempt to get New Jersey to declare independence before the Continental Congress.[7] By 1775, he was elected a member of New Jersey's provisional congress.

Boudinot viewed his personal involvement in the American Revolution as directed by Providence—Providence both inspired the war and placed Boudinot in a position to be useful. During the war, political responsibilities kept pulling him into deeper public service.[8] Against the backdrop of the Continental Army's presence in New Jersey, Boudinot worked to supply the army as a private citizen. Those services led George Washington to appoint Boudinot as commissary of prisoners.[9] In this capacity, Boudinot visited American prisoners of war held by the British to insure that they were properly supplied. When finances from Congress ran low, Boudinot even provided for the prisoners from his own pocket.[10] While serving in these capacities, he wrote his wife often, reminding her that events happened in the will of God. "I must confess," he told her, "I do not enjoy my present wandering life with any degree of relish, but what arises from a conviction of its not only being duty, but the path marked out by divine Providence. . . . God & our Country call to a different exercise of our Talent."[11] Boudinot saw a providential involvement on behalf of the American cause, that God was actively encouraging the establishment of the new nation.[12] This reinforced his vision that America was a land chosen and blessed with good government and Christianity. It also raised the stakes when those two institutions seemed in jeopardy.

Boudinot served as commissary during 1777 and 1778. At that time, he laid aside his commission because he had been elected as a New Jersey delegate to the Continental Congress. There he pursued useful activity as an expression of his Christian duty to serve God and man. Boudinot expressed this motivation after he had tasted a little of the duties of Congress, writing his wife, "My desire is to be usefull, and as my gracious God has in his all wise Providence been pleased to favour me beyond the common Lott of the Children of Men . . . with the means & hopes of eternal Life, so I would endeavour at the Risque of every earthly comfort & Enjoyment, to do his will under every circumstance of Life."[13] Because he believed that God was providentially working through the American Revolution to bring about republican government, his duty was to be involved in the process, despite personal sacrifices.

Boudinot remained in Congress, and in November 1782, Congress elected him its president for the next year. Although the post had few powers, it was the highest office in the land, invested with the duties of running Congress and corresponding with American ambassadors. His responsibilities overseeing congressional business included issuing a call for a national day of thanksgiving. The proclamation thanked God "that he hath been pleased to continue to us the light of the blessed gospel, and secured to us in the fullest extent the rights of conscience in faith and worship," and went on to offer the prayer that "it may please him to pardon all our offences" and "to cause pure religion and virtue to flourish, to give peace to all nations and to fill the world with his glory." These sentiments showed that Boudinot had no difficulty combining the concerns of Christianity and the republic.[14] Boudinot also received both the preliminary articles of peace and the final peace treaty from Paris.[15] With the coming of peace, Boudinot looked hopefully into the future, writing, "A new Empire rising into Existence with such extensive Views, must attract the attention of the whole World."[16] To Boudinot, the new nation held the possibility of being an exemplar of liberty, promoting political rebirth around the globe.

Despite such hopes, Boudinot still had to lead Congress through the dangerous shoals of a lack of finances and a still-mobilized army. Boudinot wrote to Washington, "Perhaps there has not been a more critical delicate and interesting Period during the war. Our Finances are in the most Deplorable situation and it will take a considerable Time before they can be replenished."[17] On this front, Boudinot could only request funds from the states while urging the American diplomats in Europe to continue seeking loans. Boudinot also faced an immediate danger when in June 1783, several hundred Pennsylvania militiamen left their barracks near Lancaster and marched to Philadelphia to demand their back wages. The danger of military coercion loomed, and Boudinot was distressed at how little help Congress received.[18] Refusing to allow military interference to overawe civil power, Boudinot quickly moved Congress from Philadelphia to Princeton, where it could conduct business in peace.[19] Dealing with both finances and a military threat undoubtedly heightened Boudinot's fears of anarchy and his belief in the need for a strong government. Boudinot left Congress at the end of 1783 to return to private life.

In Boudinot's revolutionary career, an evangelical Presbyterian piety motivated him early and stayed with him throughout his endeavors. Boudinot believed that God was providentially working through the American Revolution to bring about the good of republican government. To further this providential plan, Boudinot sought to produce the best government possible. His experiences with a weak Confederation Congress reinforced his belief that government needed additional powers, and he carried that belief into his public service under the new Constitution.

Serving the Federal Government and Creating a Combative Federalism

Boudinot also saw Providence working in the establishment of the federal government, even though he was not involved in writing the federal Constitution or New Jersey's quick ratification.[20] Under the new federal government, Boudinot's district elected him to the House of Representatives. Arriving in Congress, he announced to his wife, "I profess to be directed by the kind overruling Providence of that God who has led by the hand ever since I have had my being, and therefore do Eye his Providence as my great pole Star, to follow where it shall lead me." Boudinot was selected as part of the House's delegation to welcome Washington, who breakfasted at Boudinot's home in Elizabethtown before being accompanied by Boudinot into the city by ferry.[21]

Serving in the first three Congresses, Boudinot emerged as a "friend of government." He supported the administration in the assumption of state debts, funding the national debt, establishing the Bank of the United States, and putting a tariff in place, in the process siding with Fisher Ames, Theodore Sedgwick, and other Federalists.[22] On several occasions, Boudinot's moral and religious impulses came through. On the tariff, he attempted (unsuccessfully) to place a high tax on rum to discourage its consumption and attendant problems.[23] He also pressed for the House to receive the original petitions from the Pennsylvania Society for Promoting the Abolition of Slavery. In an address to Congress on the subject, he asserted that, although eliminating the slave trade was prohibited until 1808 by the Constitution, it did not mean that petitions could not be received, especially if the petitions expressed Congress's opposition to slavery. To his mind, defending the African slave trade proved "an arduous task in this day of light and knowledge." Boudinot's principled opposition to slavery would continue until the end of his life. In the same speech, Boudinot asserted it was Congress's "duty of our exalted station to do everything in our power to remove every obstruction to public righteousness."[24] Boudinot was asserting the possibility of "public righteousness," that is, a corporate establishment of justice rooted in biblical norms. If the government embodied "public righteousness," then Boudinot's stance as a "friend of government" was a natural outgrowth of his religious commitments.

Public righteousness to Boudinot included offering corporate thanksgiving to God, as a recognition of divine favor and a means of inculcating belief in future generations. Boudinot was the first congressman to

advocate a national day of thanksgiving, attempting to continue the practice from the Confederation period. Boudinot "said he could not think
of letting the session pass over without offering an opportunity to all the
citizens of the United States, of joining, with one voice, in returning to
Almighty God their sincere thanks for the many blessings he had poured
down upon them." He therefore proposed that Congress wait upon the
president to declare "a day of public Thanksgiving and Prayer, to be observed by acknowledging with grateful hearts, the many signal favors of
Almighty God, especially by affording them an opportunity peaceably to
establish a constitution of government for their safety and happiness." Although South Carolinians Aedanus Burke and Thomas Tucker opposed
the motion, it carried "by a great majority," and Boudinot was appointed
to transmit it to the president. Washington agreed and began a tradition
that both he and John Adams would observe—and which Thomas Jefferson would intentionally allow to lapse.[25]

In 1793, while serving as a U.S. representative, Boudinot delivered a
striking address to the Society of the Cincinnati that revealed his positive vision for a Republican alignment of patriotic ideals with evangelical
religion. Focusing on political rights, the nature of representation, and
the duties of citizenship, Boudinot offered an optimistic interpretation
of the revolution. He quickly moved from honoring the occasion and
eulogizing the fallen to describing the political principles that justified
their sacrifice. These rights were those he considered "*natural, essential,*
and *unalienable;* such as the security of *life, liberty,* and *property.*" He was
quick to assert that he did not mean men were equal in acquired position,
since "men must and do continually differ in their genius, knowledge,
industry, integrity, and activity." Boudinot's second principle was the
right of the people to govern themselves. This topic allowed him to speak
about the proper place of representatives in such government. Boudinot believed some suspicion was always warranted, but that normally,
representatives should be allowed "a fair and candid experiment of the
plans they form, and the laws they enact for the public weal."[26] In short,
Boudinot was expressing the Federalist notion of representation, that the
people should vote and then leave their chosen representatives alone to
govern.

Because of the great opportunity Americans possessed, a commen-
surate duty fell on them. They could not be "careless, indolent, or in-
attentive in the exercise of any right of citizenship." To Boudinot, morality was necessary to support the republic, since, "if the moral character of
a people once degenerate, their political character must soon follow." The

experiment of republican government was a cooperative event in which both rulers and citizens had responsibilities. This political endeavor was ultimately tied to a religious vision. America, "the country for which we have fought and bled," had the possibility of becoming "a theatre of greater events than yet have been known to mankind," the possible fulfillment of both Old and New Testament prophecies. Thus, Boudinot concluded his peroration with a vision of how the political principles he had described might help to bring about "that happy state of the world, when, from every human breast, joined by the grand chorus of the skies, shall arise with the profoundest reverence, that divinely celestial anthem of universal praise,— 'Glory to God in the highest,—Peace on earth—Good will towards men.'"²⁷ In short, America had an immediately positive role to play, which, if fulfilled, carried even greater promise. In his first few years in Congress, Boudinot acted under an optimistic belief that the nation could be the instrument to bring about the kingdom of God.

Under the growing pressure of foreign affairs and political conflict at home, however, Boudinot's positive vision of America grew darker— a position colored by the apocalyptic and prophetic books he had been reading for several years past. Perhaps tribulation, rather than millennial joy, was immediately ahead. These darker visions were reflected in a 1794 letter he wrote to his brother, where he observed, "I foresee great Evils coming on the World, from which we cannot expect to be wholly exempt. It becomes therefore every serious & considerate Person to pray earnestly to be hidden till the Indignation be over past."²⁸ With the danger of great evils ahead, Boudinot did not despair, but his labors on both political and religious fronts grew more grimly determined.²⁹

A large part of the shift in Boudinot's vision came from America's interactions with other nations and consequent political polarization. European events—especially the French Revolution and the clash of England and France on land and sea—increasingly crowded into Americans' political consciousness and actions. Varying American reactions to these foreign conflicts helped to fuel the growth of domestic political parties and partisan animosities. Boudinot witnessed and participated in the party struggles of the 1790s. During the third Congress, Boudinot supported the president's policy of neutrality toward Britain. He opposed a bill in the House to cut off trade with Great Britain, because he believed it could easily precipitate a war. The country was in no condition to either stop trading with Britain or enter a new war.³⁰

The debate over the Jay Treaty highlighted for Boudinot the political divides in the country. While Federalists including Boudinot welcomed the treaty, the Democratic-Republicans lambasted it as a surrender of American independence. To oppose it, Democrats rallied popular support through mass meetings. To Boudinot's mind, this tactic was both uninformed and dangerous. "The disorganizing Democrats," he told a friend, "no sooner heard of the arrival of the Treaty, than they began without knowing its Contents, to rouse the lower People into a flame agt. it." Boudinot singled out Benjamin Franklin Bache, who rode through the country "blowing up the coals of faction." He concluded that "Every Effort was attempted, that ingenuity could devise, and the most violent resolutions were obtained from the Populace, before one in fifty had read it."[31] Instead of standing unified during a time of national danger, the Democrats (to Boudinot's mind) were threatening to tear the nation apart by "disorganizing" it and creating factions—without even knowing what the treaty said. For Boudinot, the ratification of the Jay Treaty was positive. Despite its faults, the treaty was going to benefit the country as a whole. It would bring "Pleasure" to the "Friends of our Government" (not just of the administration but of the entire constitutional order) because of the good it would do.[32] Its opponents clearly could not be interested in the good of the country.

If Boudinot hoped the furor would die down after the political decision about ratification was made, he would be disappointed. The Democratic-Republicans continued to organize and oppose the administration, and Boudinot believed these actions aimed to destabilize the entire American government. Surely some nefarious purpose was at work. "I have but little doubt," he wrote, "but that a scheme has been, and is still on foot, among the Enemies of our happy Government, to bring about a dissolution of it." Such political organization seemed to Boudinot intentionally designed to bring about the downfall of the republic for which he had been working. In the face of such danger, Boudinot continued to trust in divine protection, believing, "God in his Providence has not yet left our Country to destruction, but he seems to be counteracting the devices of the secretly wicked & persevering Enemies to our Peace, in a remarkable manner."[33] Boudinot could hold onto hope if divine aid was still being extended to the republic.

Still, the party conflicts wore on Boudinot. By the end of his third term, he felt ready to leave Congress. He was sickened by the attacks on the "happy Government" then in place, which could only bring about "Anarchy & Confusion."[34] Despite Boudinot's weariness, George Washington prevailed on him to become the director of the U.S. Mint, a position that had opened in 1795. Serving until 1805, Boudinot proved to be an efficient administrator, and the post allowed him time to read, write, and keep in contact with other Federalists.[35]

Given Boudinot's position as a "friend of government," his support for Adams in the 1796 election is not surprising. He was genuinely disturbed by the "Anarchy & Confusion" he saw around him. To answer it, he asserted the need for greater activity to counter the Democratic exertions. "There must be more exertions made by the Friends of Order & good Government, or all will be lost at last," he told his brother. "A few People calling themselves a democratic Society or other Club," he continued, "disappointed at every Election & not able to lead the People as they please, may easily command a printing Press, and make as much Noise & abuse, as a whole People." Boudinot thus presented the strident Jeffersonian editors as slanderous, factious, and disgruntled. The noise they made was disproportionate to their numbers, largely because of their access to print. Their danger lay in the way they reduced their approach "to a system" and spread it nationwide. In the same letter, though, Boudinot expressed hope that "Providence will bring about the designs of his Government, by these very means, tho his Enemies do not mean it."[36] Again, Boudinot cast his opponents not only as political enemies but as adversaries to God's will, which intended continued Federalist control.

Although Providence may have been in charge, Boudinot still followed the election closely and was mostly satisfied with the results.[37] Only one element—Jefferson's appeal despite his religious beliefs—troubled him. He wrote a friend, "It is a most remarkable event and one that soon cannot be forgotten, that in the year 1796, on the first disputed election for a President of the United States, the State of Pennsylvania who values herself on her attachment to the christian character should give 13 votes out of 15 for a President & Vice President who are open & professed Deists." To Boudinot, the idea of electing both a president and vice president who were Deists was too much. Because Boudinot drew such a close connection between belief and proper political behavior, dangerous beliefs would necessarily lead to dangerous political actions. Boudinot found this shocking turn of events a manifest sign of national declension. "These facts," he continued, "are too remarkable to escape the Pen of our future Historians & I confess they give such substantial evidence of our degenerating from the zeal of our forefathers. . . . Those who retain any of their spirit have their fears greatly alarmed for the consequences."[38] Himself "greatly alarmed," Boudinot would seek to avert the threatening collapse by working for an aggressively Combative approach for religion's role in politics.

During Adams's administration, Boudinot watched as the French continued their dangerous machinations. He supported Adams's move for a strong defense and welcomed the firm response of his country-men, which offered a possibility for restoring national unity.[39] Against the backdrop of Quasi-War with France, Boudinot wrote to Samuel Bayard, "When the News [of troubles with France] first was announced, the friends of the Government had very well founded fears, arising from the Body of Jacobins & Democrats." Boudinot's identification of Democratic-Republicans in America with the Jacobin party in France revealed why the stakes were so high. Boudinot truly believed that if the Democratic "faction" prevailed, they would plunge America into a new revolution every bit as bloody as the French. Despite such fears, Boudinot could report a positive turn. "But it is a pleasing Consideration," he announced, "that the imprudent Conduct of the french Directory have so convinced the Judgment even of our violent People, that a political Change has taken Place which augurs well & gives pleasing Expectations that a happy unanimity will prevail."[40] The French had overplayed their hand and turned many Americans against them. The tide seemed to be turning in the Federalists' favor—including the possibility of renewed national harmony.

In the midst of this political struggle, Boudinot encountered Thomas Paine's incendiary salvo against Christianity, *The Age of Reason*. Shortly after Boudinot read it, he began working on a response, which he completed in 1795 and published in 1801. Boudinot's *The Age of Revelation* provides a valuable window into his concern over the spread, influence, and results of religious beliefs he—following the lead of Timothy Dwight and Jedidiah Morse—termed "infidelity."[41] This infidelity carried both spiritual dangers (leading people away from belief) and political dangers (preparing for the destruction of self-government). In combating infidelity, Boudinot's work served to defend both the religious and political orders.

Boudinot expressed shock at finding that Paine had written for "the youth of America, and her unlearned citizens." He feared Paine's strategy was to find "the best inlet to infidelity" by preying on the uneducated. Boudinot did not believe that Paine's arguments were persuasive, but he worried that Paine's rhetoric could sway the unstudied. Boudinot responded vigorously because he believed the stakes were high: Paine's religious ideas could undermine the belief in Christianity that served as the foundation of sound republican government. Paine's arguments would strip his readers of their beliefs, which would then ruin their morals and virtue, making them unfit to be republican citizens. Boudinot's theological work was thus also a practical work meant to preserve the republic for the next generation. This concern for posterity explains his dedicating the work to his daughter, Susan.[42] By educating the next generation in the principles of right religion and sound government, Boudinot believed the ideas advanced by Paine could be countered.

In the preface, Boudinot related his concerns for the public consequences of Paine's work. Specifically, he observed that in Philadelphia, *The Age of Reason* was sold for 1½ cents, to tempt "children, servants, and the lowest people" into buying such an affordable book. Boudinot did not know who had sponsored this sale, but he reported, "I was soon convinced that a principle of the illuminati in Europe had been adopted by some unknown persons in this country, viz.—that of fixing on the rising generation, and the lower orders of the people, as the chief objects of an attack, for spreading the principles of infidelity." Boudinot's mention of the Illuminati shows that he had been listening closely to the cries raised by ministers such as Morse and Dwight in the previous years. He accepted their warnings as valid and was concerned that Paine's work might have come from the same nefarious circle of illuminists. If such a scheme to promote infidelity succeeded, it would lead to the destruction of society. Boudinot's willingness to publish came from, as he said, "an anxious desire that our country should be preserved from the dreadful evil of becoming enemies to the religion of the Gospel, which I have no doubt, but would be introductive of the dissolution of government and the bonds of society." If any doubted the seriousness of the ways infidel religion could lead to political turmoil, Boudinot pointed to France, the model for what America would become if the American "Jacobins" took over.[43]

Boudinot began by attempting to undermine the trust people had in Paine because of *Common Sense.* He claimed that Paine "has proved himself to be totally ignorant of the subject he has undertaken to elucidate, not only as to the intrinsic merit of the question, but also the ideas and terms, which its advocates have been known always to hold up and use."[44] Boudinot attacked the specific points Paine had raised in sections on Christ's virgin birth, resurrection, and ascension; the Trinity; the reliability of the Gospels; and the authenticity of the Pentateuch.[45] In each section, Boudinot described Paine's assertion and then attacked it with references to a number of writers meant to disprove either Paine's logic or his historical assertions.

Boudinot's method points to a significant point of contention between himself and Paine: the place of rationalism in their conflicting

systems. They were both fighting to capture the high ground of true reason—and common sense.[46] Boudinot could thus claim, "It is my present
design then, to make a few observations . . . in a manner that may serve
as a trial of its merits by the rules of *common sense,* and to this the author ought not to have any reasonable objection, as all his pretensions to
celebrity are founded on the assumption of that title."[47] What counted as
common sense, however, differed. Boudinot was much more inclined to
make a historical argument—for instance, that the reliability of the Gospels was attested to by both the earliest Christian writers and by pagan
writers, and that their value had been reaffirmed by the Church in every
generation. Paine, however, posited a much higher standard of rational
proof—one that virtually ruled out any mediated tradition or authority.
This standard frustrated Boudinot since he believed that the biblical writings were more attested to than any other ancient source. Boudinot went
so far as to argue that Paine was demanding an immediate revelation of
God to himself.[48] In these arguments, Boudinot was involved in the great
eighteenth-century debates over the powers and limits of human reason.

While Boudinot was wrestling with infidelity in print, he followed the
election of 1800 with great concern. Boudinot continued his support for
Adams, whom he believed had done much to strengthen the republic.
When it became apparent that Jefferson would win, Boudinot predicted
dire consequences. He had no doubts that, "with the present success &
sanguine views of the republicans, this will pervade the union and nothing short of fatal experience, will open the Eyes of the deluded Multi-
tude." He blamed Federalist selfishness and lack of unity for their defeat
and hoped that the Federalists would help to smooth the transition of
government. Since Jefferson was "certainly the Choice of the People,"
the Federalists should, however reluctantly, support him. "By acting on
their professed principles," Boudinot believed, "the Federalists would
now show a real difference between themselves & the Jacobins." Once
the disputed election had been settled by the House of Representatives,
Boudinot conceded the validity of the election and insisted that republican principles demanded its acceptance. The duty of Federalists was
to restrain the Democrats in power from going too far. As he observed,
"These people will have a tryal, and it had better be made when there is a
federal Majority in both Houses, than when every branch of the Government might be democratical."[49]

Examining the election through his evangelical Federalist lens,
Boudinot perceived God's allowing evil to come to purify his people. He
observed to his brother, "This untoward Event of the general Success of

the Republicans, may be permitted to try & purify the Friends of government; as they certainly stand in need of it."[50] The election was thus first a judgment on the Federalist party. Because its own faults had led to this election, perhaps the party would receive correction and thereby be prepared for renewed success. Boudinot also saw in the election a token of God's coming judgment on the whole nation, remarking, "I have observed in the history of God's dealing with his people, when in his providence, he has, what may be called dirty work, to be done, or rather when he intends to punish his people for their follies and wickedness, he does not employ his own Children, who are not fit for work of this kind, but calls in those who despise his Name."[51] Boudinot saw God's dealings with Christians in America as parallel to God's dealing with Israel. Jefferson's election was a judgment, but one that could produce purification. In the short run, Boudinot was not optimistic. Instead, Jefferson's ascent to the presidency strengthened Boudinot's belief in the approach of apocalyptic times.

During his service in the federal government, his millennial beliefs colored how he approached politics and produced an urgent, Combative use of religion. Early in the new administration, millennial optimism energized his address to the Society of the Cincinnati. It also motivated his involvement in the first Congresses. Under the pressures of religious infidelity and apostasy (from Paine and others), foreign threats, and domestic dangers (as Democrats combined irreligion with a penchant for Francophilia), Boudinot's vision darkened. Still, duty mandated his continued political engagement to keep the ship of state from foundering on rocks that would endanger Christianity, the government, and the nation.

Political Retirement, Social Engagement, and Voluntarist Strategies

In his retirement, Boudinot remained busy. This final period of his life saw an elaboration on his earlier activities. Boudinot followed politics, traveled, wrote several books, and worked with voluntary societies, focusing his efforts on opposing slavery and encouraging Bible societies. Boudinot's turn to voluntary societies makes sense when considered in light of his millennial thinking. The ascendancy of Jefferson and James Madison seemed to him a continued divine judgment on American politics, a providential national punishment. Such a reading of Providence prompted two responses, a push and a pull. Boudinot and other evangelical Federalists felt pushed out of politics, and the entire political endeavor increasingly seemed a curse, rather than a blessing (whether they held office or not).[52] If that was the case, reform in the moral realm seemed more compelling. Second, Boudinot and his compatriots felt pulled back to the basic principle they had enumerated, that underlying republican virtue was a morality inspired by Christianity. They accordingly invested their efforts into renewing the wellspring of political virtue for the good of their fellow citizens. Boudinot's actions, therefore, represent a hybridization of his earlier endeavors: he found a way to use federal principles to spiritual ends and spiritual means to Federalist ends. In so doing, Boudinot illustrated how political ideals could influence religious actions and vice versa. He thereby furthered the transformation from a Combative spirituality to a Voluntarist one.

In retirement, Boudinot traveled, maintaining connections with religious and political allies. In 1809, he accompanied his daughter and a family friend on their journey to Boston. Along the way, Boudinot met with a number of friends who were often evangelicals, often Federalists, and, in many cases, both. For instance, after leaving New York City, Boudinot and his party traveled to New Haven. There Boudinot called on Timothy Dwight ("the President of the College, with whom I was acquainted"), and they together toured Eli Whitney's gun factory.[53] That Sunday, Boudinot listened to Dwight preach "an excellent Sermon." Similarly, after visiting Boston, Boudinot toured Andover and the newly established evangelical seminary there, which he supported. While at Andover, he listened to the preaching of theology professor Rev. Leonard Woods and took Communion. Boudinot also conversed with Jedidiah Morse, specifically on the topic of how evangelicals should treat Unitarians.[54] Boudinot's connections with these New England evangelicals would prove useful in his own labors in the years to come. Meanwhile, Boudinot renewed ties forged during the revolution and Federalist administrations. While in Boston, he had tea with arch-Federalists Timothy Pickering, George Cabot, and Harrison Gray Otis. He also had a chance to visit with John and Abigail Adams, who received him "with great affection."[55] Boudinot's travels and writings kept him in touch with important figures throughout the union. He was thus connected with the personal networks that helped to define both religion and politics in the early republic. Boudinot clearly knew how to operate in an era when politics was still largely personal. If getting results was dependent on whom someone knew, then Boudinot's connections made him well-positioned to get his message out and form organizations with national reach.

One political stance that Boudinot took was to oppose slavery's expansion. This remained an issue for him, from his time in the House down to his later years. When the possibility of the expansion of slavery into the Missouri Territory loomed, Boudinot again roused himself to political action. He gathered likeminded citizens together for a public meeting in Trenton in October 1819. They voiced their opposition to slavery's expansion and urged opposition to any attempt for Missouri statehood. Boudinot saw this as part of a national campaign. As chairman, he sent the meeting's resolutions to his contacts throughout the nation, including John Jay.[56] The campaign tapped popular concern, and Boudinot wrote his nephew, "We have been a good deal agitated here on the dispute relating to once more (and if it should be forever) establishing slavery in the Missouri and of consequence in the United States—It seems to have run like a flaming fire through our middle States and causes great anxiety."[57]

The possible spread of slavery alarmed Boudinot because it would make slavery much more difficult ever to remove from the nation. As he argued, "If it is difficult to get rid of negro slavery now when there are but a little over one million what will it be when they are 10 Millions." Given Boudinot's opposition to slavery, such a thought was understandably fearful. Boudinot also realized that the growth of slavery would further strengthen the Southern bloc in Congress. In his observation that "the Southern & western States would have the sole Government of the union," Boudinot's fear of the "three-fifths compromise" run amuck sounded much like the concern of Timothy Pickering and other Federalist leaders.[58]

By January 1820, Boudinot had been driven to accept (if necessary) dissolution of the union over further acceptance of slavery. He wrote to John Pintard, "Tho I should devoutly deprecate such a distressing Circumstance, yet on the whole I should prefer a quick & peaceable division of the Union, and let each division enjoy their anxious desires." Perhaps it was better to let the South go its own way, to let them increase their slaves, rather than allow their practices to spoil the North. In contrast, Boudinot hoped that the North would continue their "imperishable Enjoyment of a rational Liberty, with a moderate portion of the good things of this Life, obtained by the sweat of our own Brows, under the inestimable blessings of our national & inherent rights of Life, Liberty, Property & the pursuit of happiness, while there will be none to make us afraid."[59] In a remarkable conflation, Boudinot had managed to harmonize John Locke's vision of natural rights, Jefferson's description of them in the Declaration of Independence, and Micah 4:4, a traditional Protestant definition of liberty. The North retained its desire for "a rational Liberty"—not license, but the freedom to benefit both one's self and one's neighbors, while the selfish Southerners were threatening to dissolve the structures that made rational liberty possible. By the time the Missouri question was settled, Boudinot would appreciate that the Missouri Compromise had not solved anything, merely delayed the final settlement of the question.

Boudinot also wrote and published several works, including his popular *Memoir of the Rev. William Tennent* in 1806. Boudinot seemed to sense the increasing importance of print for the new nation.[60] The year 1815 saw the completion of Boudinot's longest book, *The Second Advent,* in which Boudinot revealed how much his belief in biblical prophecy and millennialism had come to shape his thinking about history and the world. Boudinot reported that his interest in prophecy began "some time about the year 1790," when "the important events of that day made a deep impression on the author's mind and led him to examine the Scriptures with great attention." The result was a desire to compare biblical prophecies with the events of the day.[61]

In his conclusion to *The Second Advent,* Boudinot moved into a prophetic mode, calling for America to repent lest it become cursed like European nations. Boudinot asked rhetorically, "But has not America greatly departed from her original principles, and left her first love? Has she not also many amongst her chief citizens, of every party, who have forsaken the God of their fathers[?]" This falling away was attested to by the infidelity still common in the land. Boudinot also condemned the evils of slavery. While boasting of the Declaration of Independence, the nation had for many years countenanced the slave trade, was still protecting slavery, and was cruelly enslaving both Africans and Indians. In short, America was by no means protected from the danger that Boudinot envisioned coming upon Europe. The nation was at a crossroads. America "has been raised up in the course of divine Providence, at a very important crisis, and for no very inconsiderable purposes. She stands on a pinnacle—She cannot act a trifling or undecided part."[62] To Boudinot, America's situation at the "pinnacle" meant either great accomplishments or great judgment. He hoped that the nation would improve, and that his work was a contribution to such improvement. Boudinot would consciously devote the rest of his life to helping America avoid judgment and attain its earlier promise.

Besides writing, Boudinot's key strategy for rescuing the nation was the institution of Bible societies, into which he poured much of his remaining strength. Beginning at the state level, Boudinot helped to form the New Jersey Bible Society in 1809. On its second anniversary, Boudinot addressed the society. He began with a brief history designed to show what an unprecedented opportunity the Bible Society possessed: never before had it been as easy to distribute "the clear and only *written* revelation of the will of God to man." Boudinot believed the scriptures had great power to save souls. Moreover, the spread of scriptures through Bible societies would assist the nation's understaffed ministers, especially on the frontier. In the light of Christ's imminent return, all available means needed to be used, and all Protestant Christians were to be recruited for this goal. Boudinot's stress in the address was on the energy necessary to accomplish it: "We must be zealous and diligent," he proclaimed. Impressed with the efforts of the Massachusetts, Philadelphia, and British and Foreign Bible societies, Boudinot hoped to emulate them.[63] Through his readings, Boudinot stayed connected to religious developments on both sides of the Atlantic. This allowed him to build on the accomplishments of others to push for further organization and outreach. To do this, he advocated allying with other societies to multiply their mutual endeavors.

Inspired by the success of the Federalist plan of using the Constitution to organize disparate groups for national purposes, Boudinot hoped to harness the same energy for spiritual purposes. In 1814, Boudinot and the New Jersey Bible Society issued a call for a convention of Bible societies to form a national organization. Another prominent Bible society, the Philadelphia society, objected. They argued such a call was unseasonable (the United States was fighting a war), unprecedented, and impractical. They thought the informal cooperation of individual societies was sufficient. Philadelphia's answer—especially its accusation of "mistaken zeal"—bothered Boudinot. He insisted to a ministerial ally that "to interfere & endeavour to prejudice all the other Societies & forestall their Sentiments, against so important a Measure for the spread of the gospel of the Son of God, was in my opinion extremely wrong."[64] As president of the New Jersey Society, the duty to answer these objections fell to Boudinot. Like a lawyer, he dissected their assertions and found them wanting. He argued that the task was so great (both in America and beyond her borders) that a strong organization was needed.[65] The terms of this debate were familiar: Boudinot and the Philadelphia Society were replaying larger questions of the period, harkening back to the debates over the Constitution. In contrast to the Philadelphia Society's decentralized vision, Boudinot's approach was fundamentally a Federalist one. He wanted a national organization that would have the energy to accomplish great (spiritual) objects of national interest.

Despite the objections from Philadelphia, most Bible societies were interested. In preparing for the meeting, Boudinot wrote William Jay about making sure the constitution was wisely constructed. Here, too, Boudinot's conservative Federalist vision shone through when he wrote, "Experience &c. will be our best Teacher."[66] Although Boudinot was unable to attend the meeting because of illness, the delegates assembled in New York City in May 1816. Significant individuals in attendance included Jedidiah Morse; Peter Augustus Jay; William Jay; Connecticut Congregationalist Lyman Beecher; minister and theologian N. W. Taylor; Eliphalet Nott, the president of Union College; Presbyterian Gardiner Spring; and New York minister John Mitchell Mason—many of whom had Federalist ties. These delegates and the others in attendance formed the American Bible Society (ABS) and elected Boudinot its first president.[67]

For the next five years, Boudinot worked to expand the ABS's ability to distribute scriptures freely "without note or comment." This strategy revealed both the interdenominationally Protestant character of the ABS and its *sola scriptura* presupposition—merely reading the scriptures was enough to bring people to belief. Apart from spiritual intentions, the ABS definitely contributed to the increased role that print—especially religious writings—had for large segments of the population.[68] Further, by uniting with other Federalists, Boudinot helped to advance the vision of a national republic unified under a Protestant banner. They agreed with Boudinot that the ABS could be a site where religious activity would produce important cultural and even political effects.[69]

Among these effects, the first was to craft a Protestant nationalism among the participants. Insofar as the nation possessed little ability to affect citizens' daily lives and little tradition of forming loyalties to itself, voluntary societies helped to structure a civil society through which citizens could both imagine and participate in national-level endeavors. At a time when political and ethnic groups were also attempting to organize and express nationalist sentiments through print and public performances, religious voluntary societies led the way in creating accessible national sentiment. They enabled participants to imagine a community of Christians connected throughout the nation. The ABS and similar societies fostered a distinctive type of nationalism, one deeply inflected with Protestant Christianity. If the republic had not been founded as a "Christian nation," these Federalists hoped to create just such a nation subsequently. Not only preserving the republic, evangelical Federalists fostered the solidification and growth of the nation, which they worked to make a Protestant one.[70]

Next, these voluntary societies helped to create a popular attachment to the nation through creating a citizenship accessible by common people. This nationalist strategy involved thousands of men and women who joined the local societies—from Vermont to Georgia and into Ohio, Kentucky, and Tennessee.[71] This democratized citizenship would have political, organizational, and religious ramifications. Politically, national citizenship could be expressed locally, as members felt connected to much larger endeavors. These societies helped to build social capital in a fluid nation and thereby promote societal trust during a time of uncertainty. Organizationally, national purpose could be coordinated with local strategies, allowing local groups to work out the best strategies for their areas, a federalism in action.[72] Religiously, the local Bible societies (along with other societies patterned on the ABS) became sites for expressing piety in new, interdenominational settings. Within such pious contexts, feedback to politics could happen, and ordinary citizens could articulate new, moralistic politics. In this new world, democratic participation could be channeled into the Federalist goals of defending both religion and the republic.[73]

Third, these societies opened up public spaces for women's involvement at a time when other public activities were becoming less acceptable for women. Through women's auxiliary societies, women could demonstrate active involvement and participation in national endeavors.[74] Thus, whether women were involved in a society in Cincinnati, Ohio; Rutherford County, Tennessee; or New Castle, Delaware, they could tie into the national movement through correspondence and coordinated activity.[75] These auxiliaries allowed space for elite women's leadership. Maria Jay Banyer—Jay's eldest daughter—attended American Bible Society meetings, and Elizabeth Booth, the daughter of Delaware Federalist politician James Booth, gave leadership to her local Bible society. Boudinot's daughter, Susan, found herself involved with several reform societies.[76] Such groups also opened spaces for ordinary women to participate. In the process, their involvement helped women to craft female identities, public voices, and models of public participation. From these sources would come subsequent women's involvement in their own moralistic political crusades.[77]

Whether or not Boudinot fully grasped all these implications, his designs *were* ultimately global. Beginning with a "national superstructure of

Heavenly charity [the ABS]," he hoped to influence the entire world, as he told the New Jersey Society in the year after the formation of the ABS. He hoped the effort would endure "till every region of the earth shall be enlightened by the Sun of Righteousness." Boudinot returned to this point later: "This day . . . we renew our engagements . . . to make vigorous exertions to gospelize the world. . . . *Union is our Motto.*"[78] Just as political union was necessary for the country's survival, so spiritual union would insure the health and strength of the Church in America. Thus unified, evangelical Christians should attempt to "gospelize the world" as the best safeguard against political and social revolution. The formation of the ABS was important enough to use language that embraced the entire earth and pointed to a golden millennial future.

The success of the ABS encouraged Boudinot so much that some of his earlier enthusiasm returned. The possibility of the growth of the gospel through the dissemination of the scriptures cheered Boudinot, so that by 1821, his address to the ABS was altogether expectant of Christ's speedy return. "Every reflecting Man who hears me this day, must acknowledge that we have arrived at a most eventful period in the history of Mankind," he proclaimed momentously. "Every part of the world appears . . . to announce that Providence is about to bring forth some great event, that will astonish the World. . . . By disseminating the Bible, without Note or Comment, throughout the known World, we are bringing about the great, the eventful period."[79] Although dangers still remained and vigilance was necessary, the ABS—along with the tract societies, Sunday schools, and other voluntary religious meetings—offered great encouragement. In fact, the success of these organizations might even help Christ to return sooner. Perhaps the end would not be as dark or as fiery as Boudinot had once feared. He remained at his post as head of the ABS until his death later in 1821. He would be succeeded by John Jay. By that time, the ABS had become a premier example of the voluntary societies that would do so much to reorganize America in the first half of the nineteenth century, create a Voluntarist religious culture, and develop a compelling Protestant nationalism. Boudinot's contribution was both a Federalist and a federalizing one.

Throughout his life, Boudinot worked to create a united, evangelically Protestant nation, believing that both his life and the life of the nation were guided by an active Providence. In his political involvement, Boudinot was a "friend of government," believing the Federalists offered the only sound approach to governing and opened the possibility of establishing "public righteousness" in the nation. Through his writings, especially his polemical ones, Boudinot worked to defend and expand the plausibility of and confidence in Christianity among American citizens. Such a defense was necessary, since an irreligious republic was to Boudinot an impossibility. Only Protestant Christianity could engender the morality necessary for the virtue on which republics depended, while a republican government would form the environment within which true religion could flourish. To foster both vital religion and virtuous republicanism, Boudinot pioneered the establishment of the ABS, the preeminent voluntary society in the early republic.

Boudinot's work altered the relationship of religion and politics in the early republic. In an attempt to defend an older Republican vision, Boudinot worked innovatively and contributed to the evolution of religious and political practice. The first result was a Combative stance toward religion in the new nation. In the conflict over Paine and in the party conflicts of the 1790s, Boudinot worked to create a public Christianity and political culture that would together unify the nation. The second result, a Voluntarist strategy, came about when, in his retirement, Boudinot turned away from building up the Federalist party. He instead devoted himself to something he deemed even more significant: working for religious renewal and social reform. He thus hoped to preserve the nation by the most permanent means he could think of—conversion. As others followed him, they devoted less energy to a struggling Federalist party and channeled their labors into religious reform movements. The result was a more active religiosity among the laity, more concern about moral matters in politics, but less interest in party affiliation or full political engagement. Boudinot's efforts precipitated the issue-driven moral reforms and voluntaristic movements that would characterize antebellum political culture.

II

ALTERNATIVES TO THE EVANGELICAL PARTY

5 Unitarian Politics and the Splintering of the Federalist Coalition

IN THE ELECTION OF 1800, FEDERALISTS BELIEVED THE RELIGIOUS qualifications of the major candidates made the choice between them easy. The *Gazette of the United States* challenged readers with the "Grand Question" of whether they would "continue in allegiance to GOD—AND A RELIGIOUS PRESIDENT" or declare for "Jefferson—AND NO GOD!"[1] That "religious president" was none other than John Adams. This appeal carried weight. Not only did William Linn and John Mitchell Mason weigh in (see chapter 2), but laity echoed their concerns. In Delaware, "A Christian Federalist" portrayed Adams as the defender of "the order of government" and Thomas Jefferson as an irreligious Jacobin. "Like the prince of darkness," this pamphleteer declared, Jacobins "are capable of assuming every shape." Thus Americans should not be deceived by Jefferson's positive reputation. Instead, if Jefferson were elected, "those morals which protect our lives . . . which guard the chastity of our wives and daughters from seduction and violence—defend our property from plunder and devastation, and shield our religion from contempt and profanation" would be trampled. The defender of such morals would be Adams, the very president championing morality and public religion for the past four years. Thus, the writer concluded by calling for his "Fellow-Citizens, who profess the religion of Christ," to realize the weight of the election and choose Adams over Jefferson.[2]

Adams's standing as the "religious president" arose from Federalist articulation of public religious ideals and from establishing Adams as the counter to the specter of Jefferson and the "Jacobin" Republicans. Whereas Jefferson had publicly speculated on religious matters, as in his *Notes on the State of Virginia,* Adams had kept his personal (Unitarian) opinions to himself. His public pronouncements had encouraged a public religiosity closely tied to morality and social order. In this stance, Adams demonstrated the strand of rationalist Unitarian religion within Federalism, a position seemingly compatible with, but diverging from, evangelical Federalist attitudes toward religion in public life. In 1800, Unitarians and evangelical Federalists could agree that Adams was the best choice for president (many evangelical supporters of Jefferson, of course, disagreed). Ironically, the two groups would never again be so united. In the years following Adams's defeat, political alliances would strain and break over theological differences.

In contrast to the evangelicals, Unitarians represented a complementary strain of religious belief within Federalism. Unitarians and evangelicals shared some similar concerns, valuing an orderly society, the rule of the best, and public religiosity. In Massachusetts until 1820, both sides continued to support the state church establishment. In matters of emphasis, however, they differed strongly. The Unitarians held a stronger hierarchical view of society. As Unitarianism was a religion for elites in New England society, their social vision emphasized the power of those elites. Further, Unitarians obsessed over the concept of morality for individuals and society. Morality became a Unitarian touchstone that was much stronger than in the conversion-oriented evangelical camp.[3] Finally, Unitarians maintained a public role for religion, but it was a more rationalist religion, with less emotional appeal.

In the course of the Federalists' existence, Unitarians held most closely to the arrangements worked out in the revolution and so continued to hold a Republican view of religion's role in society. They largely avoided the contested, Combative language popular among the evangelicals. Although they did adopt some Voluntarist strategies at the end of the period, they never did so as energetically as did the evangelicals. Their taking up of voluntarism was limited by their elitist vision, which favored top-down activity. For the Federalist party's future, the question remained whether the shared social and political concerns of the various branches could be held together across theological differences. As theological conflict grew—urged on by evangelicals but assented to by Unitarians—political alliances became harder to sustain.

As a movement, Unitarianism had been in development for a long time—John Adams identified pre-revolutionary Congregational ministers Samuel Bryant and Jonathan Mayhew as early proponents.[4] Philosophically, Unitarianism had its origins in a rationalist approach to religion derived from the English Enlightenment. Before the American Revolution, this had produced liberal Congregationalists who questioned Calvinism. After the revolution, the movement produced Charles Chauncy's belief in universal salvation and further questions about the divinity of Jesus and the Trinity.[5] Unitarianism developed as part of a larger religious ferment in the post-revolutionary period, when it convinced many well-to-do New Englanders. Although most influential in eastern Massachusetts, Unitarianism also spread to the western part of the state. Federalist politician Theodore Sedgwick converted to Unitarianism, and his daughter Catherine Maria Sedgwick emphasized Unitarian morality in her novels. Many rationalist clergy adopted Unitarianism, while some, like William Bentley, moved to even more radical positions.[6]

The major theological issues for Unitarians were the character of Christ, the nature of man, and the relation of emotion to religion. Theologically, their identity came from their denial of the Trinity. Asserting the Trinity developed as a later accretion, they rejected it in an attempt to purify Christianity. If Christ was not equally divine, he yet held an exalted place, whether as a super-angelic created being (an Arian position) or as a specially honored human (a Socinian position). Connected to this was a high respect for human reason and human capacities. Unitarians promoted a rational piety rather than an emotive one.[7]

Unitarians also promoted unique attitudes to church and society. First, Unitarians emphasized morality and moral formation as part of spiritual development, rather than individual conversion. In this they differed from the evangelicals, who insisted on a new birth. The resulting Unitarian stance toward society was affirming and positive. Further, since they also developed from the colonial Congregational establishment, they retained a comprehensive attitude of stewardship toward society. Unitarian pastors continued to serve as both the "spiritual leader of the church" and the "minister of the town." In opposition to the increasingly particularistic evangelical churches, Unitarians maintained an interest in society; they felt "a responsibility for the spiritual well being of the whole society, not just their own communicants." Unitarians approached politics as stewards of society and emphasized the significance of morality as especially important for the republic.[8]

To trace the contours of Unitarian politics, John Adams and Henry Ware, Sr., provide particularly good resources. Adams as a political leader and Ware as a minister and then a professor at Harvard College occupied significant positions within Federalist Massachusetts. In their lives, writings, activities, and offices, they demonstrate how Unitarianism shaped emphases for Federalist politics. They also delineate areas of agreement with evangelical Federalists and the potential for discord. Whereas Adams kept the Federalists together through a rationalist appropriation of religion, Ware was close to the heart of the post-1800 theological disputes that roiled the Federalists and weakened their movement. These disputes received further fuel as Jedidiah Morse publicly protested against both Ware and the female author Hannah Adams.

The Unitarian Federalist Politics of John Adams

As one of the best-known and nationally recognized Federalists, John Adams's treatment of religion in public life gave national exposure to Federalist attitudes about religion.[9] As president and party leader, Adams could (largely) serve as a rallying cry for his party.[10] Although Adams's religious beliefs evolved throughout his life, it is fair to describe him as a rationalist Christian and a Unitarian.[11] Still, his core beliefs about religion and society remained relatively constant, even if emphases differed during his long political career.[12] Adams demonstrated a rationalist Unitarian politics on both state and national levels. He argued for the political benefit of public religiosity and practiced it throughout his career.

Adams's Unitarian public religion took three forms, roughly corresponding with three phases of his public life. First, in the lead-up to the revolution, Adams demonstrated an accommodation of religious and revolutionary principles. Rather than opposing the spirit of Protestant Christianity and the spirit of liberty, Adams tied them together. Second, in the years of Constitution-making, Adams worked to continue a public Christianity, while securing toleration—not full religious liberty—for other religious groups in Massachusetts. Fully in support of the Congregational establishment, Adams allowed for spaces where other religious beliefs might flourish. Third, in his presidency, Adams made use of public expressions of religion as a support of his Federalist administration. In these ways, Adams attempted to secure public acknowledgment of corporate religion and to unite religious believers for political ends. These strategies all supported the Republican outlook on religion forged by the revolution.

Religion and Liberty in the Imperial Struggle

Adams was powerfully shaped by the religious character of the New England society in which he was raised. More than just growing up in a devout Congregationalist family, Adams personally took a moralistic and even religious stance toward his political involvement. He carried on, in secularized form, the seriousness of New England Puritanism.[13] Further, Adams grasped the deeply religious character of New England's public culture. To rally support against Britain he drew upon the region's history and culture and crafted an account of New England's religion in alliance with rationalist, Republican principles. This would lay the groundwork for his subsequent activities as a Federalist politician and president.

This rationalist strategy is evident in Adams's early *Dissertation on the Canon and Feudal Law* (1765). In the *Dissertation*, Adams decried the oppression of the Middle Ages, in which church ("canon law") and state ("feudal law") combined to subjugate the entire population. He then traced a history by which "God in his benign providence" directed the Reformation to overthrow that combination. The work was carried further by "a sensible people," the Puritans.[14] Hence New England society was shaped by a commitment to "universal liberty." In these formulations, Adams combined religion and rationalism. New England society "was founded in revelation, and in reason too"; it was built "on the foundation of the Bible and common sense."[15] Adams placed his republican values of liberty squarely in the center of New England's religious experience. In his language, he constantly treated religious and civil rights as inseparable. Because of this alignment, he could deliver his moral: "Be it remembered, however, that liberty must at all hazards be supported. We have a right to it derived from our maker. But if we had not, our fathers have earned and bought it for us."[16] Adams placed this liberty at the heart of New England's history and tied it firmly to New England's religious mission.

Adams continued this attack in subsequent years, again using religion to support American liberty in his "John Winthrop" letters. Taking the voice of Massachusetts's Puritan first governor, Adams rooted his case in the region's history and religion. Adams argued that the region had been founded on "English, humane, and Christian principles"—again harmonizing rationalism and religion. The end result was to create a proper "constitution" for both "church and state" that defended liberty. Religion supported liberty, but in Adams's treatment, liberty itself took on religious meaning. "The world, the flesh, and the devil," Adams warned, "have always maintained a confederacy against her [liberty], from the fall of Adam to this hour."[17] Liberty became a spiritual good for New Englanders to support. Those who would oppose it, such as the British, were clearly taking a demonic role. It became a spiritual duty to oppose encroachments on American liberties. Adams's rhetorical redefinition of things would work well as a rationalist attempt to rally New Englanders to oppose England.

Religion and Constitution-Making

During the revolutionary era, Adams was also involved in the process of constitution-making and therefore had to struggle with the formal place of religion in his native state of Massachusetts. While actively supporting the continued Congregational establishment, Adams showed some concern for the rights of religious minorities. In this way, he demonstrated a rationalist public religiosity that allowed a public role for religion while permitting freedom of thought (though not freedom of the purse) for other groups.

Although Adams had run across opposition to the Massachusetts establishment earlier—he confronted Baptist and Quaker opposition in the lead-up to independence, for example—his major contribution to the cause of a constitutional, legally supported place for public religion came in 1779.[18] In that year, he served as part of the Massachusetts Constitutional Convention. Adams became the prime actor in the subcommittee charged with drafting the text of the entire constitution—the same committee Caleb Strong worked on. In addition to implementing his theories about government and the balancing of interests within society, drafting the constitution gave Adams the power to institutionalize public Congregationalism. Adams began with a statement of the necessity of public religion: "It is the Duty of all men in society, publickly, and at stated seasons to worship the SUPREME BEING, the great Creator and preserver of the Universe."[19] Adams clearly intended religious belief to be part of the commonwealth, and other provisions would clarify how it would function.[20] Adams proposed a religious test of Christian belief for the governor, legislators, and all state officials.[21] Although the convention restricted these requirements—requiring the religious test and oath only for the governor, lieutenant governor, and legislators—Adams's suggestion of these provisions should not be overlooked. Adams clearly believed a general Protestantism needed to have a substantial public presence in society. On the other hand, Adams also made some provisions for the rights of individual religious conscience. The same article guaranteed that "no subject shall be hurt, molested, or restrained, in his person, liberty, or estate, for worshipping GOD in the manner most agreeable to the dictates of his own conscience; or, for his religious profession or sentiments."[22] Adams opposed an oath (later approved) that would specifically ban Roman Catholic participation in government.

Despite these protections, they were not enough for Baptists and other groups outside of the establishment, who still found such arrangements burdensome. These evangelical groups instead opposed all religious establishments, believing that churches and individuals functioned best as free responses to the Christian message. To them, the presence of religious taxes—even if they could be evaded—hurt both the churches and the state. This would later incline them toward supporting the Democratic-Republicans.[23]

Adams declined writing the most controversial element of the constitution, the actual establishment clause in article 3. "I could not satisfy my own Judgment with any Article that I thought would be accepted," he confessed. "Some of the Clergy, or older and graver persons than myself would be more likely to hit the Taste of the Public."[24] Still, once drafted by others, Adams fully supported it and defended it in debate. When the constitution was approved, Adams believed he had succeeded in both guaranteeing public religiosity and the rights of conscience for other groups, even if those outsider groups disagreed.

Religion and the Presidency

As president, Adams was confronted with numerous challenges, including conflict with the French republic abroad and tension with the Democratic-Republicans at home. One of Adams's responses to these challenges was to draw on religious sensibilities to strengthen the connection felt between himself and the populace. The political end would be to cement the people's connection to the Federalist administration, for the continued prevalence (to his mind) of order, good government, and public religiosity.

Adams's attempt to continue public religious language in the presidency began with his inaugural address. Opening with a quick survey of the history of the nation, Adams asserted that those who pushed for independence had done so "under an overruling Providence, which had so signally protected this country from the first." Although perhaps a customary observation, Adams did not leave that as his only statement about religion. Rather, he highlighted at several additional points his commitment to a public religion. In this vein, it made sense that Adams would close with a prayer, asking, "May that Being, who is supreme over all, the patron of order, the fountain of justice, and the protector, in all the ages of the world of virtuous liberty, continue his blessing upon this nation and its government, and give it all possible success and duration, consistent with the ends of his providence!" Adams's characterization of God as the source of order, justice, and virtuous liberty shows a strong grounding of his public politics on theistic belief, which explains why he would acknowledge providential involvement with the nation's affairs.[25]

Adams also used the inaugural to highlight his belief that religion would support the republic. He voiced his desire "to patronize . . . every institution for propagating knowledge, virtue, and religion among all classes of people." Adams reiterated that, not only would such institutions provide "benign influence on the happiness of life," but more importantly, they were "the only means of preserving our constitution from its natural enemies," including party, intrigue, corruption, and foreign influence. Seeing religion, virtue, and knowledge as intertwined categories, Adams wished to encourage them for a political purpose—the defense of the Constitution. They thus served a very significant civic purpose. Adams later observed his "veneration for the religion of a people, who profess and call themselves Christians, and a fixed resolution to consider a decent respect for Christianity among the best recommendations for public service." Adams thus presented himself as respectful toward the institutions of Christianity. For Adams, this was not only a personal opinion but a decided qualification for serving as a chief executive and a principle that would guide his conduct.[26] Although himself a rationalist, Adams was willing to import public religion to the national stage.

Adams continued to use such religious language in subsequent addresses to Congress. For example, later in 1797, Adams would indicate his pleasure at Americans' continued commitment to "a rational spirit of civil and religious liberty, and a calm but steady determination to support our sovereignty, as well as our moral and religious principles." Again, political and religious liberty went together, and the presence of both morality and religion could serve as defenses against threats to the republic, such as the French. Observing that "the state of society has so long been disturbed," Adams hoped that morality and religion would work together to buttress civil society, and as president he worked to encourage that.[27]

Nowhere was this strategy more prominent than in his use of national fast day proclamations. As conflict with France rose, Adams called two national fasts in March 1798 and March 1799 respectively. In this, Adams was reflecting the traditions of New England, as well as carrying on actions instituted by George Washington. He thereby created the public environment in which Timothy Dwight and Jedidiah Morse could issue warnings about the dangers of infidelity and the Illuminati. The language of these fast proclamations is noteworthy and decidedly evangelical. The 1798 fast, for instance, instructed Americans to "Acknowledge before God the manifold sins and transgressions with which we are justly chargeable as individuals and as a nation; beseeching him at the same time, of his infinite grace, through the Redeemer of the world, freely to remit all our offences, and to incline us, by his Holy Spirit, to that sincere repentance and reformation which may afford us reason to hope for his inestimable favor and heavenly benediction."[28]

With these fasts given under Adams's signature, most Americans freely assumed that Adams was comfortable using such devout language. Only many years later did Presbyterian Ashbel Green reveal that, in fact, he was the coauthor with the other chaplain of Congress, Episcopal Bishop William White. Green observed that he had written the fast proclamation "to remove the complaint which I knew the religious community of our country had made, namely, that the [previous] proclamation calling them to the duty of thanksgiving or fasting lacked a decidedly Christian spirit, I resolved to write one of an evangelical character." Green recounted that Adams only changed a few words and then released it, producing "ardent and general" praise from American Christians. Green recognized but ultimately excused Adams's oratorical sleight of hand, claiming that "the sanction given it [the proclamation] by the President made it virtually his own act."[29] By allowing Green to write the proclamation, Adams stood to gain in his standing among religious Americans—as he did—without revealing his own more rationalist beliefs.

Adams also employed religious language in his responses to the petitions and addresses that flooded the capital during the "War Fever" of 1798. Federalists across the country organized these petitions as a means of expressing support for the government, and many included religious language. Adams's ability to respond with a religious sensibility strengthened his appeal.[30] In one particularly pointed address to the grand jurors of Hampshire, Massachusetts, Adams attacked the religious reforms and process of dechristianization in the French Revolution. Observing that "a new order of things has commenced," he warned that "it behoves us to be cautious, that it may not be for the worse." Adams told the jurors that he was open to processes that would diminish the abuse of Christianity. Yet, he suggested, "This will not be accomplished by the abolition of Christianity and the introduction of Grecian mythology, . . . by erecting statues of idolatry to reason or virtue, to beauty or to taste." In referencing Jacobin attempts to institute the "Festival of Reason" and other secular celebrations, Adams saw not advance but political and religious oppression, as he decried "the present reign of pretended philosophy in France."[31] This "pretended philosophy" was just another form of tyranny. By opposing French religious innovation, Adams cast doubt on their entire system and implicitly pledged himself to the defense of American religious practice.

In his replies, Adams used religious language to articulate religious and political principles. This went far beyond merely referring to God as "the Source of light and power," the "God of armies," or "the God of our fathers."[32] Instead, Adams described the importance of religious and political liberty and the close connection of religion and public morality. Moreover, public morality could not be supported without religion. As Adams told the students of Princeton, "You may find that the moral principles, sanctified and sanctioned by religion, are the only bond of union, the only ground of confidence of the people in one another, of the people in the government, and the government in the people."[33] Such ideas continued the rationalist instrumentalism that Adams had pioneered in previous years.

In these replies, Adams also laid out a political vision that connected religion to his larger concern for resistance to revolutionary change. In contrasting the French and American experiences, he asserted that the French constitution, laws, and experience were "essentially different from ours." The French had experienced "the prostitution of morals and depravation of manners." These declines prepared them to be misled by "the wildest philosophy which was ever professed in this world." This speculative attempt at reform had produced in France a "rage for innovation," which Adams decried because it threatened to overturn delicate balances within society that had protected citizens.[34] Adams associated ideology with unhealthy innovation and wild philosophy. Lacking an empirical foundation, false thinking was bound to produce confusion and destruction.

Adams insisted that "justice, morality, or piety" were necessary for the United States: "Nothing is more certain and demonstrable than that free republicanism cannot exist without these."[35] Further, Adams praised the importance of law for protecting liberty—a safeguard that the French had trampled roughshod. As he told the grand jury of Morris County, New Jersey, "That the laws must be obeyed in a government of laws, is an all important lesson. For what can be more destructive of liberty and property than government without law?"[36] Once laws and constitutions were established, they needed to be respected. To protect them, Adams suggested not only the military defense of the country—which Americans were preparing in 1798—but the avoidance of the "principles and manners which are now producing desolation in so many parts of the world." The best inoculation against those dangers was a renewal of morality and religion. As Adams insisted, "Our Constitution was made only for a moral and religious people. It is wholly inadequate to the government of any other."[37] While decrying the politics of the French Revolution, Adams was simultaneously encouraging a virtuous and religious American republic, and Adams was willing to use both ideals for political ends in his appeal to the nation.

All of Adams's pronouncements—his addresses, his fast day proclamations, his responses to petitions in 1798–1799—demonstrate why Federalists in 1800 could champion him as the "religious president," the candidate of public religion. For Federalists of either Unitarian or evangelical stripe, Adams's public religion was a compelling reason to support him. Although the appeal may have swayed some, it failed to convince voters—many of whom were also evangelicals—in Democratic-Republican strongholds. Adams lost and found himself forcibly returned to private life—a fate awaiting many other Federalists.

Henry Ware and the Unitarian Federalist Clergy

In a manner similar to John Adams, Henry Ware, Sr., rose from a farming family to become a Unitarian leader. Born in 1764 to a yeoman family in Sherburne, Massachusetts, Ware had little chance of formal schooling until his brothers pooled their inheritances so he could attend college. Ware matriculated at Harvard, graduating in 1785. He then read theology with Timothy Hilliard, the pastor of the First Church, Cambridge, and in 1787, he accepted the pastorate at the First Church in Hingham.[38]

Ware's ministry demonstrates both a Unitarian allegiance to Federalist politics and the distinctions of Unitarian outlooks from evangelical Federalists. Ware emphasized four elements in common with other Unitarians. First, morality became a central feature of religion. In contrast to an evangelical focus on conversion, Ware saw moral formation and training as necessary for developing Christians. Second, Ware connected this morality with the health of the republic. Drawing on a Republican strategy that dated to the revolution, Ware insisted that the moral condition of the nation would determine its political success. To encourage this, Ware endorsed, third, a public religiosity like John Adams. This accorded with the New England tradition of public religion, but its purposes were more moralistic and civil-religious than the evangelical outlook. Finally,

Henry Ware, Sr., the Hollis Chair of Divinity at Harvard. James Frothingham. *Henry Ware, Sr. (1764–1845),* c. 1810. Oil on canvas. (Harvard Art Museums/ Fogg Museum, Harvard University Portrait Collection. Gift of John F. Langmaid, Jr., in memory of his wife, Dorothea Ware Langmaid, great-great-granddaughter of Henry Ware, Sr. H729. Photo: Imaging Department © President and Fellows of Harvard College)

Ware endorsed social order and hierarchy as necessary for political good, a tribute to the elitist outlook of many Unitarians, despite his own humble background.

Ware's two published sermons of the 1790s both addressed political themes. In 1795, Ware published his thanksgiving sermon, preached in response to Washington's thanksgiving proclamation. Ware's sermon shows his similarities to evangelical Federalists, while also revealing differences in emphasis. In common with other Federalists, Ware celebrated the establishment of the constitutions of both the United States and the state of Massachusetts and believed they should fill the citizens' "lips with praise to the benign Author of all good." Ware's comment pointed to the way he cast a religious mantle over public activities. "For all these public blessings and marks of private prosperity, which distinguish our condition as a people and as individuals," he told his congregants, "let the just tribute of our united thanks ascend this day, as an acceptable sacrifice to that God, by whose providence we enjoy them all." Ware would willingly acknowledge a divine involvement in both the nation's formation and continuation. He invited his hearers to notice "the footsteps of a kind providence in our national concerns."[39] Ware's language carried forward religious content from the revolutionary period, and he used it to embrace the still-young constitutional order.

Along with evangelicals, Ware saw dangers arising from both French principles and French sympathizers in America. Ware pointed out that he, along with many other Americans, had sympathized with the French and even overlooked some of their excesses of violence, but he now repudiated their actions, especially since they had taken to abusing American friendship. Further, Ware warned against the antireligious stance of the revolution. He suggested that the French had gone to the extreme of conflating all religion with oppressive superstition. As a result, Ware warned against "the atheistic sentiments so openly avowed and publicly countenanced," and celebrated how Washington's thanksgiving proclamation worked against those sentiments. In addition to dangers from abroad, Ware warned about domestic threats. He saw great danger in the "societies in imitation of the jacobin clubs in France." He decried how these groups endeavored "by seditious and inflammatory publications . . . to poison the public mind,—to deceive the people . . . and rouse their passions." By wrongfully claiming to defend the liberties of the people, they were invidiously undermining the Washington administration.[40] In seeing a religious element to the conflict with France—and by extension to their American sympathizers—Ware had much in common with evangelical Federalists.

At the same time, Ware revealed differences in emphases that marked potential future divergence. Ware throughout the sermon celebrated public order to a much greater extent than some evangelical Federalists. He wanted to defend "the present order of things," and to him the Federalists were the "firm friends to *liberty with order.*" Ware thus revealed his passion for the social and political order that he believed constitutionally preserved republican liberties, thereby holding "liberty with order" in creative tension. For Ware, the danger was "licentiousness and disorder," and disorder was linked to moral decline. Because "freedom and order can be supported only in an enlightened and virtuous community," Ware stressed the importance of moral training. Moral formation would happen through the process of education to form "habits of *sobriety, order, morality and piety*."[41] This moral formation would occur alongside religious training, but it was not linked to conversion per se. Ware's emphasis on moral training would only grow in subsequent years.

Ware again addressed the public with a sermon commemorating the death of Washington. As with many other Federalist clergy, he used the opportunity not only to memorialize Washington but to advance Federalist political ideals. The primary instruction that Ware took from Washington's life was the need to support established governors. He asserted that Washington had achieved his great success because of the public confidence he possessed. Rulers' "best plans for promoting the public good may be prevented . . . unless we their constituents, after putting the administration of government into their hands, are ready to aid them in it with our cheerful confidence and firm support." This call to support rulers echoed Federalist claims that rulers, once installed, be allowed to govern with minimal interference. Ware took it a step farther, however, by making an explicit statement in favor of the Adams administration.[42] Ware thus articulated a view of public support of religion similar to many other religious Federalists, but his attention to public morality was definitely more pronounced.

Even after Adams's electoral loss, Ware remained in his pastoral role while confronting a fragmenting Congregationalist establishment. With the death of minister and Professor of Divinity David Tappan, the Trinitarians lost their moderate Calvinist voice at Harvard. The college's governing body, the Corporation, confronted serious disagreements in filling the Hollis Chair of Divinity, which Tappan had held. When the more liberal and rationalist party came to dominate, they elected Ware to the chair. Ware would spend the rest of his life at Harvard College and Harvard Divinity School, teaching theology and moral theory. For many at the time, Ware's election signified the triumph of Unitarians at Harvard.[43]

Ware's presence at Harvard provided him with a firm position to advance Unitarian ideals through ecclesiastical activity, theological polemics, and the nurturing of Harvard's Unitarian character. The year 1806, for instance, found him involved in an ordination service for Rev. Charles Lowell at the West Church in Boston, surrounded by rationalists and Unitarians. Unitarian Eliphalet Porter preached the main sermon, and prominent Unitarian minister Joseph Stevens Buckminster offered "the right hand of fellowship." It fell to Ware to charge the candidate to his duties, and he challenged Lowell to receive "the plain unequivocal doctrines of the bible alone." The Unitarian interpretation of scripture, however, had by this time clearly diverged from that of Trinitarian Congregationalists, even as both groups claimed the scriptures as their source of inspiration.[44] This divergent appeal to scripture and reason appeared strongly in Ware's sparring with Andover Seminary's professor of theology Leonard Woods in the famed "Woods and Ware Debate" (1819–23). In this extensive exchange of books and pamphlets that set forth the best arguments of both sides, Ware appealed both to scripture and to an Enlightened sense of morality to argue against Trinitarianism.[45] Ware also became deeply committed to the life of Harvard College and helped to found Harvard Divinity School, where he encouraged "liberal and enlightened" doctrines.[46] As Ware stressed virtue in private life as the distinguishing mark of religion, such emphasis tended to downplay political engagement. At this point, Ware had accepted the state of society and merely hoped for virtuous individuals to preserve and improve it incrementally.

In 1821, Ware was invited to deliver the Election Day sermon for the state, and he used it to lecture public officials on the ties between universal benevolence produced by Christianity and good governance. Addressing John Brooks—Caleb Strong's Federalist successor—and the legislature, Ware set out to give advice to the "assembly of christian rulers" to guide them "in all their endeavors to promote the public good." After laying down some general principles, Ware turned to particular policy advice, emphasizing the value of education. He claimed that "it should be the great object of a christian government" to educate all its citizenry. This equitable aid to all citizens would encourage "intellectual, moral, and religious education."[47] Ware's support for education is not surprising, given his position at Harvard. Nonetheless, it was a continuation of themes he had earlier insisted on, as he saw in state-sponsored education the proper means of maintaining morality and a "christian" society.

At the same time, Ware approved of the continued Federalist disposition of the state of Massachusetts. Citizens continued to elect Federalists to office and support the Massachusetts constitution. "We have learned," Ware intoned, "that there is not in [the citizens] that restlessness and love of change, which would make them willing, in pursuit of an unattainable object, to put at hazard all that is valuable in their civic institutions." Ware found the source of this success in the institutions "for religious instruction, for general education, and for the general diffusions of knowledge and virtue," and in the "general respect paid to the Christian Sabbath, and the worship of God in public assemblies."[48] Because Massachusetts remained faithful to its public religiosity and educational institutions, it maintained the virtues necessary to continue a self-governing Federalist state.

In many ways, then, Ware maintained a general Federalist political outlook even as the party had dissolved across the nation. Only in eastern Massachusetts, with its strong Federalist character, could the illusion be maintained that this approach could permanently succeed. At the same time, his emphases pointed in a Unitarian direction. As a Harvard professor, his focus on education seems obvious, but that direction also stemmed from a Unitarian sense of education as the grounds for moral formation. Further, only because of his experiences in elite eastern Massachusetts society could he believe that social order and harmony were not threatened. Most remarkable is his chastened yet optimistic tone for the state. Even as the period of Federalist politics receded, he hoped for an orderly, moral political order to continue.

Theological and Political Controversies

It is conceivable that the differences between evangelicals and Unitarians within the Federalist party could have been contained, relegated to differences in emphasis or preference. Instead, because the Federalists had tied religious and political matters together, religious differences had incredible capacity for becoming political differences. Indeed, this is exactly what happened, first in conflict over Harvard College, then over a publishing dispute between Hannah Adams and Jedidiah Morse. Through these controversies in Massachusetts, the theological differences of the camps became exposed. In working for separation, both sides alienated their political allies. The pursuit of purity worked to fragment the party and drain the energy it would need to beat back the surging Democrats.

The first conflict, over Harvard College's professor of divinity, would test whether these competing versions of religious Federalism could continue cooperating with each other in the nineteenth century. They decidedly failed the challenge. The controversy, which spanned 1804 and 1805, revealed differing goals not only for Harvard but for society. Henry Ware's appointment to the Hollis Chair of Divinity was thus much more than an academic decision or a theological triumph. These battles contributed to strong schisms among religious Federalists.

Jedidiah Morse's evangelical goals for Harvard aimed for a continued orthodox institution that would possess religious weight to shape society. In his pamphlet published shortly after Ware's appointment, Morse complained about Ware's writings—they could be accepted by "an Arminian, Arian, or a Universalist"—and that Ware's appointment violated the spirit of the bequest by Thomas Hollis for an orthodox Calvinist to hold his chair. Even more troubling to Morse was the effect such a Unitarian professor of divinity would have "on the religious and moral character of our citizens." He bemoaned how "the faith of our churches should become less pure" and "the standard of christian morality lowered."[49] Morse feared both the inevitable religious decline and the resulting moral decline: bad theology would trouble society. As Morse confided to a fellow clergyman, "Unitarianism dissolves all the bond of Christian union & deprives religion of all its efficacy and influence upon society."[50] These concerns were echoed by Morse's Trinitarian ally Eliphalet Pearson, who in private debates about the Hollis Chair urged that "the University stands in some such relation to the body politic & the church of Christ, as the heart does to the body natural."[51] Because the ideas and beliefs would circulate through all of society just as a heart transmits blood, the central teaching posts at Harvard needed to be protected by the orthodox.

By contrast, Unitarians argued for a broader, more tolerant religious vision that could embrace a diversifying commercial society. Morse's approach was an annoyance and distraction to this larger cultural agenda. This was best expressed by "Constant Reader" who wrote to the *Centinel* to declare, "Whether the candidates for the President and Theological Chairs, be Calvinists, Arians, Socinians, or Latitudinarians, is not of so much importance as whether they are learned, pious, moral men."[52] Piety and morality, with minimal regard for a specific theological position— this broadly suited the Unitarians who pushed for changes at Harvard. Valuing social and political stability, Unitarian Federalist leaders hoped to preserve Harvard's "existing cultural and institutional identity" and its capacity for "readying a new Federalist generation for the moment when 'political fortune' might smile once again."[53] To this end, a theological precisionist would unduly narrow the character of the institution, while someone like Henry Ware could seem very appealing.

Both sides brought their outlooks from political battles to the Harvard controversy, but Morse especially viewed the Harvard cause as akin to the

political battles he had waged in the previous decade. Morse worried that
the college was "most imminently threatened with a revolution which
will deeply & lastingly affect the cause of evangelical truth."[54] Revolution
in college governance presaged a revolution in theological truth, and he
opposed both. In another letter, Morse declared, "I consider Unitarianism as the *democracy* of Christianity."[55] That political categories could be
imported into this theological debate demonstrates the salience of both
for Morse's thought and explains how religious conflict could generate
political conflict. By coming to view longstanding allies in Federalist politics as more like their political opponents than relevant friends, Morse
demonstrated how much ground had been traversed.

The result was to drive a significant wedge between evangelical and
Unitarian Federalists. In statements by the evangelicals, a definite sense
of betrayal emerged. Morse was most impassioned, declaring, "It is un-
fortunate that a number of the ablest federalists are engaged (with truly
Jacobinic arts) in revolutionizing [Harvard] college."[56] To use the arts of
the French Jacobins, their longtime enemies, was the final insult. Similarly, Eliphalet Pearson wondered, "Can Federalists then adopt a policy
and make use of weapons in the cause of *religion*, which they so justly
brand with infamy in the cause of politics?"[57] This was a *cri de coeur* over
the betrayal of one Federalist by another. Because this split occurred *between* Federalist groups, the result was particularly bitter.[58] Moreover,
this religious split contributed to a breakdown of party cooperation at a
time when it could be least afforded in the political realm.

The subsequent activities of Morse and the evangelicals would keep
theological conflict alive and simultaneously poison the possibility of
political cooperation. Evangelical responses took several forms. Calvinists of several stripes put their differences aside to found Andover Seminary, to be led by Leonard Woods, the future theological sparring partner
of Henry Ware.[59] Trinitarians founded Park Street Church on Boston
Common, creating a beachhead for orthodox theology in Unitarian-
dominated Boston. Finally, Morse created the *Panoplist* magazine as a
means of keeping continued attention on Unitarian malfeasance.[60] These
activities, which stretched for a decade after the controversy over Harvard, produced ongoing tensions for Federalists and demonstrated that
religion could be a hindrance to partisan cooperation as well as a help.

Just as the dispute at Harvard was coming to a head, Morse became
involved in another controversy that further soured his standing in Boston society and contributed to even larger divisions between evangelical
and Unitarian Federalists. In this case, Morse became embroiled in a dis-

pute over legal and literary responsibilities with the female writer Hannah Adams, a distant cousin of John Adams. Hannah Adams was one of the first American women to make her living by her pen as a nonfiction writer on historical and religious subjects. Religiously, Adams was most at home among Boston's genteel Unitarians, although she herself never wrote as an outright Unitarian.[61] In 1799, Adams had published her *Summary History of New-England*, which focused extensively on New England in the American Revolution.[62] She likely intended to abridge it for use in schools at some point in the future. In 1804, though, she received news that Jedidiah Morse and his fellow Federalist clergyman Elijah Parish had published their own history of New England, *A Compendious History of New England*, a work with a religious emphasis (and hence a different organizing principle than Adams's).[63] Adams felt her authorial territory had been violated, and she was worried that Morse and Parish's history would be purchased by schools, depriving her of potential future income on which she had been depending. Adams approached Morse after a sermon and awkwardly asked if he would object to her printing an abridgement of her history. Morse assured her that he was "perfectly willing" to allow her to publish such a work. The two left with utterly different interpretations of the conversation. Morse believed he had indicated he had no power to stop her from publishing another book in competition to his; Adams believed this was an assurance that Morse would remove his history from the market. The misinterpretations of this exchange would reverberate for a decade.[64]

The trouble arising from this misunderstanding began almost at once. Morse quickly sent Adams a letter clarifying that, although she was free to publish an abridgement, he and Parish still retained the right to publish their own. Adams objected on the grounds that she was a poor woman with a moral right to possible future income. Supported by Unitarians such as Joseph Stevens Buckminster and wealthy layman William Shaw, Adams went ahead with her *Abridgement of the History of New-England*.[65] Morse and Parish responded with their own revision, and Adams turned to powerful male advocates for help, including Buckminster, Shaw, and most importantly socially prominent Stephen Higginson, Jr. As biographer Gary Schmidt summarizes this conflict, "What might have been a small, if bitter rivalry turned into a battle between Adams and the religious liberal establishment of Boston, against Morse and the Calvinistic establishment of Boston. It became a miniature version of the larger battle for New England's theological soul."[66]

This controversy escalated as letters flew between the principals, but

Morse and Adams never once met face to face after their first encounter. The controversy soon reached print. In 1805, the Unitarian *Monthly Anthology* reviewed both histories in a single essay, praising Adams's and demeaning Morse's. Liberal Boston came to despise Morse, and frustration from the struggle over Ware's appointment to Harvard continued to poison perceptions. To clear his reputation, Morse submitted the case to three referees. The individuals selected were all Federalists, but all members of the liberal party: John Davis, Thomas Dawes, and Samuel Dexter. Morse went ahead with this plan despite the concern raised by friends, including Timothy Dwight, that this was a dangerous escalation which limited Morse's ability to respond. The resulting decision granted that, legally, Morse and Parish owed nothing to Adams, but the referees insisted that she was owed "attention and respect" as a result of "moral concerns"—a Unitarian construction of the award. Morse refused to accept that this included financial compensation, and Adams refused to settle for anything short of financial remuneration and recognition of her being wronged.[67]

The controversy renewed in 1812, with Morse taking new steps to clear his reputation. He pushed unsuccessfully for a personal meeting with Adams. Morse was growing desperate to remove a possible financial penalty at a time when he had suffered several business reversals. He continued to deny any financial compensation was due to Adams, but behind this assertion lay his straitened economic standing, which made it impossible to pay her anything. He continued to pester the original referees until they forthrightly told him that they believed some financial recompense was due.[68] Morse's final contribution came in the summer of 1814 with an almost two-hundred-page book, and Adams answered with a quiet pamphlet of her own. The controversy finally died, unresolved, in 1815. Although he had paid no money, Morse's reputation had been badly damaged.[69]

Although the Hannah Adams dispute was not immediately connected to the Unitarian controversies, Morse and his allies connected them in their minds. The full title of Morse's final book was *An Appeal to the Public, on the Controversy Respecting the Revolution in Harvard College, and the Events Which Have Followed It; Occasioned by the Use Which Has Been Made of Certain Complaints and Accusations of Miss Hannah Adams, against the Author.* Morse believed that the Adams controversy flowed from the Harvard conflict. Adams herself was just a pawn, controlled by more powerful Unitarian forces. Further, in writing to Adams, Morse identified her protectors as "my enemies," and he insinuated that she was being duped into attacking him.[70] Morse was correct that some of the animus involved in the controversy arose from the Harvard controversy, but he missed the ways in which his actions and attitudes also worsened it. Still, this perception of religious conflict would lead to greater polarization between the camps.[71]

Moreover, this conflict had a political component, as is evident in a booklet published anonymously but written by Morse's son Sidney. Sidney began his presentation by denying that the works of his father and Adams were similar enough to impinge on each other. With different emphases, they would not interfere. He then went on to examine what he considered the real motivations of Jedidiah's antagonists, and he found that the claims "have been magnified, inflamed and distorted for *religious* purposes and to destroy his influence in the *religious* world"—hearkening back to the entire Unitarian controversy.[72] In this attack, Sidney framed the debate around rightful claims of Federalists. Just as the Federalists held to a strict interpretation of the Constitution, so a strict interpretation of Harvard's founding and the Hollis professorship was required. To deny both was a "liberal" approach. In rebutting a review of Morse's *Appeal to the Public,* Sidney concluded, "We have now done with this man's *politics.* They may be summed up in one word; He is a *true Jacobin.*" By cutting present action apart from founding principles, Boston's Federalist elite had opened themselves up to the very principles of French Jacobinism. The underlying reason for this shift was religious. "We may add too," Sidney continued, "that the *Unitarianism* which he advocates is the genuine *Jacobinism* of Christianity."[73] Repeating Jedidiah's claims, Sidney was tying the dangers of the "liberal" party in religious matters to revolutionary political radicalism. The Morse family and their evangelical friends could not imagine how potential political allies could tolerate such heterodox opinions, and this undermined political trust and willingness to work together. Religious heresy presaged a descent into political heresy, away from the principles of Federalism.

The Morses' continued attacks on Unitarian religion thus also had a political logic to them. This combined religious and political outlook drove Jedidiah—while the Hannah Adams controversy was unresolved—to open one more significant attack on Unitarians. In 1815, Morse used the publication of a biography of the English Unitarian Theophilus Lindsey to paint all of Massachusetts's liberal rationalists as Unitarians of the worst sort. The doctrinal "defection had proceeded in the downward course," wrote Morse, "to the very borders of . . . infidelity."[74] Morse claimed that Unitarianism had spread secretly, just like Jacobinism, and he believed countering it required public controversy to illuminate the different religious beliefs. At stake was nothing less than "whether Christianity shall exist in any thing more than a name in our country, or be supplanted by the new philosophy." If Christianity itself was at stake, strong measures were required, and this prompted his call to "let the orthodox separate in worship and communion from Unitarians."[75] Morse's attacks stirred up liberal opinion in Boston and caused a number of responses, most articulately from the younger Unitarian William Ellery Channing.[76] Through these attacks, Morse succeeded in driving a wedge between moderate Congregationalists and Unitarians. Historian Conrad Wright reflected on the ironic result, commenting, "So in a curious inverted way, Jedidiah Morse was the founder of American Unitarianism as a distinct religious denomination."[77] In this campaign to drive Unitarians apart from Congregationalists, Morse succeeded. Politically, though, he managed to sour relations between two wings of a weakening Federalist party badly in need of all the cooperation it could muster, not only in Massachusetts but throughout the country.

By the end of these debates, the religious and political landscape within the Federalist party had shifted radically. Gone were the days when liberals and evangelicals could unite on political matters, giving hearty support to the Federalists. Not only did the two camps have differing emphases, but they had proven to each other that they had two opposing theologies. The groups did not drift apart but were instead pried apart by partisans. Both sides demonstrated that even in New England, the cultural unity that Federalists hoped for could not last. Together they had weakened their political position at a time when their entire party was fragmenting. The theological rifts between evangelicals and Unitarians put added strain on the party in their New England heartland. If the party could not succeed there, it had little hope of advancing elsewhere.

6 Religion and Federalism with a South Carolina Accent

IN EARLY 1788, THE SOUTH CAROLINA LAWYER HENRY WILLIAM DE Saussure wrote to maintain a connection established the year before with a visitor from the North—Jedidiah Morse. De Saussure informed Morse of the efforts undertaken to guarantee ratification of the Constitution in his state, since they shared a commitment to its acceptance. "My Situation in the middle states during the four years of life when the principles are fixed, made me a federalist almost involuntarily. Reflection has fixed me so," he wrote. The correspondence continued for years afterward. In 1793, De Saussure celebrated "the adoption of the Constitution & the wise administration of the Government have secured us Internal good order, with the enjoyment of the most Compleat Freedom." The Constitution they had both supported had provided the advantages they had promised its opponents. Yet De Saussure had cause for worry, observing that in France, "the convulsions of dying despotism & of Crumbling Superstition are so violent as to threaten ruin to the Infant liberties of France."[1] Foreign affairs were definitely a concern for commercially minded Charlestonians. When he wrote several years later, De Saussure declared, "It is a pleasure to me to learn that your Sentiments in relation to our political affairs coincide with mine, and that we both appreciate the blessings of a wise & virtuous government, & deprecate a change which might put to extreme hazard those blessings."[2] In 1800, Federalists North and South shared many opinions, as well as fears, about the possible direction of the nation. Constitutional, political, and religious concerns could potentially make De Saussure open to the type of evangelical and Combative Federalism Jedidiah Morse, Timothy Dwight, and other Northerners were developing.

Differing political, social, and economic settings, however, meant that Southern Federalism developed differently than its Northern counterpart.[3] Much of Southern Federalism's character emerged independent of

Northern Federalism, as few connections tied the sectional wings of the party together. Still, a few individuals such as De Saussure and Charles Cotesworth Pinckney attained national prominence or traveled enough to make strategic connections with other Federalists. These South Carolinians illustrate the character of Southern Federalist conservatism, the possibilities for the operation of religion within Southern Federalism, and the limits of those opportunities.

Religion intersected politics differently in the South than the North. Although there was not a direct linkage between denomination and party in the South, historian James Broussard has observed, "there were subsidiary ways in which religion affected the first party system." He has further suggested links existed among certain denominational outlooks and the Federalists, describing a greater affinity for Federalism among Presbyterians, Episcopalians, and the German Reformed. "In spite of these possible relationships between religion and party loyalty," Broussard has observed, "this question has been investigated very little in the South."[4] No historian has subsequently taken up Broussard's challenge. This chapter traces the personal and ideological connections between religious belief and politics for two important South Carolina Federalists, Henry William De Saussure (a Congregationalist and Presbyterian) and Charles Cotesworth Pinckney (an Episcopalian). While allowing for variations within southern Federalism, these two figures offer insights into how religion shaped Southern Federalism and how that process differed from its influence on Northern Federalists.[5] For them, religion was present but not centrally constitutive for their Federalist politics. Religion and politics were both present in their lives but never integrated.

Two significant differences in political context created variation from Northern Federalism. The first was the differing role of religious establishment. In South Carolina, the 1778 state constitution created a multiple establishment for all Protestant denominations, but this practice was ended in the 1790 constitution, leaving complete disestablishment.[6] All groups within the state seemed to accept this arrangement, so the formal power of a state church was never debated during the party struggles of the 1790s through 1810s. This shifted the religious ground in South Carolina by removing a potentially bitter issue and thereby blurring the lines of religio-political dispute. Thus, "establishmentarian" in the South Carolina context meant not supporting an official denominational establishment but rather nurturing a custodial outlook that undergirded the established order in society. Second, the presence of slavery dramatically shaped South Carolina politics. In the early republic, South Carolina functioned as a slave society, where every institution was influenced by and forced to relate to slavery. The concern for slavery ran throughout Federalist politics in the state and limited the religious influences possible by shutting out opinions that would question slavery's standing.

As a result, religion for Southern Federalists functioned in ways different than in New England or the Mid-Atlantic states. The primary mode in which Southern Federalists operated reflected the Republican religious outlook demonstrated by Northern Federalists. For the most part, Southerners never varied far from the approach begun in the revolution. Religion was important and valuable for supporting the social order, but it had only a limited role in Federalist politics. Whereas in the 1790s, Northern Federalists had developed a Combative outlook of impassioned religious politics, this style received only a faint echo in the South. Southerners borrowed some language from Northern Federalists, but it was never delivered with the same passion as farther north. Then, as Northern Federalists developed Voluntarist strategies, Southerners also adopted them but at a slower pace and with less gusto. The result was that by the time Southern Federalism dissolved—and it disappeared at a quicker rate than in the North—the dominant outlook on religion's place in society was still a Republican approach, with a light overlay of Voluntarism.

Politics and Religion in the Career of Henry William De Saussure

De Saussure's life connected at a young age to the events of the American Revolution. Born in 1763, he came of age as the imperial crisis grew. His father was an ardent patriot who traveled in South Carolina and Georgia recruiting for the war. When the British besieged Charleston in 1779, sixteen-year-old Henry William volunteered for its defense. When the city capitulated, he was among the soldiers captured. The British interned him for a time on a prison ship in Charleston Harbor and then paroled him to Philadelphia, where he was reunited with his family and studied law.[7] De Saussure, then, was a young but committed patriot. As he developed his Federalist principles in later years, he would see them within the revolutionary tradition for which he had fought.

De Saussure soon entered professional life as a lawyer. He was admitted to the Philadelphia bar in 1784, and the next year he married Elizabeth Ford of Morristown, New Jersey. They soon sailed for Charleston, where De Saussure established his legal practice. With them traveled Elizabeth's brother, Timothy Ford. Together, De Saussure and Ford formed a legal partnership that—with Elizabeth providing significant practical support—proved financially successful.[8] While practicing law, De Saussure regularly encountered other South Carolina Federalist leaders, such as Charles Cotesworth Pinckney, Thomas Pinckney, and Edward Rutledge.[9]

Just beginning his career, De Saussure expressed proto-Federalist concerns about the weakness of the Confederation government. "We are it is true Independent. But we are not yet a happy people," he told a friend. He located the problems in both the nation's debts and the unwillingness of states to share power with the central government. "Others withhold their assent to measures of general and extensive utility; and necessity, on trifling & local pretences." Given these conditions, he hoped for reform. "We shall either see our folly, and mend, or we shall fall into Anarchy, from which an Energetic Government of some kind must necessarily arise." Here, De Saussure was not using "Energetic" in a positive sense, but with the fear of a government no longer republican. When the Constitution was written, De Saussure approved and actively supported its ratification. As he told Morse, he was "a federalist almost involuntarily." Still, he hoped that "a Spirit of federalism" would spread throughout the union.[10] This commitment to union and constitutional government would long characterize De Saussure's Federalism.

Religious Background

De Saussure came from a strong Protestant heritage, and his activities showed an ongoing commitment to Reformed churches. The De Saussure family traced its roots to Huguenot refugees who migrated to South Carolina in the 1730s.[11] The De Saussures found a religious home in Congregational and Presbyterian churches. In Charleston, Henry William and his wife were members of the Independent Congregational Church, also called the Circular Church. This church had a decidedly evangelical flavor to it, having been founded by William Tennent.[12] One of their ministers, Isaac Keith, corresponded with both Ashbel Green and Jedidiah Morse and so was another connection to Northern evangelicals.[13] When De Saussure moved his family to Columbia, South Carolina, the De Saussures were instrumental in the formation of the First Presbyterian Church. In 1813, he shepherded the church's incorporation documents through the state legislature. Only three years later, he reported to Timothy Ford, "The Presbytery is now sitting here, and our little Church filled up."[14] De Saussure also served on building and pastoral search committees, and he presided over the church's corporation board in the years 1823–28 and 1831–33.[15]

De Saussure's expressions of personal religious belief in his letters and comments indicate traditional Protestant commitments. His friend William Harper described him as "habitually and devoutly religious, according to the faith of his fathers."[16] In reflecting on the death of his wife in 1821, De Saussure praised her piety. She was "a genuine disciple of our God & Saviour. . . . Her sole reliance . . . was on the merits of the Saviour & on the atonement made for fallen man, by his blood shed on the Cross." De Saussure thus identified himself and his family with enunciated Protestant beliefs about salvation. Moreover, he told his friend Judge Thomas Waties that seeing his wife's pious death gave "a genuine & an honest Consolation," which he hoped would stir up himself and his family to Christian obedience and preparation for a similarly devout death.[17]

De Saussure also spoke of God's providential involvement in both the nation and his family. In 1806, De Saussure observed, "The times are becoming very Critical, and I am fearful we shall have trouble in this land, so long favored with peace & prosperity. God in his providence may avert the Evil; & I pray that he may."[18] De Saussure's use of providence went beyond merely the national providentialism so common in the new nation, rising instead to John Jay's belief in God's active involvement in the affairs of both nations and individuals. Through his active church life and reflections on mortality and providence, De Saussure lived out a Southern Reformed faith.[19]

Federalist Politics in the 1790s

Due to a severe "attack of rheumatism," De Saussure and his wife traveled north to New York in 1794. While recuperating there, De Saussure's reputation as a Southern Federalist led to his nomination to direct the U.S. Mint—part of a Federalist strategy to build patronage arrangements with Southerners. He accepted the position in 1795, and on George Washington's suggestion minted the first gold coins for the new nation.[20] After only a few months, he resigned the position. Not only had his health recovered but he complained that the business distracted him from studying law.[21] De Saussure turned the position over to Elias Boudinot. Although the position itself received little public attention, it was important for the nation's finances and had significant effects on De Saussure's Federalism. It reaffirmed his connection to the "friends of government" and brought him into working relationships with many Northern Federalists—not only Washington but also Timothy Pickering and Elias Boudinot. These connections further cemented De Saussure's opinions in support of the Federalists.[22]

Returning to South Carolina, De Saussure soon became engaged with state politics.[23] Writing as Phocion in 1795, he argued in extended newspaper essays against the growing demands of the Upcountry for greater representation in the legislation, based on their larger population.[24] In this case, a writer named Appius (Robert Goodloe Harper) had advanced the argument with the approval of a committee of Upcountry immigrants.[25] De Saussure defended the current arrangement by which the Lowcountry received much greater representation than their population as a result of their wealth.[26] Throughout his argument, he showed an overriding concern for order and stability in governance. He sounded this note in his dedication to Charles Cotesworth Pinckney and Edward Rutledge, in which he stated his essays were designed for "the support of the constitution and the laws, and to advocate the true and permanent interests of the community." Further, in his opening paragraph, De Saussure declared himself "strongly attached to order and good government, well instructed in the happy results of union and social order, and as well apprised of the infinite evils of civil dissentions." This overriding concern for orderly government disposed De Saussure against change. Accepting that the current arrangement was reasonably just, he declined to consider reforms that he believed would cause "dissentions" for only marginal gains.[27]

De Saussure also denounced the plan of equalizing representation because it seemed an abuse of "general theorems or axioms." De Saussure decried the misapplication of political theory. "Perhaps no greater misfortunes have befallen the human race," he asserted, "than those which have resulted from this disposition to carry principles into extremes, and to mistake or abuse their application." In this case, the misapplication came in the principle of equality. De Saussure rejected Appius's contention that equality meant strict numerical equality. When communities attempted to apply theories without proper attention to existing conditions, the results could be disastrous. This fear pushed De Saussure to take a strong antiphilosophical stand, claiming "it may be asserted with safety that there never was a government erected solely on these [axiomatic] foundations, and that many have been reared happily and usefully, without paying the least attention to them." Sounding like Edmund Burke, De Saussure adopted an antitheoretical approach to politics, and, not surprisingly, the negative example he held up was the French

Revolutionaries, who had erred by "too boldly launching into the sea of experiment." Further, De Saussure worried that this misapplication of theory originated from groups who misunderstood South Carolina.[28] Not grasping the wisdom of traditional arrangements, these men would rush to make changes according to theory, rather than the sound practices that had promoted tangible happiness and prosperity. De Saussure's argument may have made sense to Lowcountry Federalists, but it was unlikely to convince many emerging Democratic-Republicans who supported Thomas Jefferson and who were quickly building their numbers in the Upcountry.

In an unexpected diversion, De Saussure also commented on the place of religion in society. He described state-established churches and the oppression of religious sects as examples of theories carried to extremes. This misapplication of valuable beliefs produced misery across Europe. He celebrated, however, that "mankind . . . have just learnt that this union of church and state, and this uniformity in public worship, however plausible and desirable in theory, were utterly destructive of civil and religious liberty, when carried into practice." Experience had taught the overwhelmingly negative consequences of establishments. Instead, De Saussure celebrated "that society exists more harmoniously, happily, and even honestly, when religion is left to operate on men by herself, undefiled and uncorrupted by an impure union with politics, and when individuals are allowed to worship God after their own heart."[29] With South Carolina having disestablished the Anglican Church, De Saussure felt no need to defend it or any establishment. This very different setting than New England produced a contrasting outlook on religion in public matters. If De Saussure was wary of any "impure union" of religion with politics, he would be less likely to use it as a political weapon—as indeed proved the case. He did not abandon the religious polemic strategy entirely, but its presence was more muted than it was in New England.

De Saussure's Phocion letters thus do a remarkable job describing the emphases of South Carolina Federalists. Their primary concern was to maintain a stable social order. Within that, they wanted to continue the prosperity of the state and the protection of property. What they would only grudgingly admit was that that property was inextricably linked with slavery. These Federalists also cherished republican liberty, but they believed that liberty could exist alongside inequality. Indeed they were willing to argue that inequality in a number of realms was not only necessary but natural. To reach this conclusion, they argued from conditions as they were, rather than ideological "axioms." A respect for religion fit within this larger conception of society. Living in a post-establishment environment, they could be tolerant of multiple Protestant Christian denominations, which they expected to support the social order. Although not central, religion remained significant for society.

Conflict with France

The year 1798 saw De Saussure concerned with practical matters involving the threatening war with France. This responsibility was greater since De Saussure had become intendant (mayor) of Charleston and hence responsible for its safety. Writing to Senator Jacob Read, he was direct in his assessment: "War seems inevitable, unless we will submit to a foreign yoke." Fortunately, "Neither the government nor people seem prepared for this degradation. A high national spirit has arisen, to vindicate our Country; & maintain her Independence."[30] This "high national spirit" was magnified in South Carolina due to the indignities Charles Cotesworth Pinckney had suffered at the hands of Talleyrand and the French Directory in the XYZ Affair, as the French demanded bribes in exchange for negotiations. Loyal to its native son, South Carolina showed a marked opposition to France. De Saussure reported to Timothy Pickering, "The language, the Conduct, the authority of Genl. Pinckney's high Character will have a prodigious effect, & be of the utmost utility."[31] The "utility" was to swell—briefly—Federalist ranks, producing both confidence and belligerency.

De Saussure helped to lead the Federalist attempt to channel popular opposition to France. The American Revolution Society invited De Saussure to deliver its Fourth of July oration. The scheduled event was cancelled at the last minute when De Saussure's father died. Instead, the society published the address and distributed it throughout the city. De Saussure's oration made the most of the moment. Echoing other July 4 orations, he recounted the political conflicts of the revolutionary era, the genius of the Declaration of Independence, and the military glory of the heroes of the war. The Constitution was a welcome attempt to "infuse new energies into her government." After delineating the American dreams of peace and prosperity, De Saussure shifted to the controversies with France that had disrupted the 1790s, from Citizen Genet to the XYZ Affair. His call for action showed his explicit linking of the sacrifice of the American Revolution to Federalist calls for military preparedness to counter France in the present: "It only remains for [America] to re-act the heroic part she performed in her revolutionary struggle, and under the protection of God, the same result will follow." To defend the American way of life, De Saussure called for political and military resistance to French oppressions.[32]

Within this context, De Saussure's political use of religion emerged in two ways: as an inherent part of the republic and as a call for action. First, De Saussure praised the national attitude toward religion, claiming "it is of a milder temper, and promises fairer fruit than a harsher system." By abandoning a religious establishment, the nation leaves religious belief "a matter between God and every man's conscience," apart from government interference. Further, De Saussure happily reported, "The Citizen is neither excluded, nor advanced, by his profession of any particular creed." For De Saussure and his South Carolina readers, religious identification counted for less than it did in Northern states. De Saussure concluded his observation by praising the "fruit" of this arrangement: "Bigotry does not exist, and superstition is not known." Religion would inform individuals but not trouble the state.[33]

Second, De Saussure used religious language to call for resistance to France. He made reference to Jacobin projects of dechristianization, arguing, "I would arouse the piety of religious men, by pointing to their altars, in danger of demolition or pollution." Rather than being a central concern for De Saussure, however, it was only one in a long list of reasons to stir his readers to action. De Saussure also closed on a religious note. After taking an oath in God's name to defend the nation's liberties, De Saussure concluded with a prayer: "May the God of our fathers sustain, protect and bless us in the defence of our rights of our country; and may her liberties and independence be immortal." God supported the republican endeavor, although not in an immediate way.[34]

De Saussure's oration clearly contrasts with some of the more religiously charged orations given further North, such as Timothy Dwight's *Duty of Americans, at the Present Crisis*, preached the same day that De Saussure's was to be delivered. Religious concerns were much less central for De Saussure, with his focus more on the political liberties Americans needed to defend.[35] Whereas other evangelical Federalists were moving into a decidedly Combative combination of religion with politics, De Saussure remained within a Republican approach—even at a time when it was likely he would go further. This one oration at the height of tension with France demonstrates a real divergence in how South Carolina Federalists dealt with religion in contrast to their Northern evangelical peers.

Federalist exertions were successful in the short run. By November, De Saussure could inform Timothy Pickering that "thousands who were deluded by French artifices have been enlightened . . . and have turned with loathing from their foreign attachments to the Government of their own Country."[36] De Saussure nurtured the Federalist hope that these energies could be channeled into permanent support of Federalist leadership. When the crisis with France passed, however, much of this energy dissipated.

The Election of 1800 and Afterward

The political conflicts of 1795–1800 sharpened De Saussure's estimation of his opponents as dangerous. He identified them as "our Jacobins." No longer just a faction, they were acting as a fifth column and sending "unwise advice and Communications" to France. "What a lamentable misfortune it is to our country that she bred & nourished such vipers in her bosom," he exclaimed. Since no "Virtuous man" could "be prejudiced agst. his own Country," these opponents clearly lacked virtue and deserved an impassioned political resistance. In 1800, De Saussure declared that the election was between Federalists who wanted "to preserve our Country in peaceful & prosperous neutrality, agst. the Efforts of those who would yoke us to France, & plunge us into war."[37] Again, the notion of Democratic-Republicans as pro-French took the shape for De Saussure that they wanted an active alliance with France, which would produce war with Britain.

De Saussure threw himself into working for Adams and Pinckney in the election of 1800. As he assured Jedidiah Morse, "We are taking measures here to secure the election of Mr. Adams & Genl. Pinckney."[38] By August, he had grown concerned that Federalists were operating "not with as much industry as the opposite party." De Saussure recommitted himself that "no fair exertions will be wasting on our part. We shall converse freely and write fully." He did this, because, as he told Federalist Congressman John Rutledge, Jr., "I have not been able to resist my own impressions of the necessity of exertion, & of ev'ry man's putting his shoulder to the wheel, on this occasion, when the best interests if not the peace & existence of the Country are at stake."[39] Aware of both the stakes and the Democratic opposition, De Saussure worked to match their energy.

As a significant part of that effort, De Saussure contributed to the print controversies of 1800 with two electioneering pamphlets. In one, he responded to a newspaper attack from "Republican," because he deemed the charges leveled against Adams and Pinckney no more than "men of straw." In so doing, De Saussure revealed his Federalist concerns for society and for the implications of the election. He attacked Republican's preference for a change in administration, claiming that it smacked of "that pure democratic spirit" unmixed with constitutional concerns for good government and stability. Instead, De Saussure worried that Republican would promote change as an experiment, not knowing what the outcome would be. De Saussure wanted to hold on to the advantages that the Federalists had produced, proclaiming, "It is not in matters which so immediately concern their best interests, that you will persuade a sensible and thinking people, to become speculators, or to exchange the benefits they possess, for the problematical advantages of experimental theory." The Republicans were advocating undoing the substantive accomplishments of the Federalists in exchange for unknown possibilities.[40]

De Saussure believed this opposition came from longstanding resistance to the government, and like other Federalists, he identified the Republicans with Anti-Federalists. They were "An opposition bottomed party" who intended the election as a means of weakening the constitutional order.[41] Jefferson, as the head of the "party," most fully embodied these dangers. To De Saussure's mind, "He appears to be too much of the theoretical, and too little of the practical statesman. . . . He does not appear to be friendly to our constitution. . . . His being placed in the office of president, added to the election of our federal legislature, of men possessing the same sentiments, would probably be productive of the evils of a revolution."[42] De Saussure feared that Jefferson would undo Federalist successes, including the establishment of the Bank of the United States and the wise policy of diplomatic neutrality. Further, Jefferson would do this as a speculative philosopher, unconcerned with practical consequences.[43] De Saussure suggested that much of Jefferson's theorizing came from his time in France, "where he resided nearly seven years . . . [and] his disposition to theory, and his scepticism in religion, morals, and government acquired full strength and vigor."[44] Jefferson's time in Paris allowed De Saussure to connect him again to the evils of the French Revolution, including its irreligion, and suggest why he was such a dangerous candidate.

Simultaneously, De Saussure supported both Adams and Pinckney. Unstinting in his support for the president, De Saussure praised Adams as fully worthy of "confidence."[45] In his second pamphlet, De Saussure spent multiple pages praising Adams's career and his administration, even defending the Alien and Sedition Acts. Nor did De Saussure limit his praise of Pinckney, whose most important qualities were personal: his "heart . . . zeal for the public welfare . . . spirit . . . experience of men and things ripened and complete . . . [and] judgment."[46] De Saussure thus concurred with other Federalists in making a personal rather than a policy argument.[47]

De Saussure's election-year writings reveal his Federalist outlook at a time when the contest was heaviest. He was clearly worried about both Jefferson and Jefferson's Republican followers. They seemed ready to undermine the stable political order produced by the Federalists. De Saussure was less concerned about Jefferson's religion, although he did touch on the matter in an extended and revealing footnote. Reflecting on Jefferson's comments in *Notes on the State of Virginia*, De Saussure observed that Jefferson's right to hold any religious beliefs or none were protected by the law, yet that did not mean voters should ignore them. "But when one of these believers in *twenty* gods, or unbelievers in *any* God, claims the supreme magistracy in a country, where only *one true and ever living God* is worshipped, the people of that country, surely have a right to object to being ruled by such." De Saussure thus rooted his opposition to Jefferson's religion in the religious beliefs of his own South Carolina community. As part of the social order he was defending, De Saussure wanted to defend Christianity and elect Christian—and Federalist—rulers. He concluded that Jefferson "abhors the christian system, and it is an unwise experiment, for a religious people, to elevate to the chief magistracy any man who has expressed such entire indifference to all religions."[48] De Saussure revealed something of the texture of religious argument for South Carolina Federalists. At a time when John Mitchell Mason and William Linn were attacking Jefferson's religious credentials at length, De Saussure was more reserved. Arguments of Northern evangelical Federalists had made their way into the South but received less attention there, as religion remained one of several factors that contributed to a stable community order.

The election proved that De Saussure was right to be concerned about Democratic-Republican activities. Although the Federalists continued their electoral success in Charleston, they had much less success in the Upcountry. Once the votes were cast, De Saussure was close to the center of action in the state legislature in Columbia, which determined the allocation of the state's electoral votes. Although there were some suggestions that the state might split its votes between Pinckney and Jefferson, this was never seriously a possibility. Further, Pinckney refused this compromise, feeling honor-bound to remain linked to Adams.[49] South Carolina's votes guaranteed the election would go to Jefferson and Burr. Reflecting on this defeat, De Saussure expressed dire warnings to John Rutledge, Jr., that America faced "a great crisis in our affairs." De

Saussure prayed he would be wrong in his gloomy outlook, however, since "I would rather enjoy the prosperity of my country contrary to my expectations, than . . . share in its Misery."⁵⁰

In the wake of the defeat, De Saussure would struggle to carry his Federalist ideals forward. De Saussure hoped for "virtuous & moderate" government, but he feared that the initial signs from the new administration promised neither. As the months progressed, his mood grew darker still. He confided to Rutledge, "I am so disgusted that nothing but a sense of duty prevents my abandoning politics for ever. I remain firmly attached to republicanism, as modelled by our Constitution. . . . [The leaders and principles of the present] government are visionary. Man is imperfect; and all best institutions must partake of his imperfection." In avoiding monarchy, the Constitution had opened itself up to an overabundance of democracy. Those "considerable vices" would remove leadership from wise gentlemen informed by experience and wisdom—conditions that left De Saussure with little confidence.⁵¹

In the following years, De Saussure worked to advance Federalism by considering the power of print and nurturing further ties with Northern Federalists through travel. He was very impressed with Jedidiah Morse's *New-England Palladium,* calling it "an excellent paper" and promising to "endeavour to extend the subscription for it." De Saussure saw the paper as a possible Federalist weapon. He noted "the great attention paid by the democrats, to the support & diffusion of the Aurora [of Benjamin Franklin Bache] and a few other papers which procured them the small majority they had in the Election, which decided the fate of the Presidency." The *Aurora* had undermined popular support of the government by "the eternal repetition of alarming falsehoods." The best weapon, therefore, was truth, setting forth clearly what the Federalists intended and what negative measures the Republicans were enacting. The *Palladium* could thus serve as an anti-*Aurora* to reach the entire country and make a difference in South Carolina.⁵²

Travel also helped to connect De Saussure to other Federalists, encouraging him that a Federalist resurgence might be in the offing. In the fall of 1802, De Saussure traveled to New England, a journey for health, amusement, and political strategy. Arriving in Boston, he was most impressed with New Englanders, observing, "all the men of character are highly correct in their principles & politics." De Saussure mentioned that he had visited Timothy Pickering and "found him . . . rich in his Integrity & strong in his principles." Building further support for Pinckney, De Saussure reported that Massachusetts Federalists "honor his Character highly" and would support him in a future election. Traveling south, De Saussure stopped in Hartford, where he witnessed the local elections—the Federalists won a small majority—in the company of Federalist lawyers Chauncey Goodrich and Theodore Dwight, Timothy Dwight's brother. De Saussure was happy to report that they "inform me that the state remains sound, & that the federalists are even stronger than they were."[53] Through these personal contacts, De Saussure could share Federalist opinions and strategies. Perhaps the Connecticut model of Federalists' organizing and succeeding in the face of partisan challenges could have helped South Carolina Federalists. In such a visit, De Saussure was unusual, as few others in the South ever received such a Federalist reinforcement.

De Saussure's political involvement was curtailed after 1808, when he was elected a chancellor of the state, despite his Federalist credentials. By this point, De Saussure was bemoaning the small presence of Federalists in the state legislature, observing, "party spirit governs so absolutely that it sweeps away every other consideration."[54] As chancellor, he served on the state courts of equity and oversaw equity appeals. To fulfill his duties, he moved to Columbia and lived there for the next twenty-nine years, although he maintained connections with family and friends in Charleston. De Saussure would serve on the bench in a legal, not political, role until ill health forced his resignation in 1837.[55] Meanwhile, the Federalist Party in South Carolina would collapse. Having very little presence in the booming Upcountry, its appeal was limited to its bastions in Charleston and among the Lowcountry planter elite, an ever-shrinking percentage of the state's vote.

Voluntarism and Federalism

De Saussure also participated in religiously motivated voluntary societies. As soon as the Bible Society of Charleston was formed, De Saussure became a contributor. Other Circular Church members involved were Isaac Keith, Timothy Ford, and David Ramsay.[56] More than just interested in contributing, De Saussure actively involved himself in Bible distribution. After moving to Columbia, he reported to Ford that "I am distributing [Bibles from Charleston] gradually & I hope usefully."[57] The Circular Church in Charleston took the lead in setting up (in 1789) the Society for Elderly and Disabled Ministers, and De Saussure served as one of the five founding committee members.[58] He also supported the Society for Promoting the Interest of Religion, contributing $25.[59] As late as 1835, De Saussure was serving as president of the Columbia-based Society for the

Advancement of Learning.[60] Altogether, these demonstrate De Saussure's interest in decidedly religious voluntary societies and his willingness to support them with time and money over many years. De Saussure valued both the spiritual and social benefits they provided.

The connections De Saussure saw between piety and society emerged in a eulogy for a fellow jurist, Judge Thomas Waties. De Saussure depicted him not only as an ideal jurist but as a model Christian and citizen. Waties was never seduced by abstract theorists. Rather, he applied the law to protect society, giving order and stability to South Carolina, inspired by his Episcopalianism. De Saussure attested that Waties's "piety was strong and uniform; that it was in the true spirit of the gospel, fervent, benevolent, humble, and unpretending." While believing strongly, Waties also demonstrated nonsectarian openness, calling all Protestants "his *christian* brethren." De Saussure thus portrayed Waties as his model Christian. As part of this ideal, De Saussure praised Waties for "Knowing the intimate relation which subsists between religion and the well being of society, as well as its influence on individual character and happiness."[61] Waties accorded perfectly with De Saussure's outlook: when Christianity was embraced and practiced, it could support the "well being of society." De Saussure thus embraced a generic Republican construction of religion within society coupled with Voluntarist practice.

Charles Cotesworth Pinckney and the Disconnect between Religion and Politics

Charles Cotesworth Pinckney's treatment of religion and politics reveals that De Saussure was not anomalous among South Carolina Federalists. It would be hard to find a more prominent South Carolinian than Pinckney, whose life was wrapped up with both state and national Federalist politics. Born to a leading family in the state, Pinckney was educated in England as a lawyer, even attending lectures given by William Blackstone. Returning to America, he supported the patriot cause in the American Revolution. He served in the Continental Army, though he never saw significant action. Like De Saussure, the fall of Charleston ended his war involvement, but he still achieved the rank of general at the war's end. South Carolina sent Pinckney to the Constitutional Convention, where he argued from "Experience" rather than abstract theoretical principles. He supported the Constitution and worked for South Carolina's ratification.[62]

Like most South Carolinians, Pinckney retained attitudes friendly

Charles Cotesworth Pinckney, emphasizing his military credentials. James Earl. *Major General Charles Cotesworth Pinckney,* 1795–96. (Worcester Art Museum, Worcester, Massachusetts, accession #1921.86. Image © Worcester Art Museum, all rights reserved)

to France and even hosted Citizen Genet during his visit to Charleston. The events of the 1790s, though, turned Pinckney against France and into a decided "friend of government." Washington had repeatedly invited Pinckney into the federal government, and Pinckney finally relented when President Adams asked him to serve as a special minister to France, along with John Marshall and Elbridge Gerry. There, the three of them were the subjects of the plotting of the XYZ Affair and French requests for bribes in exchange for diplomacy. Pinckney first gained national exposure with his refusal to compromise with French demands. Returning to America, he was feted by the Federalists. When a new army formed in 1798 in anticipation of a French invasion, he was third in command, behind Washington and Alexander Hamilton. Pinckney's standing led to his being named Adams's running mate in 1800. Ironically, it was Pinckney's refusal to accept votes not also committed to Adams that guaranteed all of South Carolina's votes would go to Jefferson and Burr. Pinckney's honorable actions raised his standing among Federalists nationwide, and he became the Federalist presidential nominee in both 1804 and 1808. Pinckney lost badly in both elections—even failing to win South Carolina either time—and retired from political life to nurture the religious and voluntary societies then developing in Charleston.[63]

During his years as a national figure, Pinckney voiced political views very typical for other Federalists. Writing to Timothy Pickering, Pinckney looked for a re-creation of American unity. "I most ardently wish that we would banish all party distinctions and foreign influence," he wrote, hoping that everyone would "think and act only as Americans."[64] Pinckney's experiences in France solidified his hostility to "foreign influence," which he equated with French influence. He reported from France that Talleyrand and the Directory intended to gain "the direction of American measures," and to accomplish these ends, "they mean to exert themselves to keep up their party in America."[65] Pinckney thus portrayed the Democrats as the instruments of French policy. With other Federalists, he determined not to let agents of a foreign government make any inroads on the republic. Despite such attitudes, his army responsibilities kept him out of active politics during the election of 1800.[66]

After Adams's defeat, Pinckney worried about the dangers he sensed. "Attempts are making," he warned Theodore Sedgwick, "to construe away the Energy of our Constitution, to unnerve our Government, & to overthrow that system by which we have risen to our present prosperity."[67] Democratic policies would strip away Federalist successes and undermine American stability. Nor were politics in South Carolina much better. In witnessing state politics, Pinckney decried the actions of the "Demos." Once in the state legislature, they had advocated a "Jacobin proposition" to issue a "General Ticket" for the state, where presidential electors would be assigned to the single winning party rather than by voting districts. "The openly avowed principles of this measure," he observed, "was to stifle the voice of federalism."[68] Facing defeat in the 1808 election, he remained defiant, telling John Rutledge, Jr., "I however think [exertions] ought to be vigorously made, in order to shew that federalism is not extinct, and that there is in the Union a formidable party of the old Washingtonian School, alert to detect & expose any weak or visionary plan which may endanger the prosperity or safety of our Country."[69] Pinckney thus fought on, defending the "Washingtonian School" against Democratic visionaries, speculative theorists like Jefferson and James Madison who ignored both human experience and the practical interests of the nation—even if the success of these measures was less and less likely.

In addition to his Federalist credentials, Pinckney was, from all accounts, a very devout individual. Educated to Anglican piety, one of his eulogists reported that he remained throughout his life "a Christian from conviction. His judgment and affections were with the Church of his fathers, and his influence in support of its faith, worship, and discipline, in their primitive excellence and integrity, was usefully exerted." Pinckney could accurately defend Trinitarianism, for instance.[70] Always attached to the Episcopal Church, he attended and regularly partook of the Eucharist. When in Charleston, he worshipped at St. Philip's Episcopal Church, and this local attachment led to many opportunities for service. He repeatedly filled the office of vestryman for the church, elected for the first time in 1774 and during the entire period of 1784–95. He appears to have participated actively whenever he was in Charleston.[71] As an Episcopalian, Pinckney also participated in the Protestant Episcopal Society for the Advancement of Christianity in South Carolina, collecting donations from others and contributing himself. One particular gift he made was of a large theological library that he had imported from London, printed by the Society for Promoting Christian Knowledge.[72]

Such devotion to Episcopalianism did not limit his religious contacts. Rather, he enjoyed friendships with ministers of many denominations, and he warmly participated in a variety of nondenominational voluntary societies. He was particularly engaged in the Bible Society of Charleston. Not only did he become its first president, but he actively participated over the years and hosted its meetings in his home. The society happily reelected him from the founding of the society until his death.[73]

With Pinckney's decided Federalism and his clear piety, he might present a useful figure for understanding their connection in the South Carolina environment. He does, but only insofar as he demonstrates a definite separation of those categories. In neither public declarations nor private correspondence did he connect his religious and political beliefs. Whereas De Saussure showed brief connections between the two, echoing faintly Northern Federalist attitudes, the connections are completely absent for Pinckney.

Perhaps behind Pinckney's reticence was his strong commitment to disestablishment and his friendship with Baptists. As one of his eulogists pointed out, he was a quick supporter of the 1790 move for complete disestablishment, rising to second the proposal advanced by the Presbyterian minister William Tennent. Pinckney had "advocated the change, with a force of liberal reasoning, that carried conviction to every bosom, and caused its adoption by a decided majority of the members."[74] Rejecting an Episcopal establishment in the state marked Pinckney's unwillingness to connect political and religious outlooks. Pinckney also cultivated the friendship of some Baptists, such as Rev. Richard Furman.[75] Influenced by Baptist opposition to establishments, Pinckney was less willing to connect religious arguments to politics, especially if it meant dividing denominations in the South. Having worked to disestablish South Carolina so shortly after the revolution, Pinckney continued to leave the two arenas entirely separate.

Pro-Slavery Federalism

In a major difference from Northern Federalists, De Saussure, Pinckney, and other South Carolina Federalists possessed a strong commitment to the institution of slavery. Slavery was an ongoing reality in De Saussure's life, thought, and activities. His family owned slaves, as did he in Charleston and Columbia. Slavery was also a significant element in his writings. As early as his 1795 Phocion letters about state representation, slavery impinged on his political principles. In attacking the principle of equality as a basis for political decisions, De Saussure wryly observed that, if it were applied fully, all slaves in South Carolina would immediately be freed and placed on the same level as their masters. Clearly he did not believe this would happen, and he envisioned the result that "this fine country would be deluged with blood, and desolated by fire and sword." To De Saussure it was self-evident that this was a misapplication of the principle of equality. Further, De Saussure suggested that inequalities in representation could be justified because of the three-fifths clause of the Constitution. South Carolina benefited from it, gaining additional representatives, and to base all representation only on population would weaken South Carolina's standing in the nation.[76] Finally, De Saussure's discussion of "property" obscured the reality of what much of that property represented—slaves and the products of slave labor. Thus, while De Saussure attempted to ignore it, the property he was defending was inescapably linked to slavery. In a slave society, all political questions were tinged with the issue of slavery, and it was an important subtext even in this debate over the state legislature.

Further, slavery was an important element of De Saussure's polemic against Jefferson's presidential candidacy in 1800. De Saussure saw as proof of Jefferson's dangerous theorizing a commitment to slave emancipation. De Saussure claimed, "He is a *philosophe*. . . . He entertains opinions unfriendly to the property, which forms the efficient labor of a great part of the southern states." De Saussure used Jefferson's actions in Virginia, as well as Jefferson's correspondence with African American mathematician Benjamin Banneker and the radical French *philosophe* Marquis de Condorcet, to support his claim that Jefferson hoped for immediate emancipation. De Saussure exclaimed that Jefferson's plans for freeing and educating the slaves were more radical than either "the Quakers, or the Abolition Society!"[77] De Saussure understood this electioneering rhetoric would appeal to South Carolinians.

De Saussure's support of slavery advanced even farther in 1822 when, in the wake of the Denmark Vesey slave conspiracy in Charleston, he published six essays countering Northern condemnations of slavery. In his opening, De Saussure accepted slavery as an evil—"an evil not denied by intelligent persons in the southern states"—but he found the problems associated with ending slavery much greater than slavery itself.[78] In the essays, De Saussure's earlier rejection of theory and embrace of practicality came to the fore. With no Federalist party still functioning in South Carolina, De Saussure continued to defend Southern society and republican liberty, which he defined, unmistakably, as white. De Saussure considered the possibilities of emancipation with compensation, colonization to Africa, and even granting equal rights to freed slaves in America, but he rejected all of them as impractical.

In defending against Northern charges, De Saussure asserted that slavery was justifiable biblically and was not as an institution inherently cruel. On the biblical level, De Saussure claimed that slavery had been practiced by the Jews and was prohibited by neither Jesus nor the Apostles. In contrast, "In pursuance of the system of universal benevolence, preached under the new dispensation, the Apostles strenuously recommended gentle treatment by the owners of slaves, but they never expressed one word on the duty of emancipation." Although individual masters might be moved by conscience to free their slaves, De Saussure did not believe any moral principle required emancipation. De Saussure also asserted that slavery as practiced was not cruel. He insisted, "The condition of the slave in this country, with respect to the quantity of labor imposed, and to food and clothing, and with respect to the treatment experienced in health, and in sickness, is, generally speaking, as good as that of the peasant and day labourer in most countries." As cruelty became an important element of the debate over slavery, De Saussure worked to deny that the practice was cruel. Instead, such attacks originated from "a morbid affectation of humanity in many, and a mistaken conscience in others." Clearly a wrongly formed moral sense was directing slavery's opponents.[79]

De Saussure continued to reject abstract political theories—just as he had done in his Phocion letters. "We are not however going into the question of abstract right," he insisted. Although slavery in the abstract might be a useful topic for philosophers setting up a state, it made little difference given the existence of a large and growing slave population in the country. Instead, he asked that the possible solutions to slavery be considered practically. For compensated emancipation, De Saussure stated his figure at $450,000,000 ($300 per head for 1.5 million slaves). "Can this country afford this expense?" he asked, answering, "I apprehend it is not prepared for this, and cannot bear this burthen." Emancipation was simply too costly, and so he concluded it was not a practical approach. Further, the idea of transporting the freed slaves back to Africa would reach another $100,000,000. "All these views go to demonstrate the impracticability of the scheme of transportation, even on the score of expense alone," he asserted. Beyond expense, the loss of slave labor would cripple the South's economy and deprive it of the labor it needed for its agricultural production. De Saussure gave the lie to the overly optimistic schemes of colonization. Because the colonizers never seriously considered full emancipation and colonization, they never confronted the sizable difficulties the procedure might entail. De Saussure concluded that "no wise statesman would advise the experiment and no humane government would attempt it."[80] Again, this was an impractical experiment not to be tried.

Finally, De Saussure insisted that freed slaves would never be content with freedom but not political rights. Indeed, the lesson of the Vesey conspiracy was not to offer some rights to freed blacks while denying them political rights. Moreover, the freed African Americans were not ready for political rights, a point he claimed was "founded on experience." Because they lacked the "moral training" necessary for self-government, freedmen would be easy prey for demagogues. Just as Federalists had warned of Democratic-Republican demagogues, now De Saussure transmuted that fear into a specter of a mass of unthinking men controlled by "some of their own cunning and base leaders" or by "profligate white demagogues."[81]

Even while considering these difficulties, De Saussure hoped to use the question to forge greater connections among whites of all sections. De Saussure denied that there was a contradiction between slavery and republican liberty. Citing historical examples, he insisted that "domestic slavery has never been found inconsistent with the highest enjoyment of liberty by the citizens of republics." De Saussure then went on to defend a white republic in which color and liberty were intertwined. In this vision, social equality was an impossibility that endangered the liberties of all whites: "With us it is a struggle for life, for character, for colour, for dignity, for government and mastery—in short for every thing dear to men, and most especially to free white men." In this single statement, De Saussure connected his concerns over racial identity, rule, freedom, and masculinity. He was struggling for the prerogatives of "free white men." Against such danger, De Saussure called for a union of whites, North and South. He asked that Northerners consider as their friends those "who are masters, and who are united to them by every tie which binds men together—a common origin and colour, a common religion and language, similar habits and feelings, laws, governments, and institutions of all kinds."[82] Seeking a cultural connection much like Federalists had done decades earlier, De Saussure called for white unity to strengthen the republic.[83] In this appeal, De Saussure revealed how dramatically out of step he was with Northern Federalists. Not only was the Jay family opposed to slavery, but many other Northern evangelical Federalists such as Dwight, Morse, and Boudinot were as well.[84] Although little commented on at the time, this represented a serious difference in the Federalist party in regard to politics and social practice.

Similarly, given his social standing, it is no surprise that Charles Cotesworth Pinckney was enmeshed in the practice of slavery. As a plantation owner, he owned and managed hundreds of slaves. He contracted slave labor, directed their assignments, and purchased clothing for his slaves—even recording his purchase of 141 pairs of shoes.[85] As a lawyer, he dealt with many cases involving slaves, including inheritance cases probating slaves.[86] The political result was that Pinckney was a strong defender of slavery. At the Constitutional Convention, when the subject of slavery came up, he insisted, "S[outh] Carolina & Georgia cannot do without slaves."[87] He also protected the foreign slave trade, pushing the date for its elimination back to 1808 from 1800. He thought that slaves should be counted toward the South's population for representation— though not taxation—in Congress, although he would accept the three-fifths compromise.[88] He later complained when Quakers petitioned Congress, that "I don't like it at all." He would brook "no idea of their intermeddling with our Negroes," since slavery was "altogether a matter of domestic regulation."[89] Slavery to Pinckney's mind was a "domestic" matter, a fact of Southern life, an economic reality. Pinckney was open to some melioristic approaches to slave conditions, and he did adopt a paternalist approach to his slaves, but he refused to go further.[90] He contributed to several colonization efforts but thought they would do little good. For Pinckney, as for De Saussure, antislavery moralism from the North could do little. Thus Pinckney could be involved in religious voluntarism without allowing such attempts to reshape his vision of Southern society. This division of voluntarism from the structural reform of society, though, weakened both the religious energy and the overall effect of a Voluntarist strategy.

Slavery proved a clear difference between Northern and Southern Federalism. Not only would it produce different political actions on the national level—such as Pinckney's opposition to ending the slave trade—it limited South Carolina's ability generally to adopt a stance toward public religion and morality that had so energized evangelical Federalists in the North. Other elements of society also resisted this connection of religion and politics—indeed South Carolina's early disestablishment pushed for a respect for Protestant Christianity without deploying a larger concern that morals or religion shape public policy. Nonetheless, the very limited nature of connections between religion and politics in the South is striking. In minimizing such ties, Southern Federalists passed over a potentially energizing factor for their politics as well as an appeal that might have gained them some traction in the Upcountry—especially among the many Presbyterians there. The limited nature of the connections between Northern and Southern Federalists suggests another factor in the slow adoption of Northern Federalist uses of religion. Still, connections were strong enough to encourage the establishment of some voluntary societies, including several (such as the Charleston Bible Society) affiliated with national organizations. Religion for these Federalists remained an integral part of the social order but never significantly impinged on political matters. These Federalists thus ended their existence holding on to the revolutionary-era Republican synthesis of religion and society, to which they had added some practice of Voluntarism. In speaking Federalism with a Southern accent, these Carolinians limited religion in their politics.

III

RELIGION & POLITICS AFTER THE FEDERALIST PARTY

7 Peter Augustus Jay

FEDERALIST WITHDRAWAL AND THE
TURN TO VOLUNTARIST MORALITY

IN THE FIRST HALF OF THE NINETEENTH CENTURY, JOHN JAY'S TWO
sons, Peter Augustus (1776–1843) and William (1789–1858), struggled
to defend their father's attitudes about society, politics, and religion's connection to both. Beginning in a Federalist milieu, they participated in
Federalism's declining fortunes. Like their father and other older Federalists out of politics, they participated in the process of retirement from
public life, reflection on politics as outsiders, an increased attention to
religion's vitality and significance, and a reorientation to other endeavors.
As politics and society evolved in the nineteenth century, Jay's sons took
alternative courses to preserve parts of their father's Federalist legacy. Peter Augustus was most influenced by Jay's Federalist politics, vision of
an ordered society, and domestic religion. He found himself executing a
fighting retreat in politics and was eventually forced from the arena. In
his retirement, he emphasized a privatized religion and stress on public
morality. William, by contrast, was less constrained by Federalist politics
and so freer to innovate in addressing the needs he perceived in society.
Because he emphasized religious belief and the religious reform of society, politics was only one sphere in which to advance public morality and
religiosity. In different ways, both Jay brothers lost coherent visions of
religion integrated into politics and society, but developed new strategies
to cope with the changing American environment.

The Jay brothers, in pioneering different styles of Voluntarism, illuminate the development of the practice. Their lives and emphases point first
to the way voluntarism could grow out of Federalist concerns, a development that occurred throughout the North. Second, they demonstrate
how these attitudes could be portrayed as beneficial to society. Third,
they explain how various strands of abolitionism could grow from differing emphases. The end result was to develop a culture of Voluntarism.[1]

Peter Augustus Jay, as John's elder son, sought to carry on his father's work. To insure sound political principles would continue to guide the re-public, he entered the stress and strife of the politics of the early republic. His early politics thus exemplify the experience of "Young Federalists." At first, he still had confidence that Federalists could win the day. Instead, as Federalist standing waned precipitously during the first decade of the nineteenth century, his career turned into a fighting retreat. As a result, retirement was repeatedly forced upon him. His life witnessed a series of retreats and retrenchments, as Federalist politics lost any chance of suc-cess.

Even so, Peter Augustus's public activity aimed to shape society in nonpolitical ways. In emphasizing the necessity of morality for society, Jay attempted to mould it through respectable, even elitist voluntary societies. In so doing, he, like other Federalists forcibly removed from politics, recognized the power of cultural influence. Controlling cultural institutions offered a strategy to maintain order and temper democratic excesses. Authority would continue, but not through politics. Through recognizing the power of the public sphere, shaping sentiment, and in-fluencing action, the republic could be preserved through means the founding generation had not foreseen. In his actions, he contributed to the power of voluntary societies that Alexis de Tocqueville would both celebrate and analyze after his visit to America in the 1830s. Despite Jay's glum, resigned attitude, he contributed creatively to the power of volun-tarism for directing society and thereby helped to fix the alignment of public life in antebellum America.[2]

Early Years as a Young Federalist

Peter Augustus Jay developed his political consciousness at a young age. By the time he was sixteen, he was observing and commenting on his father's thwarted bid for governor of New York.[3] When his father went to England to negotiate the 1795 treaty, Peter Augustus accompanied him as his personal secretary—an appointment that only strengthened his po-litical commitments. While in England, he interacted with political men and received the British perspective on the dangers of the French Revolu-tion. He attended Parliament and listened to Edmund Burke, the scourge of revolution.[4] He also visited with William Pitt the Younger and William Wilberforce, who left a significant impression on him.[5] With England at war with France, Peter Augustus's time in England bred in him a positive assessment of the English and a sense of the danger posed by the French.

Such sentiments grew with the debate over the Jay Treaty. Even be-

Peter Augustus Jay, "Young Federalist." From John Jay, *Memorials of Peter A. Jay, Compiled for His Descendants.* (Arnheim, Netherlands: G. J. Thieme, 1905).

fore leaving England, Peter Augustus guessed that "a certain party in New York with a worthy Senator at their head have been the most forward to reprobate and oppose it." This was, of course, the Republicans, with Aaron Burr leading the charge. Jay warned, "Let them however remember that should it [the treaty] thro' their machinations be rejected, upon *their* heads will be all the Bloodshed and Calamities which must ensue." Soon thereafter, he bemoaned "the success of the Antifederal party in the Elections of Congressmen."[6] He thus revealed his political categories, portraying opponents of the government as continuing the movement that began with opposition to the Constitution and that still threatened to harm the body politic. This attitude to the Democratic-Republican opposition would only grow more pointed as the years progressed.

When John became the governor of New York, Peter Augustus managed his father's political interests. In November 1797, he warned about local elections: "From all I have been able to observe I augur well concerning the Election of Governor. But from inactivity and indecision of the Friends of Government I fear there is some reason to apprehend a new Defeat in the Choice of Representative."[7] Here, Jay echoed the common belief that Federalists were the true friends of government, the only group truly devoted to the Constitution and federal system. If they worked together, all would be well. If not, "Democratic Agents" would gain the upper hand. Several months later, he observed, "Little danger however is to be apprehended unless it be from the great Security and inactivity of our friends," and so he continued to monitor the various political meetings going on.[8]

In 1798, worries over war with France overwhelmed the excitement of the election campaign. Jay pressed his political point in that fevered summer in two ways: involvement in public meetings and participation in the militia. In both settings, he served as an exemplary "Young Federalist," and his actions provide an insight into the motivations of the younger Federalists as they sought to craft a masculine identity that would demonstrate republican virtue worthy of the "fathers" of the Revolution.[9] In public meetings in New York City, Jay fought for both Federalist political advantage and personal identity and standing. For instance, he joined a great many other Federalists at the Society for Free Debate. Peter suggested to his father that "this Society was lately instituted in all probability with the intention that it should be converted into a Jacobin Club." He based his presumption on the assertion that "a Committee of Managers was appointed consisting with only one or two Exceptions of Violent Democrats." He believed the organizers also called the meeting "with a View to influence the [upcoming] Election." To Peter Augustus, this society, although ostensibly open to the public and committed to impartial debate, was really a front for advancing Democratic notions, encouraging American Jacobins, and promoting the "Antifederal" party. To Jay, his political opponents opposed the American government and allied themselves with the French revolutionaries. At the first meeting, however, he and his friends were able to guarantee that "a vast majority were Federalists."[10]

At a subsequent public meeting organized by Federalists for their "*Young Men,*" about one thousand attended. "Every Symptom," Jay reported, "was exhibited of ardent attachment to the Govt. & violent *Hatred* to France and our Democrats." This meeting called upon Jay to write an address of support to President John Adams, and he produced a strongly anti-French appeal.[11] "Whatever might once have been thought of the Merits of our Controversy with that Republic but one Sentiment can now exist upon the Subject. The Door of Negociation has been closed, & we are even permitted to speak but upon Terms to which Freemen must disdain to submit," he wrote. Jay called for unity in defending America's liberties. In doing so, he laid claim to republican manliness, writing, "To avert that punishment [defeat by France] from ourselves is the Duty of every one who professes the Feelings of a Man or the Patriotism of a good Citizen." Active defense was a mark of manly patriotism, and success-ful defense would set Americans apart from European failures. Hence, he and his compatriots would "claim it as our Right as we know it to be our Duty to be placed foremost in Defence of our Property our Liberty our Independence and we may add our Religion." Jay thus spoke for the thousand other young Federalists who were willing to fight to fulfill their "Duty" and protect their liberties. In such a defense, he also referred to the defense of religion that would accompany resistance to France. In this resistance, he believed he had "the Consolations of Conscience, and the Approbation of God."[12] Public events provided the young Jay a stage on which to defend what he perceived as the interests of the nation, which were primarily political yet held a religious dimension as well.

Jay also took practical steps to encourage military defense. At yet an-other meeting, the "young men" agreed they would train "to acquire Mili-tary Knowledge." He went a step further and joined the New York militia, hoping to counter the false steps it might take. For instance, some wanted their militia to address the president directly. Jay rejected this because, as he wrote, "To undertake in our Military Capacity to control, condemn, or even approve the Measures of the Government or any particular Branch of it, I suppose a very pernicious Example. I take it to be our Duty to obey implicitly every Command of our Rulers however inexpedient or to resign our Commissions."[13] He believed the militia was not a policymak-ing body. Its sole assignment was to defend the existing government by obeying its orders.

Military involvement aided Jay in his own political and social iden-tification. His rank, for instance, was very important, and he wrote per-sistently to guarantee that his appointment was exactly as it should be.[14] The martial accoutrements also helped him to make a statement, as he wore the Federalist black cockade in his hat to oppose the French tri-color. He believed the black cockade was a mark of those who were the true "friends of their Country." Such actions met opposition. Jay reported that insults to the black cockade and to the Federalist anthem "Hail, Co-lumbia" had increased. He even found himself engaged in fisticuffs "with a Set of Blackguards at a late Hour of the Night." Still, he believed that such attacks served to strengthen public support. By August, he noted, "the Stream of public opinion continues to run with increasing rapidity in our Favor."[15]

While these political battles raged, Jay also revealed his political interpretations in letters suggesting his potent youthful Federalism. If war with France began, he hoped that a national spirit would break out, uniting the nation: "If . . . we shall happily unite in defence of our Independence, we shall then probably become divested of our foreign Prejudices & Partialities, & acquire a National Character & a national Pride." His concern for a national identity echoed his father's hopes from a decade earlier and looked for a strong, secure republic. On the other hand, he feared that if "the Democratic Party still continues to oppose every measure of the Govt. to distract its Counsels & to enfeeble its Measures, if they still endeavor to divide the People & to alienate their Affections from the Officers they have chosen . . . our Situation will be lamentable indeed."[16] He saw the Democrats as aiding and abetting the French and weakening the nation. He thought they were driven by ambition, aiming to advance "their own private Interests." He believed that "the final aim of the leading Men among our Jacobins is to dismember the Continent, preferring the first offices in a small state to those wh. are inferior in a great one."[17] Pride was causing the Democrats—who were nothing less than American Jacobins—to undo the very republic John Jay and other Federalists had so carefully built. The man behind these Democratic measures was Thomas Jefferson, who Peter Augustus suspected "of being the Author & Secred [secret] conductor of a system which if successful cannot fail of reducing [the nation] to subjection or at least Dependence on the will of a foreign nation."[18] Jefferson's love of France would endanger American liberties, and Jay hoped that a sufficient number of Americans would recognize this before it was too late.

After all his exertions during mid-1798, he was hopeful. By August, he could write that "Federalism is at present greatly predominant." Even more encouraging was the general tone in New York: "A Spirit of Resistance very honorable to the Country people is fast rising among them & tho' I expect serious & difficult war with the great Nation I have no doubt but it will be finally crowned with Success & I hope will eradicate that foreign Influence & their foreign partialities which have been the sources of so many evils & of so much humiliation."[19] Jay believed that the nation had prepared itself for war, which meant that war would eliminate foreign allegiances and create a national spirit among Americans. Through this political activity, he had solidified his allegiances and gained a measure both of manliness and social standing—elements threatened by subsequent Federalist defeats.

With Jefferson a candidate for the election of 1800, Jay followed events closely. He nervously watched results in New York and told his father, "The Event of the Election here has been as unexpected as it is mortifying. . . . It now appears that the Plans of the Democrats were commenced a considerable time ago & conducted with equal Secrecy & Judgment." Having learned from Federalist organization, Republicans in New York had planned ahead for the state election and made excellent progress. Moreover, the New York results presaged even more dire consequences, and Jay dreaded the possibility that "if as is supposed it insures the election of Mr Jefferson the prospect is gloomy indeed."[20] As it became apparent that a Republican would succeed John Adams, Jay slipped farther into disengagement. Once Jefferson was definitely elected, Jay had little to say. "I have scarcely been anywhere but at Court, & the only topics of Conversation are the mortifying Event of the Election."[21] For the next several years, he would be reduced to observing political affairs, rather than participating in them.

In the midst of this turmoil, Jay began his formal study of law. He studied in the office of his cousin Peter Jay Munro. Since John Jay had trained Munro in the law, John could be sure his son was receiving the type of legal education of which he approved. Peter Augustus passed the bar in 1797 and was admitted to argue before the New York Supreme Court the following year. More than just a profession, this legal training shaped him. The settled legal order was the alternative to the political storms of the 1790s. It offered retreat and calmness in contrast to the conflict of politics. Although Jay left politics, he never stopped practicing law.[22]

Jay's first political retirement came after the excitement of 1798–1800. Part of the shift was personal. He confessed to his close friend Elias Woodward, "My political ardor has somewhat cooled. . . . I feel great anxiety for the future, but think it unwise to permit that anxiety to prey upon my quiet or to renounce my tranquility, before it becomes necessary."[23] Jay could not keep the passion required for fulltime political engagement, and he seemed unable to produce the energy to worry as intensely as he had. His retirement grew more pronounced when his health became bad. On his doctor's advice, he first left the city and then traveled abroad during 1802–5, visiting Italy, France, and Bermuda. He spent the subsequent two years in seclusion at the Jay family farm at Bedford. These decisions took him out of the daily flow of New York life and removed him from political participation.[24]

In his retirement, Jay could do little more than observe what he believed to be the deteriorating political state of the republic. In 1801, he wondered whether a revolution like France's would come to America. "Combustible Materials are indeed profusely provided & ferment in secret," he observed. It only required the proper demagogue, perhaps the recently elected Jefferson. Seeing Republican success, Jay decried political conditions. "When I see that Consequence is derived not from Integrity nor even from Talent—That Morality & Honor must be abandoned by the Candidate for public favor," he was forced to agree with the writer of Ecclesiastes that "all is Vanity & Vexation."[25] Several years later, he bemoaned the fact that the Democrats had placed America in a position to be threatened by England, France, and Spain simultaneously. This untenable position arose from misplaced ambition. In their rush to get elected and gain power, they had sacrificed principle and honesty, thereby putting themselves in such an embarrassing situation.[26]

By 1810, Jay had repeated his belief that ambitious men would attempt to deceive the electorate to gain power. He wrote to a friend, "In a Government like ours essentially Democratical [mischievous misrepresentations] can only be counteracted by the unwearied united & strenuous Exertions of better men." He, of course, believed he and the Federalists *were* the better men, possessing better morals and principles. Having accepted the basic nature of the electoral process, he urged greater efforts to win others to the Federalist cause or face the dreadful consequences. "Liberty under our Constitution must be preserved by toil or anarchy will sacrifice it a victim to Despotism," he warned. In electoral work, Jay argued for careful labor. "I think it of importance however that in all public Discussions great moderation should be preserved," he observed. "The friends of real liberty are now a minority, to become a majority they must make proselytes. We are not pleading a cause before a disinterested Jury, but we are endeavoring to convert our opponents."[27] To gain converts, Jay suggested that deliberative arguments and friendly tones should be preferred to sarcasm and scorn. His realization that the "friends of real liberty" were a minority was a dramatic step. In contrast to the assertion in 1798 that they spoke for the vast majority of citizens, Federalist demeanor now had to be much more chastened. In the decade between those two instances, the political culture had shifted. Federalist success might still be possible, Jay believed, but it faced more difficult conditions.

Attempting Reentry to Society and Politics

Moving back to New York City in 1807, Jay attempted to emerge from his first retirement. This reentry to society was marked by his marrying Mary Rutherfurd Clarkson.[28] He devoted himself to his business concerns such as real estate and attempted to revive his law practice, which had languished.[29] He also began to be involved in Federalist causes again. Already in 1807, he worked to organize local Federalist political activity.[30] In 1808, he allowed himself to be nominated as a Federalist candidate to the state assembly but was defeated.[31] Jay had become an outsider, trying to force his way back into politics.

The opportunity for such reentry arrived with the war of 1812. Jay, with the rest of his family, publicly opposed the war. With his father and other Federalists, he helped form the Peace and Commerce party in New York. He then ran as that party's candidate for U.S. representative. He seemed at first to have won the election in 1812, but there were hints of foreboding. "To my own Surprize I am a Member of Congress, provided the Election is not void which many of our lawyers think it is," he wrote.[32] As he observed to his father, the legal matters of the election turned on two issues: the validity of the New York election law in light of recent legislative changes to the federal statutes and voting irregularities in several towns.[33] Jay and the party based their claim to the seat on the principle that voting irregularities in a town should invalidate the votes of the whole town, thereby neutralizing several Democratic strongholds. He and his allies petitioned Congress for his seat, although he was not optimistic. "I do not believe the House of Representatives will give us Seats," he confessed to his father.[34] The matter was referred to a committee and allowed to die. When the resignation of another representative in 1813 prompted a special election, Jay again ran and lost, this time by a larger margin. He told his sister, "At this Mary rejoices & I do not grieve."[35] Even during wartime, election to public office was no longer Jay's chief object.

While electoral matters dragged on, he tried to organize additional expressions of resistance to the war, but he bemoaned the lack of concerted effort. A false idea of patriotism had silenced many. As he told his father, "It is very certain that the great majority of this Place are in their hearts utterly opposed to it. But there is an unaccountable Timidity among the Federalists which stops their Mouths & makes them assent to the Doctrine that every Patriot must now support the Government." Federalist timidity angered him, especially if it stopped them from laying the blame at the feet of the Democrats. "That we must support our

Country & its Constitution is most true," he continued, "but that we are bound to support or to slacken our Efforts against a week [*sic*] & wicked administration because they have another folly & crime to their former list I cannot understand." Not professing loyalty to an administration that had begun a war he believed to be "folly & crime," he wanted Federalists to take some sort of action to express publicly their disapproval of the war.[36] Not only did Jay work for antiwar expressions in New York, but he tried to work with Federalists from other states to create a consistent policy. The result was a meeting in New York City, chaired by Elias Boudinot. This meeting foundered on its inability to develop a coherent strategy and fumbled toward attempting to support DeWitt Clinton for president without explicitly saying so.[37] Clinton, of course, lost the election, and the war continued. Jay had as much success in opposing the war as he had in his politics. Just as earlier political support for the Federalists had evaporated, so initial opposition to the war also disappeared. The citizenry seemed to be willfully shutting their eyes to what was obvious to Jay and other Federalists.[38]

His activities during the War of 1812, although not successful, opened doors for subsequent involvement at the war's conclusion, including his one successful foray into electoral politics. When New York City's Federal Republicans nominated him for the state assembly, he accepted the nomination and was duly elected. While in the assembly he left little mark, except for supporting the building of the Erie Canal. Instead of following up on his success, however, he avoided further involvement. He declined his next nomination as well as a Federalist nomination for governor. He demurred, citing only "circumstances, Plans, Habits, & Inclinations."[39] In his place, the Federalists nominated Rufus King.

Jay, rather than sitting out the election, campaigned for King. One electoral address he delivered revealed that he was still fighting the War of 1812. He attacked the Democrats' handling of national matters, portraying them as the greatest of hypocrites. They had attacked the national debt, a standing army, and the burden of taxes. In office, they had grown the debt, raised a ten-thousand-strong standing army still in place after the war, and doubled taxation. The only things the nation had to show for these actions was an increased national debt and tax burden. The Republicans in the state of New York were no better, having racked up large debts and lost tax revenues. In addition, "Upon examining . . . We shall find that they who have most loudly and importunately proclaimed their attachment to the people, ready to violate their rights whenever it may be necessary to gratify a sordid appetite for the emoluments of office." In his attacks on his opponents, Jay returned to his old charges. Ambition and greed were at the heart of Democratic officeseeking. The appeals to the people were but a show for baser desires. Their administration had harmed, rather than helped, the state of New York, and a change was in order.[40] But despite Jay's best efforts, King lost to the Republican candidate, Daniel Tompkins—as perhaps Jay had foreseen would be the case when he declined the nomination.

In 1819, the subsequent governor, DeWitt Clinton, appointed Jay to the office of recorder of the state of New York, even though he had never been a Clintonian. The Clintonian faction had proven amenable to some Federalists who refused to support Tammany Hall's politicians.[41] Able to fulfill the duties of the position without many difficulties, he accepted and served as recorder for two years (1819–21). By this time, as the alliance with the Clintonians suggested, the Federalist party structure in New York had largely collapsed. Reflecting on this reality, Jay wrote an elegiac note to his friend William Van Ness. "To the federal party our Country owes its Prosperity. I have been educated in their Principles & tho it is probable that in future they will only occasionally & as it were by accident have the ascendance I should be exceedingly unwilling to detach myself from them." His praise of the Federalists reflected his allegiances to his father and to his own principles. Whereas earlier he had believed the Federalists to be a majority, now he believed they would win elections only occasionally and "by accident." Still, Jay continued to identify with them. Despite efforts to maintain unity, Federalist decline by 1820 was a palpable reality.[42]

Amid such decline, Jay rallied himself for one final foray into politics, the New York Constitutional Convention of 1821. He was chosen with his cousin Peter Jay Munro to represent Westchester County. From first to last, he found the convention unpleasant, undoubtedly because he and his Federalist colleagues—men such as Senator Rufus King, Chancellor James Kent, and Judge William Van Ness—were a decided minority. Writing to his wife early in the convention, Jay sounded a dour note. "You desire me to write more particularly, but what can I tell you? . . . As yet I have scarcely spoken a word, & it is my intention to speak very little. I can do no good, & may do harm." He tried not to goad political opponents to more destructive positions. As the convention progressed, he portrayed the other delegates in increasingly negative terms, using inherited categories to understand their positions. He told his father, "In the convention there is manifestly a jacobinical party. They have decided in favor of universal suffrage."[43] Calls for expanded democratization made Jay cringe, as visions of the French Revolution's Terror danced through his mind. A week later he reported about the success of "the Jacobins": "Our prospects here grow more unpleasant the more violent members of the Convention begin to act more in a body & to gather strength." Later, "The last Division shows the strength of the radical party as it is called, who are forming themselves into a distinct section of the democratic party."[44] In tracing the rise of a "radical party" in the convention, Jay marked what he believed to be the increasingly steep decline of the process.

As to measures themselves, Jay seemed out of step with the rest of the convention on most of the dominant issues, especially suffrage. During the convention, he bemoaned the appeal of "universal suffrage." Afterward, he groused, "There seems to be a passion for universal Suffrage pervading the Union. . . . When those who possess no property shall be more numerous than those who have it, the consequence of this alteration will I fear be severely felt."[45] Jay was repeating the old Federalist contention that voting needed to be connected to having a stake in the community, which was represented by property ownership. On the other hand, he defended the rights of free African Americans against those who claimed to favor "universal suffrage" but were eager to disenfranchise New York's African American population. Jay drew on natural rights language to defend African American citizenship, asking whether it was foolish to deny the right to vote to someone "merely because he is not six feet high, or because he is of dark complexion?" Not only foolish, but wrong, he argued. Jay denied that racial prejudice was any grounds on which to base political decisions. In fact, he even marshaled a religious argument: "We are all the offspring of one common Father, and redeemed by one common Saviour—the gates of paradise are open alike to the bond and the free." On such grounds, Jay urged the committee to "never consent to incorporate into the constitution a provision which contravened the spirit of our institutions, and which was so repulsive to the dictates of justice and humanity." Religion and rights united to argue against disenfranchisement. Unfortunately, he and other Federalists fought unsuccessfully to keep race from becoming a deciding qualification for voting.[46]

The struggle over suffrage, as well as battles over the judiciary, left Jay greatly displeased with the final constitution. At the convention's conclusion, he observed, "Most of the federal members have gone away, & I shall be left in a very diminutive minority indeed upon the final vote which will be taken on the Constitution."[47] The minority *was* small, only eight delegates. Returning home, he continued to speak ill of the constitution. His one meager consolation was that it could have been worse.[48] With the resigned opposition of Federalists, the constitution was duly approved. After the experience at the convention, Jay seemed frustrated enough to swear off politics for good. He wrote his wife, "They now talk of adjourning tomorrow. . . . Then I may say with Buonaparte my political life is ended. It is long since had I much relish for politics, & what I have seen here has not made me more fond of them."[49] To a large extent, that is exactly what he did.

Private Religion

When it came to religious profession, Jay was generically orthodox. His parents saw that he was educated in Christianity, learning the catechism, hymns, and scriptures.[50] Even if they were not central to him, Jay apparently never questioned those doctrines. Instead, he offered repeated, brief references to faith throughout his life. Early in his career, he objected to Erasmus Darwin's *Zoonomia* because "he insuinates Doctrines which tend to destroy all belief in Revelation & overturn the very foundations of Morality & Religion."[51] From early on, Jay was explicitly linking religion and morality, the dominant theme in both his belief and voluntary endeavors.

Later in life, he also penned what amounted to a legal brief in favor of Christianity, a thirty-eight-page handwritten document entitled "Arguments for Belief in a Deity and the Scriptures." In this document, Jay drew on William Paley's argument from design, in which design perceived by humans argued in favor of a designer. Paley claimed that "common sense" would suggest that anyone who found a watch on a wild heath would assume someone had designed it, rather than that it had appeared spontaneously. Jay explicitly referenced the watch on the heath, and then applied Paley to refute "the atheist" and "Infidels." Jay still felt that they posed a danger, even many years after political conflict. He argued that reason could show the existence and attributes of God and could point to the validity of revelation. "The truth of Revelation is a *fact* to be proved by testimony, & when so proved not to be overthrown by syllogisms. We have a Right therefore to retort—God has given a Revelation." To follow that argument, Jay spent a great deal of time arguing for the reliability of the biblical record. He concluded that Jesus was the promised Messiah whose life made sense of both God's justice and mercy. "Revelation explains the Difficulty by the Atonement & sufferings of Christ. Man is feeble & unable to preserve his purity, how then can he ever please the holy God. Revelation promises supernatural assistance to all who ask it. How is it possible that God made a creature unable to perform his Duty?" Echoing his father's demand for human activity, Jay situated religion as a duty. He observed that pardon was available for those who demonstrated repentance, faith, and obedience. He believed it was "obvious that obedience is & ought to be a necessary condition for pardon."[52] Since obedient action was the proof of faith and necessary for belief, he ended with a call to action, especially to make use of the sacraments. While largely reiterating Protestant doctrine, Jay skewed the emphasis remarkably toward reasonableness and human activity. The stress on human activity leant itself, again, to moral behavior rather than internal reform. This characteristic of Jay's view of religion helps to make sense of his approach over time.

Additionally, Jay supported the Episcopal Church and encouraged belief in his family. For many years, he—like his father—served as a vestryman at Trinity Church. Later, when he moved further north in New York City, he helped to establish near his home the Episcopal Church of the Ascension, which he also faithfully supported. He became involved in various Episcopalian denominational activities. He served as treasurer for the Corporation of the Protestant Episcopal Church in the State of New York and as a trustee of the General Theological Seminary of the Episcopal Church. He was a delegate to the General Convention of the Episcopal Church in 1832, was a friend of Bishop Benjamin Onderdonk (active bishop of New York, 1830–45), and mixed easily with the hierarchy of the church.[53] To his family, he regularly repeated pious sentiments regarding resignation to the divine will, such as "the times are in His hands who doeth all things well, & let us hope he will bring good out of evil." Like his father, Jay often described God as providence working in the world.[54] Also like John, his faith appeared in much of the counsel he gave his family. Even in his reported last words, Jay was instructing on spiritual matters, telling his children to "read your Bible and believe it."[55]

For all of this, Jay's belief was still largely one of the private sphere. He did not keep his religious convictions a secret, but they seemed to impinge explicitly very little on his public conduct or analysis of public or political matters. Although he was involved in religious reform societies, he was also involved in a number of other societies. The religious ones were but one aspect of his life. Jay seemed to take his father's domestic faith and intensify it, while failing to adopt the public religiosity that his brother, William, demonstrated in the nineteenth century.

Moral Reform Societies, Religious and Secular

Both Peter Augustus and William Jay participated in the turn to moral reform societies as a type of social service. They thus helped to pioneer a new strategy that proved very attractive to a number of Federalists, especially young Federalists. If political influence were no longer possible, the republic could yet be shaped through voluntary activity outside the political realm. They creatively elevated the value of influencing culture and shaping sentiment, realizing their potential in a republic that increasingly celebrated the equality of all citizens. Whereas William's involvements were primarily of a religious character (see chapter 8), Peter Augustus demonstrated a mixture of activities. He found himself connected to both religious and nonreligious reform societies. In all of them, though, he stressed the significance of morality for society.

Peter Augustus joined other family members in supporting the American Bible Society. When the ABS formed in New York City in 1816, both Jay brothers attended, supporting the endeavor and voicing their father's approval. At the meeting, Peter Augustus spoke in support of the society and its plans for scripture distribution as "the means to enable all to contribute to the spiritual improvement of all." Much of his address attempted to support Bible distribution on the grounds of the temporal good it provided for people. While not rejecting the importance of scripture for conversion, he again pointed to the this-worldly benefits. "Where do you find Knowledge & Humanity & Charity?" he asked. "Where does conscience flourish—where does Liberty dwell? Nowhere but in the Christian world. Christianity enlarges the mind while it purifies the Heart."[56] Peter Augustus thus pointed to the benefits of the scriptures for moral reform. This-worldly interests were largely at the front of his mind.

In the midst of his involvements, he remained connected to the ABS, occasionally attending their meetings. He kept both John and William informed about proceedings when they were unable to attend and occasionally read his father's addresses to ABS meetings. He also supported an organization meant to help Protestants still in France, because of his family's Huguenot heritage.[57] With these groups, Peter Augustus participated without exhibiting overmuch zeal. He encouraged respectability and hoped these organizations would contribute to the temporal good of society. He thereby isolated his father's stress on morality and action and made it his central concern. The social perspective was not lost, but the explicit ties to a distinctive Christianity were. Through generational change, Federalist religiosity was transforming into Victorian morality.

Peter Augustus was committed to unified action—he praised actions of which "no politician can be alarmed, no sectary can be jealous"—for the temporal happiness of others.[58] This concern motivated his involvement in a number of other societies, both secular and religious. As early as the first decade of the 1800s, he supported the New York Hospital (and later served as its president) and the New York Society Library. In subsequent decades, he became involved in the Society for the Prevention of Pauperism, served as a trustee for Columbia College, worked for the establishment of a savings bank for the poor in New York City, contributed greatly to the New York Law Institute, and headed the New-York Historical Society. During the 1830s, he served as president of the Public School Society, which became a flashpoint due to its use of the King James Bible, a policy that upset many Roman Catholics.[59] These benevolent organizations sought to give practical aid to a variety of groups and to maintain social order.

Jay's reforming attitudes appeared also in his address to the Temperance Society, which reflected his concern for orderly moral and social reform. He opened optimistically, noting, "The good effects [reform societies] have produced on the manners and customs of society and the improvement they have made upon the social and moral condition of man have contributed much to place us on the high and exalted station which in a moral point of view we now occupy." Here again, Jay's focus was on the "moral point of view." From that perspective, temperance was commendable for being "so salutary in its moral operation" and amenable to "every well wisher of the human race." Jay emphasized the moral and social benefits of temperance, rather than focusing on individual salvation. Christian benevolence helped to support the cause, but its strength lay rather in the good it did for society. The real danger of alcohol, to his mind, was moral. "Its effects upon the mind are demoralizing. It eradicates every principle of virtue and honor." Because of its effects, he called on his hearers to "destroy this monster" of drunkenness. To do so, Jay urged total abstinence as a type of "moral evolution," an insight that would cut at the root of the curse of inebriation. Throughout the address, he repeated that temperance was the moral approach for the Christian, the patriot, and the philanthropist. Each element supported the others. Thus, in his peroration, he could make a final plea to his hearers: "Are you Patriots—your Country bids you come—Are you Christians—the interest of your Master bids you come—Are you Philanthropists—the cry of suffering thousands bid you come—Are you *Men*, then come and aid us in exterminating this *foe* of man."[60] Together, these elements justified his

moral reform activities. He and his associates were reworking the conception of civil society, so that it would will itself to control itself. Because
of the power of cultural activity, Christian benevolence could create a
powerful influence for the republic.

Final Retirement, Final Political Thoughts

The last twenty years of Jay's life were spent more or less withdrawn from
politics. Offered opportunities to reenter political life, whether to run for
Congress as a Federalist or for the chancellorship of the state, he declined
them all.[61] Years later, he even received an offer to run for Congress on
the Whig ticket in 1840. "I have been very strongly pressed to be a candidate for Congress," he told his brother, "but at my age I do not think it
worth while to begin a political life."[62] William agreed with this decision,
commenting, "Had you been elected, you would have found it difficult
to satisfy a party so many of whose leaders boast of their Jeffersonian
Republicanism."[63] That political divisions of the early republic remained
contentious several decades later is significant. Just as in 1820 when Peter
Augustus had professed his loyalty to Federalist principles, so too would
they continue to influence his analysis of events during his retirement.

In his retirement, Jay interpreted national political developments
through his earlier experiences and the principles he continued to hold.
His disinterest in democratic politics led to his distaste for any of the candidates in the 1820s.[64] Specific policies, on the other hand, engaged his
interest. The threat of Indian removal bothered him. "Georgia has succeeded in bullying the Genl. Govt. in an alliance with her for the purpose
of depriving the friendly Indians of their lands," Jay wrote to James Fenimore Cooper. "I am sorry for this, for I think it a measure wh. will injure
our nations character."[65] The concern for national morality and character
was a traditional Federalist idea. Peter feared such an act would speak
poorly of the nation. Many others agreed with him.[66] Jay took note of the
tariff debates and grew concerned when South Carolinians pushed ahead
in threatening nullification. While the crisis was going on, he compared
South Carolinians' attitudes to those of Thomas Jefferson. Jefferson possessed "qualities no good man would wish to have ascribed to him," and,
with his attacks on Federalists and on the federal government, opened
the door for nullification. "His doctrines are at this moment producing
their affect in S. Carolina & threaten to endanger the prosperity & happiness of our country." Here again was the old Federalist concern that
Democrats were working to undermine the Union. With Andrew Jack-

son's strong action, the Nullification Crisis seemed to abate, and for once Jay gave Jackson some credit.[67]

In other letters, Jay reiterated common Federalist themes. He continued to value the union's functioning, if imperfectly, under the Constitution. "We are the freest & most prosperous people on the Globe & ought to be [consistently] more thankful than we are for the blessing we receive from a beneficent providence," he wrote, with a hint of his father's providentialism.[68] Other categories from the early republic also found their way into his thinking. In discussing political upheavals in Europe, he interpreted calls for greater democracy in terms of violent Jacobinism.[69] Finally, his Democratic opponents still bore a whiff of infidelity. Martin Van Buren, a fellow New Yorker, had seemingly aligned himself with the most dangerous elements: "The union of Mr. Van Buren with the ultra Radicals & Infidels & their priests effects to excite the poor against the rich, compel all who wish well to Religion & to the stability of property to oppose him."[70] The danger of infidelity, albeit in very muted form, remained, and Democrats were still not to be trusted.

Even so, Jay could only muster tepid support for the Whigs. In 1840, he reluctantly agreed to speak at a Whig campaign rally. His actions were more motivated by opposition to Van Buren and the Democrats than by any conviction of the necessity of electing William Henry Harrison. "Whether affairs will be better managed when Harrison is Prest. no one can foretell, but as I really think the present administration a very corrupt one, I shall rejoice at its fall," was his assessment.[71] Although he was able to rejoice at Van Buren's loss, the alternative did not excite him. He predicted little would come of the Whigs. "The Whigs whose bond of union has been a common enemy, will probably divide & what measures will be pursued cannot be foreseen."[72] Jay did not believe that the Whigs offered much of a positive alternative. He did not see the Whigs, perhaps because of their ties with the Jeffersonians, as recapturing the vision of the Federalists, of moral elites respecting the Constitution and governing to produce national strength and public good. His experiences had inculcated a deep mistrust in politics, which concluded in disillusionment. In one of his last letters, he stated flatly, "I am heartily sick of politics & am so little satisfied with either of the parties which now distract our country that I can judge of them & their measures, if not wisely at least without partiality."[73] From political success to political defeat to disengagement, Jay's involvement in politics had mirrored that of many other younger Federalists. The energy that had earlier found its way into politics was now redirected into private, moralistic voluntary streams. These Volun-

tarist activities were not simply a surrender to political setbacks but became an innovative strategy to use the power of culture to shape society.

Thus, Peter Augustus Jay, although always cognizant of John's legacy,
also altered it by emphasizing only one aspect of it—its stress on moral
behavior for social improvement. His work contributed to the American
Victorian concern for morality and moral reform, apart from religious
structures. His concern for morality was an admission that he had abandoned politics. Still, his vision of elite-led, genteel social reform would
shape not only New York but much of urban America in the middle
decades of the nineteenth century.[74] By contrast, his brother, William,
would have more success in producing change, but he would do so
through religiously inspired social reform.

8 William Jay

NONPOLITICAL MORAL
AND RELIGIOUS REFORM

WHEREAS PETER AUGUSTUS JAY WAS BORN IN THE YEAR OF IN-dependence, William Jay was not born until 1789, the year the federal government went into operation. By the time he reached an age of political awareness and activity, the Federalists' influence was much diminished. He had no ties to earlier Federalist dominance, no memories of political rejection or ejection from office. To a much greater extent than his brother, the possibilities of the early republic were wide open for him. He possessed greater liberty to innovate in his political and religious opinions. His actions suggest another course of action for Federalists and their children after the Combative strategy had failed and the Federalists were no longer dominant—the use of religious Voluntarism in the realm of civil society.

His father, John, guided William's education, placing him with politically Federalist, theologically orthodox instructors. When the time came for William to attend college, John chose the most reliable Federalist institution available, Timothy Dwight's Yale.[1] At Yale, William made connections with individuals such as N. W. Taylor, Gardiner Spring, and James A. Hillhouse, Federalist scions who would become ministers and join Jay in his religious endeavors. He also strengthened his friendship with James Fenimore Cooper, two sons of Federalist fathers making their way in the world.[2] Even more important than student connections, Jay sat under the teaching of President Dwight. He would later write to Dwight, "I retain a grateful recollection of your kind attention to me, and I have, and trust will ever have, reason to acknowledge the goodness of Providence in placing me under your care, when many of my opinions were to be formed, and my principles established."[3] Jay's early recognition of Dwight's formative influence suggests a great deal about his conduct. It connects Jay with Dwight's campaign against infidelity, his evangelical pietism, and his vision of social order.

Many years later, looking back, Jay praised the New England environment embodied at Yale by its president. To several New Englanders
he reported, "Educated in one of the Colleges of New England, I early
conceived a veneration for the habits and institutions of that portion of
our country; a veneration which subsequent experience & observation
have only tended to deepen." Jay was primarily celebrating the churches'
functioning in a public role and supporting self-governing citizens and
communities. Hence, he could assert, "The good order & happiness of
New England afford many instructive lessons. They teach us that liberty
& equality when under the guidance of religion, do not lead as they did in
infidel France to anarchy & despotism . . . that the influence of the Bible
is no less conducive to the tranquility of the State than to the individual."
Jay was thus moulded by the political lessons of Dwight's idealized New
England.[4] For Jay, public happiness required both liberty and religion to
be properly understood, with the Bible applied to individual and public
matters. In such a setting, liberty and equality could genuinely flourish,
avoiding the excesses of "infidel France." Moreover, they could serve as a
counterweight to his other opponents, which by the 1830s had appeared
in the slaveholding South.

Jay reflected Dwight's strategy of social reform through moral reform
in two of his early pamphlets. In 1826, he wrote a prize-winning essay on
the importance of the Sabbath, arguing that the institution of the Sabbath
(celebrated on Sunday) was part of God's moral law and hence incumbent on human beings. Although his point was primarily religious, he
also noted the importance of the Sabbath for society. He observed that
it "has contributed more than any human institution whatever, to the
peace and good order of society . . . and that the degree of reverence with
which it is regarded, affords in general a safe and accurate criterion of
public and individual morality."[5] Sabbath-keeping indicated respect for
the entire moral law instituted by divine command and was necessary for
public happiness. In laying out his argument, Jay was directly indebted to
Dwight, drawing on material Dwight had collected and acknowledging
him in two separate footnotes.[6] Similarly, in a pamphlet attacking duel-
ing, Jay took up the same cause as had Dwight and argued in very similar
terms. In both cases, Jay was echoing his teacher.[7] His basic ideas were
thus shaped at the center of evangelical Federalism.

When Jay tried to follow his father and brother into the study of law
after college, he was initially stymied. A weakness in the eyes caused him
to break off his education with an attorney at Albany and retire to the
family home at Bedford, New York. This was his first and most significant

retirement, moving to the countryside before a public political life could really start. Jay's influence, from then on, would not be through elected office. Instead, he would turn to writing and moral suasion to advance his vision of social reform. After some rest, his eyes recovered enough that he passed the bar, and Governor Daniel Tompkins appointed him judge of Westchester County. Although this local office was of limited scope, it helped to support Jay's family, and he served in it from 1818 until 1843. He avoided obvious partisanship during the whole period he was on the bench. "For twenty years or more I have had no connection with party politics, and have attended no party meeting," he commented in 1843. "It appeared to me unbecoming a judge to be a political partisan." He renounced outright political activity, favoring instead the personally disinterested, nonpartisan approach to the law advocated by the Federalists. While not actively partisan, Jay identified with Federalist ideals: "Those [political] opinions belong to the old Washington school—I have never concealed them."[8] These political beliefs, which Jay claimed had remained unchanged through twenty years of public service, would be expressed obliquely during much of his life. Only in his later years, after politics had deprived him of his judgeship, would he enter again into political debate—and then from a very different perspective. Central to understanding Jay is his seeking moral, social, and even political reform from a nonpolitical stance. This approach offered very real influence in shaping society and correcting evils, even as holding office and using it to direct society went beyond his conceptual range.

Christian Voluntarism

Jay began to implement Dwight's vision of moral reform in Bedford, where he experimented with local reform societies, including the Bedford County Society against Intemperance and Vice. The cooperation among denominations excited Jay, as he reported that "Methodists, Presbyterians, Baptists, & [Episcopalians] all support it." Similarly, he worked with his father in the founding of the Westchester County Bible Society.[9] These endeavors prepared Jay for his activities on a national stage in the development of the American Bible Society (ABS).

He would prove a significant actor in the movement to found the ABS. In so doing, he cooperated with many evangelical Federalists to establish an important institution that would further the religious beliefs he had learned at Yale. Inspired by Elias Boudinot's call for a meeting to discuss a national Bible society, he wrote and published *A Memoir on the*

Subject of a General Bible Society for the United States of America. Writing to Boudinot, Jay reported, "Having watched with solicitude, the result of your efforts to establish a Bible Institution for the United States, it was with very great pleasure, I learned from your Circular that there was now a prospect of success."[10] In the pamphlet, he argued that scattered local societies were not sufficient to supply the need for Bibles throughout the country. His familial Federalism reappeared when he denied the ability of a loose confederacy of existing societies to meet these needs. Instead, he proposed a new, national organization to which the existing societies would become auxiliaries—just as the states had become subordinated to the federal government. The national Bible society he called for would be modeled on the British and Foreign Bible Society; in fact, Jay's proposed constitution was a barely modified version of the British society's.[11] His proposed constitution became the starting point for discussion when delegates met in New York City in May 1816.

Leading up to the convention, Boudinot and Jay worked together to clarify strategy. Boudinot strongly approved of Jay's proposal, claiming it gave him "great encouragement" and offering only minor changes. He also suggested several leaders for the national society, naming Federalists such as John Jay, Caleb Strong, Timothy Dwight, and Jedidiah Morse—individuals who would soon come to be associated with the ABS.[12] William Jay was thus operating in harmony with Boudinot when he attended the convention as a delegate from the Westchester County Bible Society. Due to the recognition of his previous work, Jay was appointed to the committee for drafting the ABS constitution. Not surprisingly, the final result closely resembled his initial proposal.[13] With the work completed, he quickly sent a copy of the constitution to Boudinot, along with his congratulations "on this great & glorious event."[14] He later reported to his father, "On the whole, it appears to me that the prospects of the Society are very flattering."[15]

Despite Jay's optimism, not all shared his approval of the new realignment of religious organizations, and his forthright support for the ABS led him into an eight-year debate with Episcopalian Bishop John Henry Hobart. With the establishment of the ABS, Hobart called on Episcopalians to support their own New York Bible and Common Prayer Book Society, instead. Hobart believed that the Book of Common Prayer should necessarily accompany biblical distribution, to keep interpretation tied to Episcopalian theology. He also feared that energy devoted to the ABS would detract from denominational endeavors. Jay answered in an anonymous pamphlet, *Dialogue between a Clergyman and a Lay-*

man, responding that participation in Bible societies would neither en-danger Episcopalian identity nor weaken support for the valid ministries of the church. Rather, the ABS was dedicated to the spread of the scrip-tures, something upon which all Christians could agree. In the process, Jay made the clergyman character look ridiculous, as well as making Bishop Hobart seem outside of the consensus of the rest of the Episcopal Church.[16]

Several years later, while John Jay was serving as the president of the ABS, Hobart again spoke out against Bible societies, in the process por-traying the elder Jay as misguided. William Jay quickly responded to de-fend the familial reputation. The debate stretched through several rounds, and in the process, the two debaters defined contrasting approaches to the Church and its relation to society. Whereas Hobart was trying to de-fend denominational particularities, Jay was arguing for participation in a Christian work that, because it was less particular, could embrace mul-tiple denominational perspectives. Inspired by the possibilities of evan-gelism, conversion, and consequent moral reform, he encouraged and labored for this reorientation of American religion—to the chagrin of his bishop.[17]

Jay's continued support of both his local Bible society and the ABS was part of his oft-repeated reliance on the scriptures. As he told his brother, "The Scriptures afford an inexhaustible field for study & investigation as well as for instruction; & we can scarcely read a single chapter with atten-tion, without discovering some new beauty or new meaning."[18] The Bible societies also formed a site where he could cooperate with other denomi-nations for agreed-upon goals that transcended denominational identity. The result was a Protestant ecumenism and support for an evangelical Christian identity, centered on conversion of spirit and holiness of life, which downplayed without eliminating denominational distinctions.[19] The Bible societies thus embodied the type of spiritually motivated social reform that Jay advocated. His professed ideals translated into his actively working for the Bible societies, attending local and national meetings well into the 1850s.[20] His original work with, and continued support of, Bible societies formed an important aspect of his life and contributed to his methods and goals for subsequent reform societies.

Christian Voluntarism and Social Reform

Jay's work with the Bible societies led him into involvement with other reform movements, particularly temperance, pacifism, and antislavery.

In each of them, he argued for moral reform from an explicitly Christian perspective. He began working against drunkenness as early as 1818, and the 1830s especially saw him active with the temperance movement. Again, his reform activity began locally, with involvement in the Westchester County Temperance Society, which he served as president. In Bedford, Jay watched as the society quickly grew to a membership of five hundred.[21] He also worked to advance temperance beliefs in the Episcopal Church, bemoaning the "great ignorance & therefore great lukewarmness" still present in the church while desiring to be "instrumental in removing it."[22] He contributed addresses to temperance meetings and attended their assemblies for many years.[23] The 1840s saw Jay grow increasingly interested in pacifism, and he even worked as the president of the American Peace Society for a decade.[24] He linked the abandonment of warfare with moral reform, as a benevolent project for all of humanity.

Most important to Jay was his work against slavery. In his taking an abolitionist position, three interpretive points stand out.[25] First, his extended effort against slavery grew from religious concerns, his concerns for morality and moral reform, and his desire to protect the Constitution. These impulses were linked together in ways that had been forged by Federalists in the previous generation.[26] Second, this beginning point formed the basis for his strategy of opposing slavery in religious terms and religious contexts. He hoped that moral suasion would succeed, which made him skeptical of political activity. Third, his desire for constitutional integrity made him worry about the state of both the antislavery movement and the country in general.

In striking language over more than thirty years, Jay spoke of the work against slavery in decidedly Christian language. The moral impulse was built on deeply held religious beliefs. In his first known objection to slavery, he corresponded with—strikingly—Elias Boudinot with whom he had worked in the ABS. In 1819, Boudinot attempted to organize Northern opposition to accepting Missouri as a slave state. Jay agreed with Boudinot, writing to him, "I have no doubt that the laws of God, and, as a necessary and inevitable consequence, the true interests of our country, forbid the extension of slavery. If our country is ever to be redeemed from the curse of slavery the present Congress must stand between the living and the dead and stay the plague. Now is the accepted time, now is the day of salvation." As in other settings, the moral law of God set the standard for public policy. Drawing on a story from Israel's wilderness wanderings, Jay pictured Congress acting like Moses's priestly brother Aaron, stopping the curse—the curse of slavery. Using New Tes-

William Jay in the 1830s, a period of great abolitionist efforts. Daniel Hunting-
ton. *William Jay*, 1838–39. Oil on canvas. (JJ.1958.304. John Jay Homestead State
Historic Site, Katonah, N.Y. New York State Office of Parks, Recreation, and
Historic Preservation)

tament language, Jay announced that opponents of slavery should act immediately, thereby creating a new political salvation for both the slaves
themselves and the American republic.[27]

Two decades later, he again stressed that Christian obedience demanded resistance to slavery. Writing to an ally he asserted, "In the affairs
of life . . . duty is I believe the true criterion of expediency. . . . If slavery
be sinful it is unquestionably the will of God that we should oppose it."
The expedient course for abolitionists to pursue was the one commanded

by God, which involved working for the good of all humanity. Jay went on to state that he believed their strategy entailed "the *exhibition of truth in christian faithfulness*," which he called "the great instrument" for their cause. He also believed that this was the true expression of "*christian* anti-Slavery." At this point, he still believed that moral persuasion, advanced by pointing out the evils of slavery and appealing to the consciences of slaveholders, was the most effective, most responsible course of action.[28] Of course, such an approach proved unworkable and ineffective—as Jay himself would come to realize. Still, he encouraged himself and others to persevere through religious assurance of their right: "In God's 'duetime' we shall reap if we faint not."[29] For over thirty years, he portrayed resistance to slavery as a religious struggle, one in which God Himself was interested.[30]

Abolition also had practical bearing for the churches in America and for Jay's own Episcopal Church. He addressed several writings to American churches and Christians in general, pointing to the sin of treating a human being as a commodity. "Slavery is the conversion of a rational, accountable, immortal being, made in the image of God and a little lower than the angels, and for whom Christ died, into a CHATTEL, an article of property, a vendible commodity." He objected to this commodification because it deprived men and women of their standing as people, of their natural rights, and of their spiritual equality with whites. He traced this failure in the churches back to a too-easy acceptance of the surrounding culture. Rather than standing for clear moral right, the church had taken the easy road of bowing to popular pressure and accepting injustice. William presented a different option, a countercultural church. "The Church militant will find her strength and safety only in unceasing conflict with the world, however dire may be the strife. . . . But when she . . . calls to her aid the selfish passions and sinful prejudices of society, she is treacherous to her Lord, and forms a truce with her enemies fatal to herself," he wrote.[31] The American Church had been unfaithful to her Lord in tolerating the sin of slavery. To change the church and fight such an evil, great zeal was required, zeal demonstrated by the abolitionists. They at least clearly understood the moral evil of slavery, and Jay hoped to convince many more in the churches.

Jay also argued against racism, which he called the sin of caste. Just as churchgoers had capitulated to popular attitudes regarding slavery, so they failed by not treating black men and women as equal with themselves. He was direct: "Hence the institution of CASTE in the Church, and the obloquy, injustice, and cruelty connected with it, . . . [rest] simply and

frankly on pecuniary interest, personal antipathy, and popular prejudice."[32] American churchmen, both Northern and Southern, could not
even find biblical support for racism. They were more motivated by their
own prejudices, self-interest, and the surrounding culture than by justice. For Jay, the problem began with religious leaders. He bemoaned the
fact that "the community has been practically taught by their political, &
alas! . . . their religious instructors, that they are released from the obligations of Christianity in their intercourse with men of dark complex-
ions."[33] In the category of moral influence, both political and religious
leaders stood high but performed poorly. In failing to condemn "caste,"
they taught that racial exclusion was acceptable. Jay grasped that abolitionists had to do more than fight slavery in the South. They also had to
confront racial exclusion closer to home. He challenged Northerners not
to rest content in their supposed moral superiority, when they showed
the same detestable attitudes to free blacks living among them as Southerners did to their slaves.[34]

Jay argued that the need for action in the church was pressing because
of the challenge of infidelity—thereby revealing one more way in which
he had been listening to Dwight. Jay believed that the church's response
to slavery opened the door to infidelity among abolitionists—a charge
he leveled directly at proslavery Episcopal bishops.[35] He decried the fact
that "the church of the living God is the great buttress of slavery and caste
in the United States. If any plea can be urged in behalf of infidelity, it
is that Christianity as represented by multitudes of its official teachers
authorizes the abrogation of all its precepts of humility, justice, and benevolence in the treatment of persons to whom God has given a coloured
skin." When the church refused to take a moral stand, abolitionists distrusted its teachings, and he sympathized with such a response. He told
a minister, "I confess, my dear sir, that were I a young man . . . I fear I
should be strongly tempted to believe that a religion such as it is practically exhibited by your cotton-parsons could not and did not proceed
from a just and benevolent being." Ministers who refused to acknowledge the evils of slavery gave credence to their opponents. Jay argued that
this tendency expressed itself in abolitionist meetings. "Antislavery con-
ventions," he observed, "are whatever the leaders present happen to be;
sometimes disgustingly irreligious, and very often Jacobinical and disorganizing."[36] Infidelity could lead once again to Jacobin tendencies—ram-
pant egalitarianism, leveling, and the disorganizing of society.[37]

To fight slavery, Jay worked with the American Anti-Slavery Society
(AASS), and several of his works were published in cooperation with the

AASS.[38] During 1838–39, he grew dissatisfied with the drift of the organization and supported a withdrawal from the society led by the evangelical reformer brothers, Arthur and Lewis Tappan. Historians have dissected the splintering of the antislavery movement, highlighting the "woman question" and personal animosities as points of dispute.[39] From Jay's correspondence over the matter, the additional theme of constitutionalism emerges. His education among Federalists, training as a lawyer, and position as a judge made him particularly defensive on matters of constitutionalism. His arguments with the AASS actually concerned two interlocking constitutions: the U.S. Constitution and the constitution of the AASS. When he felt both were being endangered, he dissociated himself from the AASS.

Jay's commitment to the U.S. Constitution contained a particular reading of the federal government's relation to slavery. He believed that Congress could legislate about slavery in the District of Columbia and so argued that slavery in the district should be abolished. Jay believed this was necessary since "the very Capital of our Republic is now the great slave mart of the U. States & large gangs of slaves fastened to long chains are frequently driven past that Hall in which the Representatives of the greatest Republic are pouring forth their Declamations on behalf of liberty and equality." He did not think, however, that Congress had any power over the states where it already existed. For Jay to support the Constitution fully, he believed he had to use other means—primarily moral persuasion—to convince slaveholders to give up their slaves. Thus, he could assert, "Having sworn to support the Constitution of the U. States, I am one of the last men, who would sanction any unconstitutional interference by Congress with Slavery."[40] The problem arose when abolitionists, led by New York lawyer Alvan Stewart, began to pass resolutions asking Congress to legislate against slavery in the states. Stewart planned to take this strategy to the national meeting of the AASS. Jay censured Stewart's suggestion, as he informed Lewis Tappan, "The measure recommended by Mr. S. is in my opinion sinful, & utterly at variance with the oath I have taken to support the Constitution of the U. States. Hence there can be no compromise on this subject."[41] Stewart's measure took on added significance because it also contradicted the constitution of the AASS, which had explicitly ruled out congressional abolition of slavery. To counter Stewart, Jay worked with Tappan to design a counter-resolution at the 1838 national meeting. When the AASS rejected that measure and actually amended the constitution along lines proposed by Stewart, Jay felt the society had abandoned him. If the AASS no longer recognized the validity of the U.S. Constitution, he had no choice but to disengage.[42]

Although rewriting the AASS constitution was the major issue for Jay, he was also disturbed by the tendency to couple antislavery with other issues, which he believed showed disrespect for the organization's constitution. Whereas the original AASS constitution had been silent on other matters to avoid distractions, Jay had recently observed "frequent attempts to use Abolition as a pack-horse to carry forth into the world some favorite notion having no legitimate connection with the Anti Slavery cause." One detour proposed by some abolitionists involved particular religious beliefs. He castigated the society for an official editorial endorsing "a decoction of dried currents [sic] as a substitute for the fermented juice of the grape in the observance of the Lord's Supper!!" William was not arguing the religious merits of the claim—although he opposed it—but rather that such detours were "dishonest in their character & dangerous in their consequences, to the continuance and efficiency of our organization."[43] An organization pontificating about the spiritual merit of dried currants could not effectively fight slavery. The problem was even worse with the woman question—and here Jay was also influenced by earlier Federalist discussions about women in society. Although he apparently was willing to let Angelina Grimké as a single Quaker woman speak against slavery, he was more suspicious of married women's serving in public offices. He believed this was an "unwarrantable attempt to alter the relative social condition of the female sex." He believed the AASS had been hijacked to become "an instrument for advancing the doctrine of the equality of the Sexes, in all the relations of life."[44] Apart from whether women's equality was a worthy goal, the AASS's constitution had said nothing about it, and imposing it on the whole membership was therefore wrong. Although Jay still believed in the moral strength of antislavery, he now doubted the efficacy of the AASS. "I am full of confidence that Providence has decreed the abolition of slavery," he told fellow New York abolitionist Joseph Pierce, "but I begin to suspect that Anti-Slavery Societies on the present plan are not the chosen instruments."[45] By 1840, he had officially left the AASS and begun to work with the Tappans' new organization, the American and Foreign Anti-Slavery Society. In the years to come, Jay's antislavery energies would find other outlets.

Antislavery Politics

In the final period of his life, Jay became increasingly concerned with the political consequences and loss of American liberties that he believed would follow the failure to oppose slavery. Slavery raised the issue of whether the constitutional order put in place by John Jay and other Federalists would continue. William Jay's rhetoric carried concerns over republicanism, liberty, and Christian responsibility. Confronting the gag-rule over antislavery petitions to Congress, Jay continued to encourage petitions, and he thanked John Quincy Adams for his battle to receive them: "In common with every true & consistent republican, I feel & acknowledge my obligations to you for your faithful & fearless resistance to the usurpations of the Slaveholding power." Jay objected to Southerners' refusal even to allow debate on the issue of slavery. He also worried about slavery's proponents at the local level, as he confronted the growing danger of antiabolitionist mobs. Shocked by the murder of abolitionist printer Elijah P. Lovejoy, Jay encouraged his son in the work "to dry up a fountain which is deluging our land with crime, & threatening to engulf our liberties." His image of a fountain was particularly apt, as he envisioned violence continuing to wash over abolitionists unless some way was found to end it. In another letter, Jay interpreted the mob actions through his belief in human depravity. As a result of this belief and the political outlook of his Federalist sire, he distrusted the reaction of the mass of people. "This thing called public sentiment is a most detestable tyrant, & a very cowardly one two [*sic*]; & he is quickly intimidated by a firm honest resistance."[46] He kept hoping for such a firm resistance, but it did not come.

Behind the mobs and political activities, Jay saw several groups conspiring. At the national level, he saw political demagogues—using the same language that John Jay had—making use of the excitement over slavery. "Patriotism now sells well in the market" was his assessment.[47] Everywhere he saw businessmen and capitalists willing to terrorize abolitionists to gain a greater share in trade, thereby calling traditional American liberties into question. Both Northerners and Southerners seemed to be selling liberty for money and the continuation of slavery, "speculating, not merely in land & banks, but in the liberties of the People."[48] Southerners were encouraging this trend. When the annexation of Texas was under consideration, he warned, "If these men triumph, our County will be converted into one wide field of cruelty, oppression & anarchy: the annexation of Texas will subject the whole Confederacy to the arrogant dominion of the Slaveholders, lynch mobs will usurp the seat of justice, & the pistol & the bowie knife be substituted for the statute book."[49] Only the cooperation of abolitionists could prevent such dire political dangers. To that end, Jay urged, "The obligations of religion & patriotism, the duties we owe to ourselves, our children, the course of freedom & the course of humanity, all require us to be faithful to our principles to persevere in our exertions & to surrender our rights only with our breath."[50] Faced with the dangers of a proslavery conspiracy, he called for abolitionists to redouble their efforts.

While making such a call, Jay's concerns for moral reform of society and moral persuasion as the means to advance abolitionism left him suspicious of political approaches to the problem and severely limited his interest in a political solution. Whereas earlier Federalists had used politics to shape society, by the 1830s, Jay saw politics as a diversion from influencing society, a marker of a loss of vision. He warned that substituting "*political* anti-Slavery" for religious and moral approaches would be disastrous. "Should they become a political party striving for office & power, they wd. be joined by a corrupt & selfish herd & losing their moral feelings & moral influence, might prove dangerous to the peace & stability of our Republic." After the splintering of the AASS, he was unsure what direction the cause should take, but he was sure it was not a political one. He bemoaned the fact that "many ... are trying to get office for themselves by persuading Abolitionists to abandon the use of moral suasion & to substitute for it a third political party. Money which ought to be spent in enlightening the consciences of Slaveholders is fruitlessly squandered in electioneering." Politics seemed a diversion that was wasting money, energy, and focus. Not surprisingly, Jay cast a jaundiced eye on James Birney's Liberty party when it entered the 1840 presidential election. "I much fear," Jay wrote to Lewis Tappan, "that Birney's canvass will render abolitionists contemptible in the eyes of politicians & perhaps in their own."[51] When Birney's party only received a paltry number of votes, these fears seemed confirmed. Jay believed that for all the energy extended, nothing positive had been accomplished.

Jay had even less confidence in the two major parties. He had no truck with Democrats, who he believed were controlled by the Southern "slave power." More of his scorn, however, was heaped upon the Whigs. In 1840, he looked down upon their populist electioneering, calling the outcome of the election "the political tornado ... raising in the whirlwind the multitudinous and discordant elements, which constitute the modern 'Whigs.'" Jay's predilection for a Federalist style of society and

politics—even if he was not a part of that politics—emerged in his satiriz-
ing of the election. "The *People* have expressed their will. . . . How far it
will advance the interest of the Country time will shew. . . . That they are
selfish, or incapable of distinguishing between a mere demagogue & a
genuine patriot, is of course an impossible supposition."[52] The results had
been attained by an appeal to the masses, and he believed such an appeal
could easily be outdone in the next election. Even more disturbing to
him was the Whigs' conduct once in office. He found the actions of Cot-
ton Whigs reprehensible, and no one received more criticism than Daniel
Webster, whom Jay believed unprincipled when it came to slavery.[53]

Events drew Jay into the Liberty party nonetheless. In 1842, members
in Ohio launched a campaign to unseat Birney and make Jay president of
the party and its candidate for president in the subsequent election. He
declined this opportunity, but he grew more interested in the party, especially as a means of opposing the annexation of Texas and the Mexican
War. By 1844, he was willing to be nominated as a Liberty party candidate
for Congress. He lost that election, just as he did when nominated for
the Senate in 1845 and 1847. Yet by 1848, he had grown optimistic about
the party's chances. As he informed his son, "Our politics are in a most
extraordinary & complicated state. The old parties are greatly disorga-
nized. . . . The *third* or free soil party, to which the abolitionists have almost unanimously attached themselves is making wonderful progress."
He hoped that many years of labor would soon bear real fruit. He later
went so far as to claim, "The AntiSlavery party under the name of the
free soil party has become formidable to the others, & will before long
be predominant in the Northern States." This comment reveals that Jay
continued to see the party as merely about antislavery. In fact, he actively
worked to keep the Liberty party interested in only that single issue,
avoiding other distractions.[54] He committed himself to the principle that
"I shall leave the Liberty party whenever it makes abolition a pack-horse
to carry favourite measures unconnected with slavery, whether those
measures are of whig or democratic origin."[55] Jay, even during his involvement in politics, never came back to a coherent political philosophy.
Rather, politics were a useful strategy to advance a moral and religious
cause.

Despite the Liberty party's existence, Jay grew increasingly discour-
aged in the last years of his life. Republican virtue seemed to have slipped
away from the nation. His worries about annexation of Texas seemed un-
heeded. As he observed, "No confidence whatever is to be placed in the
sincerity of any declarations the Slaveholders may make respecting Slav-

ery, except when they avow their determination to extend & perpetuate it. I fear there is not virtue enough in our country to avert the catastrophy with which we are threatened." Distrusting Southerners' motives and bracing for the worst, Jay could only watch events play themselves out. After annexation of Texas contributed to the war with Mexico, he remarked to his son, "Our sin will find us out, & Texas may yet prove the ruin of our confederacy." In addition to warning of danger, William penned *A Review of the Causes and Consequences of the Mexican War*, another attack on the Southern interests that had brought on the war.[56]

As Jay entered his seventh decade and the nation entered the 1850s, conditions seemed to grow even darker. Jay had known Charles Sumner before he went to Washington as a senator and even advised him. Jay was horrified at Preston Brooks's caning of Sumner and even more horrified at Southern approval of Brooks's action.[57] The expansion of slavery into Kansas seemed to trumpet the triumph of slavery. Near the end of Jay's life, he delivered a dire assessment of the republic he and his family had been so involved in for so long: "To me the prospects of our country seem gloomy in the extreme." He continued, "The plaudits bestowed on Brookes, evince a corruption, or rather an extinction of the moral sense in the Slave-holding community, which I confess both surprises & alarms me. The election of Buchanan & the consequent establishment of Slavery in Kansas will I fear seal the doom of our country, & render us the basest of Republics." Virtue had finally drained from the republic; corruption had come to dominate. The slave power seemed ascendant. In its course, it would crush American liberties.[58]

Although William Jay believed he was defending his father's life and work, in subtle ways both he and Peter Augustus had modified John's thought in response to changing conditions. Just as Peter Augustus had turned simply to elite moral reform, so William also lost the Federalist political vision, wrapped up as he was in religious reform. When William turned again to politics at the end of his life, it was as an extension of his religious reforms. His concern for an antislavery party showed that his vision of politics was piecemeal—unable to offer a holistic vision. Religion's place in the republic was preserved, even advanced, but at a loss of full integration into the political sphere. William, like his brother, illustrated and encouraged significant trends in American religion, politics, and culture, as the nation developed from the Federalist republic of the 1790s to the antebellum nation of the 1830s, 1840s, and 1850s. A Combative approach to religion and politics had dissolved, replaced by a Voluntarist vision with its own strengths and weaknesses.

Epilogue

FEDERALISTS, RELIGION,
AND AMERICAN POLITICS

No longer competitive after the War of 1812, the Federal-ist party passed out of existence. Its heirs lived long enough to see the union that Federalists had worked so hard to establish be threatened by slavery and sectionalism. The Civil War would first endanger its existence and then, through the war's conduct, transform it. Although the Federalist party failed to endure, its implications were profound for both American politics and American culture. As historian Marshall Foletta has observed, "The culture of Federalism was perhaps more powerful, and certainly more enduring, than the party. . . . [It] would persist as a vital force in American affairs."[1] In its enduring effects, Federalist religious and political culture shaped American culture. The perception of religion, politics, and their intersection in the new nation and beyond bore the imprint of Federalist activity.

The zealous actions of the Federalists point to a central reality of the early republic: it was a scene of intense religious contest. Rather than creating a homogenous, unified Protestant republic, the revolution had actually created multiple religious options. Americans from the very beginning differed on theology, establishment, and the formal presence of religion in public life. This contested religious character suggests a further reason for the general upheaval of the early republic. Not only did participants not know the likelihood of their political success; they also did not know the exact religious character of the nation they were creating. In dealing with such ultimate matters regarding not only this life but eternity, the era's passion becomes more comprehensible. Understanding the early republic as a scene of religious contest can reorient how we think about the period. With religious ferment occurring throughout the nation, conflict rather than consensus was the order of the day for religious matters. That the religious situation was uncertain puts Federalist activity and accomplishment in new perspective. Federalists had a strong hand in formulating how traditional Christianity would shape the new nation.

Religion and the Federalist Party

I have argued that religion was a significant element for the politics of the Federalist party. In a contested religious environment, Federalist leaders creatively responded to the uncertainty within the early republic, crafting a strategy that at least preserved a place for public religious expression and at most sacralized politics. They built upon the Republican attitude toward religion and politics that broadly characterized the era of the revolution, but different groups found different ways of modifying it in the early republic. Given such conditions, the creativity of the evangelical wing of Federalism was particularly striking. They developed a distinctively Combative attitude of intermingling religious with Federalist political categories. Ministers such as Timothy Dwight and Jedidiah Morse set out to defend a religious American republic, but faced with perceived threats from infidelity and Illuminatism, they developed an aggressive politics intent on restraining both religious unbelief and political revolution. Evangelical Federalist laity also furthered this vision, with varying degrees of success. John Jay's understanding of the actions of providence in the nation, coupled with his personal experiences of political passions in the 1790s, led him to adopt an increasingly strong, Combative connection. Caleb Strong—whose conduct earned him the initial moniker of "Patriotism and Piety"—attempted a political approach emphasizing his personal piety, which although insuring his reelection failed to provide a coherent framework for programmatic Federalist politics. Elias Boudinot also strongly endorsed a Combative attitude toward religion in the new nation, which he implemented during his public career. In his retirement, his work with voluntary societies helped pioneer a Voluntarist outlook that many Federalist would follow in the coming years. For these evangelicals, religion motivated their political involvement and added passion to their political activity.

Yet not all Federalists were smitten with the evangelicals' Combative approach, and these disagreements pointed to the dangers of basing a political party on religious principles that were not universally embraced. These fault lines became apparent with the Massachusetts Unitarians, including John Adams and Henry Ware, Sr. They shared with the evangelicals a concern for an orderly society and public religiosity, but they differed on the role of conversion and the place of human reason within religion, emphasizing instead morality and the rationalist reinterpretation of traditional Christian doctrines. Although seemingly ideal political allies, evangelicals and Unitarians after 1800 were divided by theological controversies, with significant political ramifications. Religious fault lines weakened the Federalist party in its New England hearth region. Unitarians moved instead to a moralistic Voluntarism that would shape their elitist vision for social reform in the decades to come. Similarly, South Carolina Federalists—even when they shared the theological tenets of the evangelicals, as Henry William De Saussure and Charles Cotesworth Pinckney did—never adopted the Combative strategy. The absence of a church establishment and the presence of slavery shifted the social dimensions for Southern Federalism. With a Southern accent, Federalism was never able to articulate the religious dialect that Northern evangelicals were advancing. They thus maintained a Republican vision of religion as one factor among many that contributed to the social order. To further this agenda, they supported some voluntarist activity.

As the Federalist party disintegrated, Federalists looked for alternatives, motivated by both the push out of politics and the pull of the potentialities for Voluntarist activity. Here the Jay family is particularly instructive. Peter Augustus, who as a young man had experienced Federalist political success, was forced from public life and grumpily watched politics deteriorate. In response, he supported a range of voluntary societies with the ideal of encouraging the growth of public morality. His elitist vision encouraged the rise of a Victorian moral outlook. William, by contrast, never experienced disillusionment and so was free to experiment. Drawing on his Yale training, he favored religiously based social reform movements, from Bible distribution to pacifism to abolition. His life truly exemplified how Federalist sons could shape the culture of the early republic after the party was no more.

This narrative demonstrates how significant religion was for the Federalist party. A reassessment of the Federalists' cultural politics is thus in order. Not merely an afterthought, religion played a motivating role for multiple groups within the party. Religious belief needs to be considered as a shaping factor for how Federalists thought about politics and society, as well as an agent for both party growth and subsequent disintegration. This approach should prompt historians to reconsider the motivations and goals of Federalist politics and to widen perspectives on what the party was about, so as to comprehend their vision of cultural and religious formation and improvement.

Federalists and American Religion

Further, the Federalist imbrication of religion in politics had a significant structural impact on the practice of religion in America. This encounter of religion and politics happened at an important time in the development of American religion, usually described as the Second Great Awakening. Although more attention has been paid to the Southern and Western manifestations of the awakening, the reenergizing and mobilizing of evangelicals in the Northeast was also part of it. They, too, attempted to Christianize the American republic—for the first time, it should be noted. Recognizing that in fact evangelical Christianity was *not* the default belief of the entire nation, they set out to make it so. Their actions forced religious matters into the public gaze and helped to establish the "Antebellum spiritual hothouse."[2]

In their active engagement in politics and development of Voluntarism, these Federalists contributed to a reorganization of religion in the early republic, a "Federalization of American Christianity." Alongside the democratizing effects of the early republic, an organizing and centralizing dynamic also occurred, which drew upon Federalist outlooks on government and society. Much of the energy of the Second Great Awakening could easily have dissipated if it had not been channeled into courses designed by Federalists. Without the Federalists, Christianity in America might not have retained its vitality. Lacking organization, it might have retreated further into an energetic pietism. Instead, the "Federalization of American Christianity" directed religious energy outward, into the world. After initial polemics, non-Federalist groups such as Methodists and some Baptists either joined in Federalist organizations or created their own denominational copies.

In concrete ways, Federalists made it possible for individual Christians to express and practice their faith. As early as the 1790s, some Federalists demonstrated that political involvement could function as a type of lived religion. For citizens of a self-governing republic, politics was a necessary concomitant of faith, not an optional practice. This clearly tied American religion into the practice of government. Further, Federalists led the way in the development of religious voluntary societies, such as the American Bible Society and others. With the nationalist vision gained as Federalists, leaders such as Elias Boudinot organized these societies on a national scale. Such national organizations reached into local auxiliary chapters and provided "on the ground" means to practice faith and demonstrate belief. There they invited men *and* women of all classes to participate, producing an accessible, zealous piety. Through Federalist actions, Protestants now had greater opportunities and new venues in which to practice their faith. As a final step, this Voluntarist development also laid the groundwork for specifically moral societies dedicated to social reform. Thus, activities such as abolition or opposition to Indian Removal took the shape they did because of religious motivations. Many American Protestants engaged in these out of specifically religious concerns. Moving into the antebellum period, the opportunities for moral reform of society existed because the Federalists had led the way.

On the other hand, these developments also meant losses, and the initial intentions of religious Federalists demonstrate the costs of these developments. As the nation became more mobile and more fragmented, Federalists were not able to hold communities together. They had lost a communal vision that could harmonize society. As the market revolution spread, the republican ideal of social harmony and mutually adaptable interests broke down, and the Federalists could provide no comprehensive answer. Similarly, as religious practice shifted and broke away from a decaying Federalist party, religious Federalists lost a holistic vision for addressing political matters. The new voluntarist societies were usually single-issue oriented. Rather than retaining an overarching social ideology, Federalism's heirs devoted their energies to one cause or another. Although effective in particular cases, this strategy left a patchwork of societies with no overarching direction. Religious Federalists had neither the numbers nor the ability to compel unanimity, but strikingly, they never tried after the party collapsed. Finally, in their Voluntarist developments, these Federalists contributed to an attenuation of denominational identity. In seeking cooperation across groups, they had to minimize denominational particularities. Thus the complaints Bishop John Henry Hobart made against the Jays had some merit. In their religious societies, they were acting as evangelical Protestants, rather than as Episcopalians or Presbyterians. The immediate success of these endeavors led to the lessening of appreciation for churchly traditions in the early republic.

Federalism, Religion, and Public Life

In addition to their effects on religion, Federalists also contributed greatly to the terms of religion's operation in American public life. In an environment with unknown horizons, they not only shepherded the Constitution to ratification but also helped to guide the nation as it found its way into living with the Constitution and building a national culture.

Although the Democratic-Republicans strongly denounced Federalist administration, they never questioned the actual constitutional regime. Further, Federalists demonstrated the wisdom of acceding to elections, even when those elections went against them. They thus demonstrated real commitment to the practices of republican self-government. Finally, when out of power, they provided a helpful counterbalance to the surging Democratic-Republican party, tempering its more extreme tendencies.

As part of their constitutional thinking, Federalists wrestled with the undefined nature of religion in the public life of the republic. Endorsing the First Amendment's rejection of an established church, the Federalists still worked for a strong presence of public religion. Denying both Thomas Jefferson's "wall of separation" and the Baptist desire for informal, personal religious influence, Federalists sought for a public religiosity, a formal recognition of the place of religion in public life as a necessary support of the republic. They idealized the moment when religious citizens simultaneously worked for their own good and the good of the community. This would be the fulfillment of Micah's prophecy that every man would sit under his own vine and fig tree, with none to make him afraid.

In doing so, they encountered opponents of contrasting religious beliefs—some who agreed on Christian theology yet differed on its place in society, some who had very different religious beliefs, and some who held to religious skepticism. The energy of the political debates in the early republic grew, at least in part, from the religious fervor that infused competing perspectives. Religious individuals brought to the public sphere both religiously motivated ideals and politically motivated attacks cloaked in religious language. In advancing a vision of a religious republic, the Federalists pioneered ideals that would continue to inform Americans and would emerge in significant ways at subsequent points—during the Civil War era, in the 1920s, and amid post–World War II religious conservatism, to name a few. Struggles over religious discussion in the public sphere are thus not new developments but part of contests that reach back to the earliest days of the American republic.

The debates about religion and the nation, then, have continued to be informed not by a single religious perspective but by multiple and often conflicting perspectives. This reality helps to explain both the ongoing salience of religion in public life and its continuing contested nature. Religious conflict in politics should be acknowledged as part of the dialectic of American public life. The Federalists, with their provocative, irascible voices, contributed to the formation of American politics and to the terms of continuing American political and religious debate.

Notes

Introduction

1. Timothy Dwight, *The Duty of Americans, at the Present Crisis, Illustrated in a Discourse, Preached on the Fourth of July, 1798* (New Haven, CT: Thomas and Samuel Green, 1798), 20–21.

2. Throughout this study, I refer to the Federalist party even though the Federalists were not as organized or self-conscious a party as later nineteenth-century parties would be. They remained more of a movement with shared political outlooks and some coordination but without much formal organization. I refer to their opponents (interchangeably) as "Democrats," "Democratic-Republicans," "Republicans," or "Jeffersonians." Although somewhat more organized, they, too, lacked significant party mechanisms. On this point, see Ronald Formisano, "Federalists and Republicans: Parties, Yes—System, No," in Paul Kleppner, ed., *The Evolution of American Electoral Systems* (Westport, CT: Greenwood Press, 1981), 33–76.

3. Examples would include Stephen Berk, *Calvinism versus Democracy: Timothy Dwight and the Origins of American Evangelical Orthodoxy* (Hamden, CT: Archon Books, 1974), and John Fitzmier, *New England's Moral Legislator: Timothy Dwight, 1752–1817* (Bloomington: Indiana University Press, 1998).

4. William Doyle, *The Oxford History of the French Revolution* (New York: Oxford University Press, 1989), 252–71.

5. For reprints of Dwight's sermon and other documents, see *The Middlesex Gazette*, September 14, September 21, and September 28, 1798; Democraticus, *The Middlesex Gazette*, September 28, 1798.

6. Caleb Strong, *Patriotism and Piety* (Newburyport, MA: Edmund M. Blunt, 1808), iii, 200–202.

7. John Murrin, "A Roof without Walls," in Richard Beeman, Stephen Botein, and Edward Carter III, eds., *Beyond Confederation: Origins of the Constitution and American National Identity* (Chapel Hill: University of North Carolina Press, 1987), 333–48.

8. For an overview of these options, see Mark Noll, *America's God: From Jonathan Edwards to Abraham Lincoln* (New York: Oxford University Press, 2002).

9. Although evangelicalism is notoriously difficult to define, many have opted for the definition provided by David Bebbington. Bebbington's "quadrilateral" emphasizes four traits: conversionism, activism, biblicism, and crucicentrism. Bebbington,

Evangelicalism in Modern Britain: A History from the 1730s to the 1980s (Grand Rapids, MI: Baker, 1989), 2–3.

10. For an extended discussion of Unitarianism, see chapter 5.

11. Christopher Grasso, "Deist Monster: On Religious Common Sense in the Wake of the American Revolution," *Journal of American History* 95 (June 2008): 43–68; Amanda Porterfield, *Conceived in Doubt: Religion and Politics in the New American Nation* (Chicago: University of Chicago Press, 2012), 14–47; Eric Schlereth, *An Age of Infidels: The Politics of Religious Controversy in the Early United States* (Philadelphia: University of Pennsylvania Press, 2013).

12. William G. McLoughlin, *Soul Liberty: The Baptists' Struggle in New England, 1630–1833* (Hanover, NH: University Press of New England, 1991); Thomas Kidd, *God of Liberty: A Religious History of the American Revolution* (New York: Basic Books, 2010), 167–86.

13. Nathan Hatch, *The Democratization of American Christianity* (New Haven, CT: Yale University Press, 1989). See also John Wigger, *Taking Heaven by Storm: Methodism and the Rise of Popular Christianity in America* (New York: Oxford University Press, 1998).

14. Although in quotation marks here, throughout the text these categories will be represented by capital letters, and so capitalized forms should be understood to refer to these specific categories, whereas lowercase usage only signals a general sense of the term.

15. Debate over republicanism is extensive. Daniel Rodgers questioned the use of term in "Republicanism: The Career of a Concept," *Journal of American History* 79 (June 1992): 11–38. Still, it is a useful category to investigate the political debates of the early republic. That religion and republicanism could coexist in the early republic is demonstrated by Isaac Kramnick, "The 'Great National Discussion': The Discourse of Politics in 1787," *William and Mary Quarterly*, third series, 45 (January 1988): 3–32, and James T. Kloppenberg, "The Virtues of Liberalism: Christianity, Republicanism, and Ethics in Early American Political Discourse," *Journal of American History* 74 (June 1987): 9–33. Mark Noll, in *America's God*, 73–92, has pointed out the prominent place republicanism had for American Christianity in this period. Marshall Foletta argues that Federalists, in fact, were better interpreters of the republican heritage than their Democratic opponents. Foletta, *Coming to Terms with Democracy: Federalist Intellectuals and the Shaping of an American Culture* (Charlottesville: University Press of Virginia, 2001), 5–7.

16. This Voluntarist perspective builds on older descriptions of voluntarism in the early republic but extends them by stressing their strong connection in origin to religious Federalism. The best recent discussion of voluntarism comes from Johann Neem, *Creating a Nation of Joiners: Democracy and Civil Society in Early National Massachusetts* (Cambridge, MA: Harvard University Press, 2008). Neem observes, "We still need to know how evangelicals learned to use voluntary associations to express their religious ideals" (212n8). By connecting voluntarism to its Federalists origins, this study provides an important answer. Older studies of voluntarism include Charles Foster, *An Errand of Mercy: The Evangelical United Front, 1790–1837* (Chapel Hill: University of North Carolina Press, 1960); Clifford Griffin, *Their Broth-*

ers' Keepers: Moral Stewardship in the United States, 1800–1865 (New Brunswick, NJ: Rutgers University Press, 1960); and Lois Banner, "The Protestant Crusade: Religious Missions, Benevolence, and Reform in the United States, 1790–1840" (Ph.D. diss., Columbia University, 1970).

17. Kenneth Minkema and Harry Stout, "The Edwardsean Tradition and the Antislavery Debate, 1740–1865," Journal of American History 92 (June 2005): 47–74; Robert Abzug, Cosmos Crumbling: American Reform and the Religious Imagination (New York: Oxford University Press, 1994), especially 30–56; Daniel Walker Howe, What Hath God Wrought? The Transformation of America, 1815–1848 (New York: Oxford University Press, 2007), 164–70, 188–95, 348–52.

18. This is best expressed in Carla Gardina Pestana, Protestant Empire: Religion and the Making of the British Atlantic World (Philadelphia: University of Pennsylvania Press, 2009). Pestana builds on Linda Colley, Britons: Forging the Nation, 1707–1837 (New Haven, CT: Yale University Press, 1992). Thomas Kidd demonstrates how this was expressed in colonial New England in The Protestant Interest: New England after Puritanism (New Haven, CT: Yale University Press, 2004), 1–73. For political and social thought, see Gerald McDermott, One Holy and Happy Society: The Public Theology of Jonathan Edwards (University Park: Pennsylvania State University Press, 1992).

19. This change in public speech is documented well in Christopher Grasso, A Speaking Aristocracy: Transforming Public Discourse in Eighteenth-Century Connecticut (Chapel Hill: University of North Carolina Press, 1999). Part of this shift was economic, as described by Joyce Appleby in Capitalism and a New Social Order: The Republican Vision of the 1790s (New York: New York University Press, 1984), and Peter S. Field, The Crisis of the Standing Order: Clerical Intellectuals and Cultural Authority in Massachusetts, 1780–1833 (Amherst: University of Massachusetts Press, 1998).

20. Nathan Hatch, The Sacred Cause of Liberty: Republican Thought and the Millennium in Revolutionary New England (New Haven, CT: Yale University Press, 1977), 55–138; Mark Noll, Christians in the American Revolution (Grand Rapids, MI: Christian University Press, 1977), 49–102; Noll, America's God, 53–137; Nicholas Guyatt, Providence and the Invention of the United States, 1607–1876 (New York: Cambridge University Press, 2007), 82–109.

21. The distinction of expansion "through time" versus the Democrats' vision of expansion "though space" comes from Drew McCoy, The Elusive Republic: Political Economy in Jeffersonian America (Chapel Hill: University of North Carolina Press, 1980), 5–11, 166–208. Recent works concerned with improvement include J. M. Opal, Beyond the Farm: National Ambitions in Rural New England (Philadelphia: University of Pennsylvania Press, 2008), and John Fea, The Way of Improvement Leads Home: Philip Vickers Fithian and the Rural Enlightenment in Early America (Philadelphia: University of Pennsylvania Press, 2008).

22. Thomas Slaughter limned political distinctions in The Whiskey Rebellion: Frontier Epilogue to the American Revolution (New York: Oxford University Press, 1986), 127–42.

23. In the past decade, historians have realized the significance of the French

Revolution for American political culture in the 1790s. Rachel Hope Cleves points to the formation of an anti-Jacobin discourse centered on the problem of violence. The contest over the French Revolution, though, carried a significant religious component that is not fully recognized in her work. Cleves, *The Reign of Terror in America: Visions of Violence from Anti-Jacobinism to Antislavery* (New York: Cambridge University Press, 2009), 58–103. Seth Cotlar has pointed to the Federalist attempt to defeat "popular cosmopolitanism" through encouraging localism. Cotlar, *Tom Paine's America: The Rise and Fall of Transatlantic Radicalism in the Early Republic* (Charlottesville: University of Virginia Press, 2011). Philipp Ziesche has examined these political debates through the lens of Americans in Paris during the Revolution. Ziesche, *Cosmopolitan Patriots: Americans in Paris in the Age of Revolution* (Charlottesville: University of Virginia Press, 2010). Finally, Andrew Robertson notes religious difference without exploring it in "'Look on This Picture . . . And on This!': Nationalism, Localism, and Partisan Images of Otherness in the United States, 1787–1820," *American Historical Review* 106 (October 2001): 1263–80. Although these studies occasionally touch on religion, they largely miss how significant it was for anti-Jacobinism and the Federalist party generally.

24. Porterfield has described this as a crisis of doubt in the early republic. Porterfield, *Conceived in Doubt*, 1–13, 78–112.

25. On honor, see Joanne Freeman, *Affairs of Honor: National Politics in the New Republic* (New Haven, CT: Yale University Press, 2001).

26. Daniel Walker Howe, *The Political Culture of the American Whigs* (Chicago: University of Chicago Press, 1979), 1–2. In tracing these connections, this study echoes the approach of J. C. D. Clark, *The Language of Liberty, 1660–1832: Political Discourse and Social Dynamics in the Anglo-American World* (New York: Cambridge University Press, 1994).

27. In my shorthand description, I am echoing Simon Newman's description of political culture in *Parades and the Politics of the Street: Festive Culture in the Early American Republic* (Philadelphia: University of Pennsylvania Press, 1997), 5–6. See also Jean Baker, *Affairs of Party: The Political Culture of Northern Democrats in the Mid-Nineteenth Century* (Ithaca, NY: Cornell University Press, 1983), 12.

28. Jeffrey Pasley, Andrew Robertson, and David Waldstreicher, "Introduction," in Pasley, Robertson, and Waldstreicher, eds., *Beyond the Founders: New Approaches to the Political History of the Early American Republic* (Chapel Hill: University of North Carolina Press, 2004), 9–11; David Waldstreicher, "Federalism, The Style of Politics, and the Politics of Style," in Doron Ben-Atar and Barbara Oberg, eds., *Federalists Reconsidered* (Charlottesville: University Press of Virginia, 1997), 99–117.

29. The benefits of this approach are suggested by Andrew R. L. Cayton, "Insufficient Woe: Sense and Sensibility in Writing Nineteenth-Century History," *Reviews in American History* 31 (September 2003): 331–41. Jean Baker's study of Democratic political culture takes a similar approach. Other scholars who have found this strategy useful include Joseph Ellis, *After the Revolution: Profiles of Early American Culture* (New York: Norton, 1979); Alan Taylor, *William Cooper's Town: Power and Persuasion on the Frontier of the Early American Republic* (New York: Knopf, 1995); Howe, *The Political Culture of the American Whigs*; and George Marsden, *Jonathan Edwards: A*

Life (New Haven, CT: Yale University Press, 2003). On contingency, see David Hackett Fischer, *Washington's Crossing* (New York: Oxford University Press, 2004), 5–6, 364–67.

30. Rosemarie Zagarri, *Revolutionary Backlash: Women and Politics in the Early American Republic* (Philadelphia: University of Pennsylvania Press, 2007); Susan Branson, *These Fiery Frenchified Dames: Women and Political Culture in Early National Philadelphia* (Philadelphia: University of Pennsylvania Press, 2001); Catherine Allgor, *Parlor Politics: In Which the Ladies of Washington Help Build a City and a Government* (Charlottesville: University Press of Virginia, 2000).

31. On Wollstonecraft, see Andrew Cayton, *Love in the Time of Revolution: Transatlantic Literary Radicalism and Historical Change, 1793–1818* (Chapel Hill: University of North Carolina Press, 2013). That issues of gender and marriage could shape partisan allegiances in the early republic is evident from Michael D. Pierson, *Free Hearts & Free Homes: Gender and American Antislavery Politics* (Chapel Hill: University of North Carolina Press, 2003).

32. Albrecht Koschnik, *"Let a Common Interest Bind Us Together": Associations, Partisanship, and Culture in Philadelphia, 1775–1840* (Charlottesville: University of Virginia Press, 2007), 153–83; Catherine O'Donnell, *Men of Letters in the Early Republic: Cultivating Forums of Citizenship* (Chapel Hill: University of North Carolina Press, 2008); Opal, *Beyond the Farm*.

33. This study builds on earlier generations of concern for the Federalists. David Hackett Fischer's *The Revolution of American Conservatism: The Federalist Party in the Era of Jefferson Democracy* (New York: Harper and Row, 1965) was monumental for its time and still proves an important starting point. Linda Kerber's *Federalists in Dissent: Imagery and Ideology in Jeffersonian America* (Ithaca, NY: Cornell University Press, 1970) makes some sense of Federalist attitudes after 1800. James Banner's *To the Hartford Convention*, with its focus on both ideology and political organization, provides context for Federalist attitudes and activities. Banner, *To the Hartford Convention: The Federalists and the Origins of Party Politics in Massachusetts, 1789–1815* (New York: Knopf, 1970). Overviews of the politics of the 1790s come from Stanley Elkins and Eric McKitrick, *The Age of Federalism* (New York: Oxford University Press, 1993); James Rogers Sharp, *American Politics in the Early Republic: The New Nation in Crisis* (New Haven, CT: Yale University Press, 1993); and Gordon Wood, *Empire of Liberty: A History of the Early Republic, 1789–1815* (New York: Oxford University Press, 2009).

34. David Waldstreicher, *In the Midst of Perpetual Fetes: The Making of American Nationalism* (Chapel Hill: University of North Carolina Press, 1997); Newman, *Parades and the Politics of the Streets*; Len Travers, *Celebrating the Fourth: Independence Day and the Rites of Nationalism in the Early Republic* (Amherst: University of Massachusetts Press, 1997); Jeffrey Pasley, "The Cheese and the Words," in Pasley, Robertson, and Waldstreicher, eds., *Beyond the Founders*, 31–56.

35. Among many examples, see Jeffrey Pasley, *"The Tyranny of Printers": Newspaper Politics in the Early American Republic* (Charlottesville: University Press of Virginia, 2001); Paul Linebaugh and Marcus Rediker, *The Many-Headed Hydra: Sailors, Slaves, Commoners, and the Hidden History of the Revolutionary Atlantic* (Boston:

Beacon Press, 2000); Paul Gilje, *Liberty on the Waterfront: American Maritime Culture in the Age of Revolution* (Philadelphia: University of Pennsylvania Press, 2004); and John Saillant, *Black Puritan, Black Republican: The Life and Thought of Lemuel Haynes, 1753–1833* (New York: Oxford University Press, 2002).

36. Strikingly, this study answers a challenge posed throughout Ben-Atar's and Oberg's collection, which was capped by James Banner, Jr.'s declaration, "The Federalists—Still in Need of Reconsideration," in Ben-Atar and Oberg, eds., *Federalists Reconsidered*, 246–53.

37. It is worth noting that even Alexander Hamilton in the last years of his life proposed a "Christian Constitutional Society" that echoed the themes developed by the religious Federalists in this work. Hamilton to James Bayard, April 16, 1802, in Harold Syrett, ed., *The Papers of Alexander Hamilton*, vol. 25 (New York: Columbia University Press, 1977), 605–10.

38. David Hackett Fischer, *Revolution of American Conservatism*, 29–49, 129–49, 182–99. Subsequent comment on Fischer's project pointed out that the splits between "Old" and "Young" Federalists were not as strongly delineated as he suggested. Shaw Livermore traced the final decline of the Federalists in *The Twilight of Federalism: The Disintegration of the Federalist Party, 1815–1830* (Princeton, NJ: Princeton University Press, 1962). Philip Lampi recently argued that Federalist decline began later than is normally assumed. Lampi, "The Federalist Party Resurgence, 1808–1816: Evidence from the New Nation Votes Database," *Journal of the Early Republic* 33 (Summer 2013): 255–81.

39. McCoy, *The Elusive Republic*. See also Lance Banning, *The Jeffersonian Persuasion: Evolution of a Party Ideology* (Ithaca, NY: Cornell University Press, 1978).

40. Jonathan Sassi in *A Republic of Righteousness: The Public Christianity of the Post-Revolutionary New England Clergy* (New York: Oxford University Press, 2001) provides the best description of the evolution of the clerical outlook on "public Christianity." Noll, *America's God*, 3–18, 447–51; Harry Stout, "Rhetoric and Reality in the Early Republic: The Case of the Federalist Clergy," in Mark Noll, ed., *Religion and American Politics: From the Colonial Period to the 1980s* (New York: Oxford University Press, 1990), 62–76; Gary B. Nash, "The American Clergy and the French Revolution," *William and Mary Quarterly*, third series, 22 (July 1965): 392–412; Ruth Bloch, *Visionary Republic: Millennial Themes in American Thought, 1756–1800* (New York: Cambridge University Press, 1985).

41. Examples include Chris Beneke and Christopher Grenda, eds., *The First Prejudice: Religious Tolerance and Intolerance in Early America* (Philadelphia: University of Pennsylvania Press, 2011), 1–20; Laurie Maffly-Kipp, Leigh E. Schmidt, and Mark Valeri, eds., *Practicing Protestants: Histories of Christian Life in America, 1630–1965* (Baltimore: Johns Hopkins University Press, 2006), 1–15; and David Hall, ed., *Lived Religion in America* (Princeton, NJ: Princeton University Press, 1997).

42. Candy Gunther Brown, *The Word in the World: Evangelical Writing, Publishing, and Reading in America, 1789–1880* (Chapel Hill: University of North Carolina Press, 2004), 18.

43. For democratization, see Hatch, *The Democratization of American Christianity*. This is not to argue that democratization as Hatch described it did not oc-

cur, but an equally significant development for Federalist-inspired organization and institution-building was also in process. Barton Price deployed this concept in a complementary way in "Evangelical Periodicals and the Making of America's Heartland, 1789–1900" (Ph.D. diss., Florida State University, 2011), 69–75.

1 John Jay and the Shift from Republican Religion to Evangelical Federalism

1. John Jay to Jedidiah Morse, August 16, 1809, John Jay Papers, Rare Book and Manuscript Library, Columbia University, New York (hereafter JJP), Box 25.

2. Although people with many different beliefs discussed Providence during the revolutionary era, Jay used the term in a decidedly orthodox fashion. David Holmes has rightly observed about Jay that "most of his language was that commonly used in the orthodox Protestant circles of his time: 'Saviour,' 'King of Heaven,' 'Author and Giver of the Gospel,' 'Lord of the Sabbath,' 'Almighty God,' 'Lord of Hosts,' 'Almighty and benevolent Being,' 'Master,' and 'Captain of our Salvation.'" Because Jay used such orthodox language, his use of terms such as "Providence" should be read as the traditional, Calvinist view of God as actively working in the world. Holmes, *The Faiths of the Founding Fathers* (New York: Oxford University Press, 2006), 158.

3. On the multiple uses of Providence in early America, see Guyatt, *Providence and the Invention of the United States*, especially 95–108, 137–57.

4. This chapter builds on the previous work of Jay biographers. The tradition began with John's son William. William Jay, *The Life and Writings of John Jay: With Selections from His Correspondence and Miscellaneous Papers*, 2 vols. (New York: J. and J. Harper, 1833). Frank Monaghan's biography became the standard work for most of the twentieth century. Monaghan, *John Jay: Defender of Liberty, against Kings & Peoples, Author of the Constitution & Governor of New York, President of the Continental Congress, Co-Author of the Federalist, Negotiator of the Peace of 1783 & the Jay Treaty of 1794, First Chief Justice of the United States* (New York: Bobbs-Merrill, 1935). Recently, Walter Stahr has published *John Jay: Founding Father* (New York: Hambledon and London, 2005).

5. As Robert Ferguson puts it, "Left behind in these [previous] treatments are the ideas and cultural beliefs that Jay actually wielded so effectively." Ferguson, "The Forgotten Publius: John Jay and the Aesthetics of Ratification," *Early American Literature* 34 (Fall 1999): 236n3. This chapter seeks to address the lack that Ferguson points out. This chapter offers a much fuller description than the one previous article that has considered Jay's religion: Patricia Bonomi, "John Jay, Religion, and the State," *New York History* 81 (January 2000): 9–18.

6. Jay, *Life*, 1:434–42; Monaghan, *John Jay*, 25; Stahr, *John Jay*, 6–12, 232–36.

7. Jay to Uzal Ogden, February 14, 1796, JJP, Box 23.

8. Jay to John Bristed, April 23, 1811, JJP, Box 26.

9. Richard Morris, "The American Revolution Comes to John Jay," in Jacob Judd and Irwin Polishook, eds., *Aspects of Early New York Society and Politics* (Tarrytown, NY: Sleepy Hollow Restorations, 1974), 96–117; Monaghan, *John Jay*, 52–61; Stahr, *John Jay*, 34–41.

10. John Jay, "Address to the People of Great Britain," in Jay, *Life*, 1:466. On reli-

gious discontents and the coming of the revolution, see Patricia Bonomi, *Under the Cope of Heaven: Religion, Society, and Politics in Colonial America* (New York: Oxford University Press, 1986), 187–216.

11. Jay, *Life*, 1:468, 473, 474; Linda Colley, *Britons*, 11–54.

12. Jay, *Life*, 1:474–75.

13. Quoted in Monaghan, *John Jay*, 85; Milton Klein, "John Jay and the Revolution," *New York History* 81 (January 2000): 19–30.

14. Monaghan, *John Jay*, 59; Stahr, *John Jay*, 37.

15. Bonomi, "John Jay, Religion, and the State," 15–16; Monaghan, *John Jay*, 94; Stahr, *John Jay*, 78.

16. Monaghan, *John Jay*, 95.

17. John Jay, *An Address of the Convention of the Representatives of the State of New-York to Their Constituents* (Fishkill, NY: S. Loudon, 1776), 3, 6, 7–9, 13, 18.

18. Ibid., 4–5, 10, 11.

19. John Jay, *The Charge Delivered by the Honourable John Jay, Esq. Chief Justice of the State of New-York, to the Grand Jury, at the Supreme Court, Held in Kingston, in Ulster County, September 9, 1777* (Kingston, NY: John Holt, 1777), 6–8.

20. Monaghan, *John Jay*, 106–24; Stahr, *John Jay*, 92–111.

21. Jay to George Washington, April 21, 1779, quoted in Jay, *Life*, 2:44–45.

22. John Jay, "Notes," in ibid., 1:96.

23. Frank Brecher, *Securing American Independence: John Jay and the French Alliance* (Westport, CT: Praeger, 2003), 159–218; Bradford Perkins, *The Cambridge History of American Foreign Relations, volume 1, The Creation of a Republican Empire, 1776–1865* (New York: Cambridge University Press, 1993), 17–54.

24. Jay to Margaret Livingston, July 12, 1783, JJP, Box 17; Jay to Robert Morris, September 12, 1783, JJP, Box 17.

25. Jay to William Livingston, July 19, 1783, JJP, Box 17.

26. Jay to Egbert Benson, September 12, 1783, JJP, Box 17; Jay to John Philip Schuyler, September 16, 1783, JJP, Box 17; Jay to Robert R. Livingston, September 12, 1783, JJP, Box 17.

27. Monaghan, *John Jay*, 245–70; Stahr, *John Jay*, 197–218. For Jay's work in Constitution-making, see John Kaminski, "Shall We Have a King? John Jay and the Politics of Union," *New York History* 81 (January 2000): 31–58.

28. Jay to John Adams, November 1, 1786, JJP, Box 19; Jay to Thomas Jefferson, October 27, 1786, JJP, Box 19; Jay to George Washington, June 27, 1786, in W. W. Abbot and Dorothy Twohig, eds., *The Papers of George Washington, Confederation Series*, vol. 4 (Charlottesville: University Press of Virginia, 1995), 130–32.

29. Jay to Thomas Jefferson, July 14, 1786, JJP, Box 19.

30. Jay to George Washington, June 27, 1786, in Abbot and Twohig, eds., *Papers of George Washington, Confederation Series*, 4:130–32; Jay to John Adams, November 1, 1786, JJP, Box 19.

31. Jay to George Washington, June 27, 1786, in Abbot and Twohig, eds., *Papers of George Washington, Confederation Series*, 4:130–32.

32. Ibid.

33. Jay to Thomas Jefferson, October 27, 1786, JJP, Box 19.

34. Jay to Thomas Jefferson, August 18, 1786, JJP, Box 19; Jay to Thomas Jefferson, December 14, 1786, JJP, Box 19; Jay to John Adams, July 4, 1787, quoted in Kaminski, "Shall We Have a King?" 50.

35. Jay to George Washington, March 16, 1786, JJP, Box 19.

36. Jay to George Washington, June 27, 1786, in Abbot and Twohig, eds., *Papers of George Washington, Confederation Series,* 4:130–32.

37. John Jay to William Petty, Lord Shelburne, Marquis of Lansdowne, April 16, 1786, Andre De Coppet Collection, Manuscripts, Archives, and Special Collections, Firestone Library, Princeton University, Princeton, NJ, Box 18.

38. Stahr, *John Jay,* 246; Monaghan, *John Jay,* 282–84; Jay to John Adams, October 16, 1787, JJP, Box 20.

39. Monaghan, *John Jay,* 284–93; Stahr, *John Jay,* 248–53. For a strong assessment of Jay's significance for ratification, see Robert Ferguson, *Reading the Early Republic* (Cambridge, MA: Harvard University Press, 2004), 151–71. On Jay's rhetoric in the *Federalist Papers,* see Todd Estes, "The Voices of Publius and the Strategies of Persuasion in *The Federalist,*" *Journal of the Early Republic* 28 (Winter 2008): 541–48.

40. John Jay, Federalist 2, *The Federalist Papers,* ed. Clinton Rossiter, rev. edn. (1961; New York: Signet, 1993), 32–33. Indeed, Jay is the only one of the three authors to refer to "Providence." James Madison makes a passing reference to "Heaven" in 20, refers to God in 18 and 43, and speaks of the Almighty and "a finger of that Almighty hand" in 37. Even so, Jay's treatment of the providential union of America is the longest religious reflection in the *Federalist Papers.*

41. John Jay, *An Address to the People of the State of New-York, on the Subject of the Constitution, Agreed upon at Philadelphia, the 17th of September, 1787* (New York: Samuel and John Loudon, 1788), 3, 6, 9, 16, 19. Jay makes reference to the biblical passages of Micah 4:4, I Kings 12:16, and Proverbs 11:14.

42. Quoted in Clarence Miner, *The Ratification of the Federal Constitution by the State of New York,* Studies in History, Economics, and Public Law, no. 214 (New York: Columbia University, 1921), 108–9.

43. For ratification, see Monaghan, *John Jay,* 294–97; Stahr, *John Jay,* 255–67; Kaminski, "Shall We Have a King?" 52–58; Linda Grant De Pauw, *The Eleventh Pillar: New York State and the Federal Constitution* (Ithaca, NY: Cornell University Press, 1966); and Stephen L. Schechter, ed., *The Reluctant Pillar: New York and the Adoption of the Federal Constitution* (Troy, NY: Russell Sage College, 1985). Pauline Maier similarly recognized Jay's importance. Maier, *Ratification: The People Debate the Constitution, 1787–1788* (New York: Simon and Schuster, 2010), 333–40, 345–400.

44. Jay to Jedidiah Morse, April 24, 1800, Jedidiah Morse Papers, Manuscripts and Archives Division, New York Public Library, Astor, Lenox, and Tilden Foundations (hereafter NYPL), Box 1.

45. For Jay's time on the Supreme Court, see William Casto, *The Supreme Court in the Early Republic: The Chief Justiceships of John Jay and Oliver Ellsworth* (Columbia: University of South Carolina Press, 1995); Sandra F. VanBurkleo, "'Honour, Justice, and Interest': John Jay's Republican Politics and Statesmanship on the Federal

Bench," in Scott Douglas Gerber, ed., *Seriatim: The Supreme Court before John Marshall* (New York: New York University Press, 1998), 26–69; and Richard Morris, *John Jay, the Nation, and the Court* (Boston: Boston University Press, 1967).

46. John Jay, *The Charge of Chief Justice Jay to the Grand Juries on the Eastern Circuit: At the Circuit Courts Held in the Districts of New-York, on the 4th, of Connecticut on the 22nd Days of April; of Massachusetts on the 4th, and of New-Hampshire on the 20th days of May, 1790* (Portsmouth, NH: George Jerry Osborne, Jr., 1790), 7, 9, 12–14.

47. Monaghan, *John Jay*, 274; Jay to Jedidiah Morse, February 28, 1797, Jedidiah Morse Papers, NYPL, Box 1.

48. John Jay, "At the Opening of the Circuit Court at Richmond," May 22, 1793, JJP, Box 57.

49. Jay to Rufus King, December 12, 1793, Rufus King Papers, New-York Historical Society (hereafter NYHS), Box 4; Jay to Rufus King, December 22, 1793, Rufus King Papers, NYHS, Box 4; Jay to Rufus King, December 19, 1793, Rufus King Papers, NYHS, Box 4. See also Elkins and McKitrick, *The Age of Federalism*, 346–65.

50. Jay to Sarah L. Jay, April 9, 1794, quoted in Landa Freeman, Louise North, and Janet Wedge, eds., *Selected Letters of John Jay and Sarah Livingston Jay: Correspondence by or to the First Chief Justice of the United States and His Wife* (Jefferson, NC: McFarland, 2005), 219; Elkins and McKitrick, *The Age of Federalism*, 388–406.

51. Jay to Sarah L. Jay, April 15, 1794, in Freeman, North, and Wedge, eds., *Selected Letters*, 220–21; Jay to Sarah L. Jay, April 20, 1794, JJP, Box 21.

52. Elkins and McKitrick, *The Age of Federalism*, 406–14; Perkins, *The Cambridge History of American Foreign Relations*, 95–105; Monaghan, *John Jay*, 364–81; Stahr, *John Jay*, 313–30; Jay to Rufus King, November 19, 1794, Rufus King Papers, NYHS, Box 5. On the treaty generally, see Todd Estes, *The Jay Treaty Debate, Public Opinion, and the Evolution of Early American Political Culture* (Amherst: University of Massachusetts Press, 2006).

53. Monaghan, *John Jay*, 385; Jay to Edmund Burke, December 12, 1795, JJP, Box 23; Jay to Rufus King, November 14, 1797, Rufus King Papers, NYHS, vol. 41; Robert Isaac Wilberforce and Samuel Wilberforce, *The Life of William Wilberforce* (London: J. Murray, 1839), 2:57.

54. Monaghan, *John Jay*, 399–403; Elkins and McKitrick, *The Age of Federalism*, 415–49; William Pencak, "From 'Salt of the Earth' to 'Poison and Curse'? The Jay and Adams Families and the Construction of American Historical Memory," *Early American Studies* 2 (Spring 2004): 235n9.

55. Todd Estes, "John Jay, The Concept of Deference, and the Transformation of Early American Political Culture," *The Historian* 65 (2003): 293–317; Jay to Edmund Randolph, August 20, 1795, quoted in Monaghan, *John Jay*, 403.

56. Jay to Sarah L. Jay, April 1792, quoted in Jay, *Life*, 1:289.

57. Jay to James Duane, September 16, 1795, JJP, Box 23; Jay to Timothy Pickering, August 17, 1795, Timothy Pickering Papers, microfilm edition, 69 reels, Massachusetts Historical Society, Boston (hereafter MHS), reel 20.

58. Jay to Timothy Pickering, November 13, 1797, Timothy Pickering Papers, MHS, reel 21.

59. Jay to William Vaughan, May 26, 1796, in Jay, *Life*, 2:272.

60. John Jay, "A Proclamation," *American Minerva and the New-York Advertiser,* November 12, 1795.

61. Ibid.

62. *Aurora General Advertiser,* November 20, 1795, November 14, 1795; Jay, *Life,* 1:385–88; Monaghan, *John Jay,* 407; *Massachusetts Mercury,* November 24, 1795.

63. State of New York, *Messages from the Governors, Comprising Executive Communications to the Legislature and Other Papers Relating to Legislation from the Organization of the First Colonial Assembly in 1683 to and Including the Year 1906,* ed. Charles Z. Lincoln, vol. 2 (Albany: J. B. Lyon, 1909), 380, 400, 467–68.

64. Jay, *Life,* 1:229–33, 401; Daniel Littlefield, "John Jay, the Revolutionary Generation, and Slavery," *New York History* 81 (January 2000): 131–32.

65. John Jay, "To the Inhabitants of Washington County, Who Convened at Hartford, by Public Notice, on the 9th of August, 1798," quoted in Jay, *Life,* 1:404–5.

66. Jay to Jedidiah Morse, September 4, 1798, Jedidiah Morse Papers, NYPL, Box 1; Jay to Jedidiah Morse, January 30, 1799, Jedidiah Morse Papers, NYPL, Box 1.

67. Jay to Jedidiah Morse, April 24, 1800, Jedidiah Morse Papers, NYPL, Box 1.

68. Jay to Lindley Murray, August 22, 1794, JJP, Box 22.

69. Jay to Rufus King, June 16, 1800, Rufus King Papers, NYHS, vol. 31.

70. Jay to Benjamin Vaughan, August 31, 1797, JJP, Box 23.

71. Jay to William Vaughan, May 26, 1796, in Jay, *Life,* 2:272.

72. As Ruth Bloch has noted, millennial language was flexible and could be used to a variety of purposes. Bloch, *Visionary Republic,* 202–32.

73. Jay to the Committee of the Federal Freeholders in New York, January 27, 1801, in Jay, *Life,* 1:422. Jay himself had earlier rejected a proposal by Alexander Hamilton to influence the outcome of the election by calling the old legislature back into session. Monaghan, *John Jay,* 421.

74. Jay to Richard Hatfield, November 8, 1800, in Jay, *Life,* 1:420.

75. Jay to Benjamin Vaughan, August 31, 1797, JJP, Box 23.

76. Jay's language would thus support the multiple-discourse interpretation offered by Kramnick in "The 'Great National Discussion.'"

2   Timothy Dwight and Jedidiah Morse

1. Jedidiah Morse, *A Sermon, Delivered at the New North Church in Boston, in the Morning, and in the Afternoon at Charlestown, May 9th, 1798, Being the Day Recommended by John Adams, President of the United States of America, for Solemn Humiliation, Fasting, and Prayer* (Boston: Samuel Hall, 1798), 20.

2. Stephen Berk in *Calvinism versus Democracy* largely takes this view, subsuming Dwight's religious concerns under political concerns. Richard Moss's *The Life of Jedidiah Morse: A Station of Peculiar Exposure* (Knoxville: University of Tennessee Press, 1995), 54–80, takes an especially functionalist view of Morse's preaching.

3. Banner, *To the Hartford Convention;* Hatch, *The Sacred Cause of Liberty;* Stout, "Rhetoric and Reality in the Early Republic"; Sassi, *A Republic of Righteousness.*

4. The best recent Dwight biography is Fitzmier, *New England's Moral Legislator.* Dwight receives extended treatment in Grasso, *A Speaking Aristocracy,* 327–85. An

even more substantial body of Morse biography exists. The most useful recent biography is Joseph Phillips, *Jedidiah Morse and New England Congregationalism* (New Brunswick, NJ: Rutgers University Press, 1983). For an article that treats Dwight and Morse together, see K. Alan Snyder, "Foundations of Liberty: The Christian Republicanism of Timothy Dwight and Jedidiah Morse," *New England Quarterly* 56 (September 1983): 382–97.

5. Fitzmier, *New England's Moral Legislator*, 34–39; Timothy Dwight, *The Conquest of Canaan* (Hartford: Elisha Babcock, 1785); Timothy Dwight, *Greenfield Hill: A Poem, in Seven Parts* (New York: Childs and Swaine, 1794).

6. Timothy Dwight, *Virtuous Rulers a National Blessing: A Sermon, Preached at the General Election, May 12th, 1791, by Timothy Dwight, D.D., Pastor of a Church in Fairfield* (Hartford: Hudson and Goodwin, 1791), 14–16, 18–19.

7. Edmund Morgan, "Ezra Stiles and Timothy Dwight," *Proceedings of the Massachusetts Historical Society* 72 (1963): 101–17.

8. Timothy Dwight, *The True Means of Establishing Public Happiness. A Sermon, Delivered on the 7th of July, 1795, before the Connecticut Society of Cincinnati, and Published at Their Request* (New Haven, CT: T. and S. Green, 1795), 13, 19, 22.

9. Ibid., 23, 39–40.

10. Phillips, *Jedidiah Morse*, 16.

11. Jedidiah Morse (hereafter JM) to Jedidiah Morse, Sr., July 27, 1786, Morse Family Papers, Sterling Memorial Library, Manuscripts and Archives, Yale University, New Haven, CT (hereafter Yale), Box 1.

12. JM to Jedidiah Morse, Sr., September 20, 1786, Morse Family Papers, Yale, Box 1.

13. JM to Jedidiah Morse, Sr., 1788, Morse Family Papers, Yale, Box 1.

14. John Eliot to Jeremy Belknap, March 13, 1783, The Belknap Papers, Massachusetts Historical Society, *Collections*, series 6, 4:248–49. Chauncy had developed his views of universal salvation as early as the 1750s, but the fullest elaboration of his thought was *The Mystery Hid from Ages and Generations, Made Manifest by the Gospel-Revelation; or, The Salvation of All Men the Grand Thing Aimed at in the Scheme of God, as Opened in the New-Testament Writings, and Entrusted with JESUS CHRIST to Bring into Effect* (London: Charles Dilly, 1784).

15. Timothy Dwight, *The Triumph of Infidelity*, 1788, in Colin Wells, *The Devil and Doctor Dwight: Satire and Theology in the Early American Republic* (Chapel Hill: University of North Carolina Press, 2002), 8–16.

16. Dwight, *Triumph of Infidelity*, lines 217–18, in Wells, *Devil and Doctor Dwight*, 191. For Edwards, see Dwight, *Triumph of Infidelity*, lines 353–80, in Wells, *Devil and Doctor Dwight*, 196–97. For Chauncy, see Dwight, *Triumph of Infidelity*, lines 405–92 in Wells, *Devil and Doctor Dwight*, 198–201. For debates over Deism in England, see Robert E. Sullivan, *John Toland and the Deist Controversy: A Study in Adaptations* (Cambridge, MA: Harvard University Press, 1982).

17. Dwight, *Triumph of Infidelity*, lines 667, 753–56, in Wells, *Devil and Doctor Dwight*, 208–9.

18. For Priestley, see *Triumph of Infidelity*, lines 331–36, in Wells, *Devil and Doctor Dwight*, 195–96. For Allen, see Dwight, *Triumph of Infidelity*, lines 387–92, in Wells,

Devil and Doctor Dwight, 197–98. Allen had recently published his *Reason the Only Oracle of Man; or, A Compenduous System of Natural Religion* (Bennington, VT: Haswell and Russell, 1784).

19. On the influence wielded by Jonathan Edwards, Jr., on ministerial trainees, see Kenneth Minkema, "Jonathan Edwards on Education and His Educational Legacy," in Oliver Crisp and Douglas Sweeney, eds., *After Jonathan Edwards: The Courses of New England Theology* (New York: Oxford University Press, 2012), 45–50.

20. Phillips, *Jedidiah Morse*, 19–32, 35. Jeremy Belknap preached at Morse's installation service. Belknap, *A Sermon Preached at the Installation of the Rev. Jedidiah Morse, A.M., to the Pastoral Care of the Church and Congregation in Charlestown, on the 30th of April, 1789* (Boston: Samuel Hall, 1789).

21. Phillips, *Jedidiah Morse*, 36–37; JM to Jedidiah Morse, Sr., April 13, 1790, Morse Family Papers, Yale, Box 1; JM to Ashbel Green, September 1, 1792, Morse Family Papers, Yale, Box 1; JM to Jedidiah Morse, Sr., August 12, 1795, quoted in Phillips, *Jedidiah Morse*, 68–69.

22. Nash, "The American Clergy and the French Revolution"; Hatch, *The Sacred Cause of Liberty*, 97–102, 132–35; Edmund Morgan, *The Gentle Puritan: A Life of Ezra Stiles* (New Haven, CT: Yale University Press, 1962), 444–56; Phillips, *Jedidiah Morse*, 39.

23. On overlapping political identities, see Robertson, "'Look on This Picture . . . And on This!'"

24. JM to Jedidiah Morse, Sr., February 28, 1794, Morse Family Papers, Yale, Box 1; Oliver Wolcott to JM, June 22, 1794, Jedidiah Morse Papers, NYPL, Box 1; Oliver Wolcott to JM, February 22, 1796, Morse Family Papers, Yale, Box 2.

25. Nash, "The American Clergy and the French Revolution," 405–7; Noah Webster, *The Revolution in France Considered in Respect to Its Progress and Effects. By an American* (New York: George Bunce, 1794); Noah Webster to JM, January 22, 1794, Morse Family Papers, Yale, Box 1; Noah Webster to JM, November 21, 1796, Jedidiah Morse Papers, NYPL, Box 1.

26. JM to Oliver Wolcott, December 23, 1796, quoted in Phillips, *Jedidiah Morse*, 72.

27. Fitzmier, *New England's Moral Legislator*, 59; Grasso, *A Speaking Aristocracy*, 338–47.

28. Timothy Dwight to Ebenezer Huntington, January 31, 1795, quoted in Fitzmier, *New England's Moral Legislator*, 61.

29. Timothy Dwight, *The Nature, and Danger, of Infidel Philosophy, Exhibited in Two Discourses, Addressed to the Candidates for the Baccalaureate, in Yale College, by the Rev. Timothy Dwight, D.D. President of Yale College; September 9th, 1797* (New Haven, CT: George Bunce, 1798), 11.

30. See Henry May, *The Enlightenment in America* (New York: Oxford University Press, 1976), 105–49, 223–77, and Fitzmier, *New England's Moral Legislator*, 60.

31. Dwight, *Nature, and Danger, of Infidel Philosophy*, 13–35, 57.

32. Ibid., 64, 65, 78–79.

33. Ibid., 64.

34. Ibid., 89.

35. Morse, *A Sermon, Delivered at the New North Church in Boston*, 11–15, 17, 19.

36. John Robison, *Proofs of a Conspiracy against All the Religions and Governments of Europe, Carried on in the Secret Meetings of the Free Masons, Illuminati, and Reading Societies* (Philadelphia: T. Dobson and W. Cobbett, 1798). The acknowledged authority on this whole episode is Vernon Stauffer, *New England and the Bavarian Illuminati*, Studies in History, Economics, and Public Law, vol. 82, no. 1 (New York: Columbia University Press, 1918). Two recent studies commenting on the Illuminati controversy are Bryan Waterman, "The Bavarian Illuminati, the Early American Novel, and Histories of the Public Sphere," *William and Mary Quarterly*, third series, 62 (January 2005): 9–30, and Cotlar, *Tom Paine's America*, 97–111.

37. Morse, *A Sermon, Delivered at the New North Church in Boston*, 28.

38. Dwight, *The Nature, and Danger, of Infidel Philosophy*, 95.

39. Dwight, *Duty of Americans*, 10–12.

40. Timothy Dwight to JM, August 25, 1798, Jedidiah Morse Papers, NYPL, Box 1; Timothy Dwight to JM, January 4, 1799, Morse Family Papers, Yale, Box 2.

41. Dwight, *Duty of Americans*. Dwight used Revelation 16:12–16 as his text, which contains the reference to the "deceiving spirits." Although the sermon was undeniably millennial, it was very much grounded in the conflicts of 1798. On millennialism, see Hatch, *The Sacred Cause of Liberty*, 130–35, and Bloch, *Visionary Republic*, 211–17.

42. Dwight, *Duty of Americans*, 18.

43. Ibid., 22, 24.

44. Ibid., 18, 26.

45. Jedidiah Morse, *A Sermon, Preached at Charlestown, November 29, 1798, on the Anniversary Thanksgiving in Massachusetts. With an Appendix, Designed to Illustrate Some Parts of the Discourse; Exhibiting Proofs of the Early Existence, Progress, and Deleterious Effects of French Intrigue and Influence in the United States* (Boston: Samuel Hall, 1798), 11, 12, 13, 15.

46. Jedidiah Morse, *A Sermon, Exhibiting the Present Dangers, and Consequent Duties of the Citizens of the United States of America, Delivered at Charlestown, April 25, 1799, the Day of the National Fast* (Charlestown, MA: Samuel Etheridge, 1799), 15.

47. On the debates over Morse's claims, see Stauffer, *New England and the Bavarian Illuminati*, 289–321, and Morse, *A Sermon, Exhibiting the Present Dangers, and Consequent Duties of the Citizens of the United States of America*, 11, 18–19, 21.

48. David Osgood, *Some Facts Evincive of the Atheistical, Anarchical, and in Other Respects, Immoral Principles of the French Republicans, Stated in a Sermon Delivered on the 9th of May, 1798, the Day Recommended by the President of the United States for Solemn Humiliation, Fasting and Prayer* (Boston: Samuel Hall, 1798), 20–21.

49. David Tappan, *A Discourse, Delivered in the Chapel of Harvard College, June 19, 1798, Occasioned by the Approaching Departure of the Senior Class from the University* (Boston: Manning and Loring, 1798), 19–20, 27.

50. John Rodgers to JM, August 25, 1798, Jedidiah Morse Papers, NYPL, Box 1.

51. George Washington to JM, February 2, 1799, Jedidiah Morse Papers, NYPL, Box 1; Timothy Pickering to JM, January 30, 1799, Jedidiah Morse Papers, NYPL, Box 1; John Jay to JM, September 4, 1798, Jedidiah Morse Papers, NYPL, Box 1; John Jay to

JM, January 30, 1799, Jedidiah Morse Papers, NYPL, Box 1; John Jay to JM, April 24, 1800, Jedidiah Morse Papers, NYPL, Box 1. For the connection to Wolcott, see Phillips, *Jedidiah Morse*, 80–84.

52. John Abeel to JM, August 15, 1798, Jedidiah Morse Papers, NYPL, Box 1; Abiel Abbott to JM, December 9, 1799, Jedidiah Morse Papers, NYPL, Box 1; William Gordon to JM, May 8, 1799, Correspondence and Papers of Jedidiah Morse from Various Collections of the New-York Historical Society, NYHS, Miscellaneous Microfilm, reel 10A; William Wilberforce to JM, February 12, 1800, Jedidiah Morse Papers, NYPL, Box 1.

53. John Cosens Ogden, *An Appeal to the Candid* (Litchfield, CT?: N.p., 1798), 9, 18–19.

54. John Cosens Ogden, *A View of the New-England Illuminati: Who Are Indefatigably Engaged in Destroying the Religion and Government of the United States; under a Feigned Regard for Their Safety—and under an Impious Abuse of True Religion* (Philadelphia: James Carey, 1799), 3, 5, 16, 19–20. See Robert Imholt, "Timothy Dwight, Federalist Pope of Connecticut," *New England Quarterly* 73 (September 2000): 386–411, for Ogden's motives and additional examples of attacks on Dwight.

55. "Illuminati Sermons," New London *Bee*, June 19, 1799; "On Political Sermons," New London *Bee*, May 8, 1799; An Old Friend, "To the Rev. Doctor Dwight," New London *Bee*, May 22, 1799; "To the Clergy of New-England," New London *Bee*, September 16, 1801.

56. "On Political Sermons"; "To the Rev. Doctor Dwight"; A Sincere Christian, "On Infidelity," New London *Bee*, June 5, 1799.

57. For Adams and the Alien and Sedition Acts, see Elkins and McKitrick, *The Age of Federalism*, 581–641, and Joseph Ellis, *Founding Brothers: The Revolutionary Generation* (New York: Knopf, 2000), 190–201. Jonathan Sassi agrees that the Illuminati claims could have wide appeal. Sassi, *A Republic of Righteousness*, 79–82.

58. Stauffer, *New England and the Bavarian Illuminati*, 302–60; Phillips, *Jedidiah Morse*, 85–89; Fitzmier, *New England's Moral Legislator*, 95.

59. Nathan Strong, *A Sermon Preached on the State Fast, April 6th, 1798* (Hartford: Hudson and Goodwin, 1798), 16; Jedidiah Nash and Jacob Foster for the New England Association in Hampshire County to JM, July 29, 1799, Correspondence and Papers of Jedidiah Morse from Various Collections of the New-York Historical Society, NYHS, Miscellaneous Microfilm, reel 10A.

60. Timothy Dwight, *A Discourse on Some Events of the Last Century, Delivered in the Brick Church in New Haven, on Wednesday, January 7, 1801* (New Haven, CT: Ezra Read, 1801), 19, 21.

61. Ibid., 42–47; Dwight, "A Thanksgiving Sermon," November 26, 1801, Dwight Family Papers, Yale, Series 2, Box 6.

62. Timothy Dwight to James Hillhouse, March 1, 1800, quoted in Fitzmier, *New England's Moral Legislator*, 61–62.

63. Morse, *A Sermon, Exhibiting the Present Dangers, and Consequent Duties of the Citizens of the United States of America*, 31–32.

64. Philip Anderson, "William Linn, 1752–1808: American Revolutionary and Anti-Jeffersonian," *Journal of Presbyterian History* 55 (Winter 1977): 381–94; William

Linn to JM, May 30, 1797, Morse Family Papers, Yale, Box 2; Rev. John Mitchell Mason to JM, July 26, 1798, Morse Family Papers, Yale, Box 2; JM to Rev. John Mitchell Mason, July 25, 1800, Morse Family Papers, Yale, Box 3.

65. John Mitchell Mason and William Linn, *Serious Considerations on the Election of a President: Addressed to the Citizens of the United States* (Trenton: Sherman, Iverson, and Thomas, 1800), 4. For the religious issues involved, see Mark Noll, "The Campaign of 1800: Fire without Light," in *One Nation Under God? Christian Faith and Political Action in America* (San Francisco: Harper and Row, 1988), 75–89; Frank Lambert, *The Founding Fathers and the Place of Religion in America* (Princeton, NJ: Princeton University Press, 2003), 265–87; and Philip Hamburger, *Separation of Church and State* (Cambridge, MA: Harvard University Press, 2002), 111–43.

66. Mason and Linn, *Serious Considerations,* 5–11, 14–16, 21–23.

67. Kidd, *God of Liberty,* 237–43.

68. Tunis Wortman, *A Solemn Address to Christians and Patriots, upon the Approaching Election of a President of the United States: In Answer to a Pamphlet, Entitled, "Serious Considerations," &c.* (New York: David Denniston, 1800), reprinted in Ellis Sandoz, ed., *Political Sermons of the American Founding Era, 1730–1805* (Indianapolis: Liberty Fund, 1991), 1481, 1484, 1486.

69. John Mason, *The Voice of Warning to Christians, The Ensuing Election of President of the United States* (New York: G. F. Hopkins, 1800), 7, 25.

70. The warnings of Mason and Linn found a strong echo in a pamphlet published by A Layman, *The Claims of Thomas Jefferson to the Presidency, Examined at the Bar of Christianity* (Philadelphia: Asbury Dickins, 1800).

71. Fitzmier suggests Dwight's turn to the Hamiltonians. Fitzmier, *New England's Moral Legislator,* 198n121. On Federalist depression, see Timothy Dwight to James Hillhouse, January 15, 1801, quoted in ibid., 62; JM to Jedidiah Morse, Sr., December 22, 1800, Morse Family Papers, Yale, Box 3; and JM to Jedidiah Morse, Sr., January 1, 1801, Morse Family Papers, Yale, Box 3.

72. Dwight, *A Discourse on Some Events of the Last Century,* 42–43.

73. Timothy Dwight to JM, December 21, 1800, Morse Family Papers, Yale, Box 3; JM to Jedidiah Morse, Sr., September 9, 1801, Morse Family Papers, Yale, Box 3.

74. Quoted in Phillips, *Jedidiah Morse,* 93.

75. Timothy Dwight, "Farmer Johnson's Political Catechism," *Mercury and New-England Palladium,* March 31, 1801. For Dwight's contribution, see also Robert Edson Lee, "Timothy Dwight and the Boston *Palladium,*" *New England Quarterly* 35 (June 1962): 229–39.

76. Timothy Dwight, "Farmer Johnson's Political Catechism," *Mercury and New-England Palladium,* April 17, 1801; Timothy Dwight, "Farmer Johnson's Political Catechism," *Mercury and New-England Palladium,* April 3, 1801.

77. Timothy Dwight, "Farmer Johnson's Political Catechism," *Mercury and New-England Palladium,* April 14, 1801.

78. Timothy Dwight, "Farmer Johnson's Political Catechism," *Mercury and New-England Palladium,* May 8, 1801. Dwight also published a series "To the Farmers and Mechanics of New-England." Dwight, "To the Farmers and Mechanics of New-

England," *Mercury and New-England Palladium,* May 12, 1801, May 15, 1801, May 26, 1801, June 5, 1801.

79. Timothy Dwight, "Morpheus," *Mercury and New-England Palladium,* November 24, 1801, December 8, 1801, December 11, 1801; Timothy Dwight, "Morpheus, Part 2," *Mercury and New-England Palladium,* March 5, 1802, March 9, 1802; Cayton, *Love in the Time of Revolution,* 217–19; Chandos Michael Brown, "Mary Wollstonecraft; or, The Female Illuminati: The Campaign against Women and 'Modern Philosophy' in the Early Republic," *Journal of the Early Republic* 15 (Fall 1995): 389–424.

80. JM to Manasseh Cutler, February 3, 1803, in William P. Cutler and Julia P. Cutler, eds., *Life, Journals and Correspondence of Rev. Manasseh Cutler, LL.D.,* 2 vols. (Cincinnati: R. Clarke, 1888), 2:129; JM to William Plumer, November 16, 1803, quoted in Phillips, *Jedidiah Morse,* 101.

81. Timothy Dwight to Rev. Doctor Ryland, March 16, 1805, Dwight Family Papers, Yale, Series 1, Box 1.

82. Elijah Parish, *A Discourse, Delivered at Byfield, on the Annual Thanksgiving, in the Commonwealth of Massachusetts, Nov. 29, 1804* (Salem, MA: Joshua Cushing, 1805), 4–9, 13–21.

83. Elijah Parish, *Ruin or Separation from Anti-Christ. A Sermon Preached at Byfield, April 7, 1808, on the Annual Fast in the Commonwealth of Massachusetts* (Newburyport, MA: E. W. and W. B. Allen, 1808), 5, 17, 20.

84. For religious responses to the War of 1812, see William Gribbin, *The Churches Militant: The War of 1812 and American Religion* (New Haven, CT: Yale University Press, 1973), 1–60.

85. John Lathrop, *The Present War Unexpected, Unnecessary, and Ruinous* (Boston: J. W. Burditt, 1812); David Osgood, *A Solemn Protest against the Late Declaration of War: In a Discourse Delivered on the Next Lord's Day after the Tidings of It Were Received* (Cambridge, MA: Hilliard and Metcalf, 1812).

86. Elijah Parish, *A Discourse, Delivered at Byfield, on the Annual Fast, April 8, 1813* (Newburyport, MA: E. W. Allen, 1813), 3–5, 17.

87. Timothy Dwight, *A Discourse, in Two Parts, Delivered July 23, 1812, on the Public Fast* (New Haven, CT: Howe and DeForest, 1812), 49.

88. Ibid., 49; Lathrop, *The Present War Unexpected, Unnecessary, and Ruinous,* 12–13.

89. Lathrop, *The Present War Unexpected, Unnecessary, and Ruinous,* 30, 34; Dwight, *A Discourse, in Two Parts, Delivered July 23, 1812,* 50, 52–53; Parish, *A Discourse, Delivered at Byfield, on the Annual Fast, April 8, 1813,* 22.

90. For an excellent, succinct summary of the questions around Dwight and the Second Great Awakening, see the bibliographic essay in Fitzmier, *New England's Moral Legislator,* 228–33. Stephen Berk argues that the revival had been "contrived." Berk, *Calvinism versus Democracy,* 161–93. Better assessments have come in Richard Shiels, "The Second Great Awakening in Connecticut: Critique of the Traditional Interpretation," *Church History* 49 (December 1980): 401–15, and David Kling, *A Field of Divine Wonders: The New Divinity and Village Revivals in Northwestern Connecticut 1792–1822* (University Park: Pennsylvania State University Press, 1993).

91. Amanda Porterfield points out that Dwight also contributed to religious renewal with his hymnody. Porterfield, *Conceived in Doubt*, 95. Dwight's work included his versification of Psalm 137, "I Love Your Kingdom, Lord," which is still included in Protestant hymnals. Dwight, *The Psalms of David, Imitated in the Language of the New Testament, and Applied to the Christian Use and Worship by I. Watts, D.D. A New Edition, in Which the Psalms Omitted by Dr. Wattes Are Versified, Local Passages Are Altered, and a Number of Psalms Are Versified Anew, in Proper Metres* (Hartford, CT: Hudson and Goodwin, 1801), 317–18.

92. Richard Hall to JM, October 7, 1811, Jedidiah Morse Papers, NYPL, Box 2; Ashbel Green to JM, April 12, 1815, Jedidiah Morse Papers, NYPL, Box 3.

93. JM to John Mitchell Mason, July 25, 1800, Morse Family Papers, Yale, Box 3; John Mitchell Mason to JM, August 19, 1800, Morse Family Papers, Yale, Box 3.

94. David Bursey to JM, June 15, 1808, Jedidiah Morse Papers, NYPL, Box 1; Houlton Church Committee to JM, October 8, 1811, Jedidiah Morse Papers, NYPL, Box 2; Grasso, *A Speaking Aristocracy*, 381.

95. Alexander Proudfit to JM, March 16, 1815, Jedidiah Morse Papers, NYPL, Box 3; American Bible Society, *Constitution of the American Bible Society, Formed by a Convention of Delegates, Held in the City of New-York, May, 1816. Together with Their Address to the People of the United States; a Notice of Their Proceedings, and a List of Their Officers* (New York: Hopkins, 1816).

96. Dwight, *A Discourse, in Two Parts, Delivered July 23, 1812*, 42.

97. James Rohrer, *Keepers of the Covenant: Frontier Missions and the Decline of Congregationalism, 1774–1818* (New York: Oxford University Press, 1995), 50, 60, 118–21.

98. Timothy Dwight, *A Sermon Delivered in Boston, Sept. 16, 1813, before the American Board of Commissioners for Foreign Missions at Their Fourth Annual Meeting* (Boston: Samuel T. Armstrong, 1813); Jedidiah Morse, *A Sermon, Delivered before the American Board of Commissioners for Foreign Missions, at Their Annual Meeting in Springfield, Massachusetts, September 19, 1821* (Washington, DC: Davis and Force, 1822).

99. Jedidiah Morse, "Journal of a Mission to the Isle of Shoals," August 5–15, 1800, Jedidiah Morse Papers, NYPL, Box 1.

100. Rev. E. Eastman to JM, January 7, 1812, Jedidiah Morse Papers, NYPL, Box 2; Alexander Proudfit to JM, October 22, 1812, Jedidiah Morse Papers, NYPL, Box 2; Robert Morrison to JM, May 1816, Jedidiah Morse Papers, NYPL, Box 3; G. Hall to JM, April 18, 1817, Correspondence and Papers of Jedidiah Morse from Various Collections of the New-York Historical Society, NYHS, Miscellaneous Microfilm, reel 10B; Thomas Shepard to JM, August 22, 1817, Jedidiah Morse Papers, NYPL, Box 4; Eli M. Ripley to JM, October 17, 1817, Jedidiah Morse Papers, NYPL, Box 4; George Bunder to JM, April 6, 1819, Jedidiah Morse Papers, NYPL, Box 4.

101. David Ramsay to JM, May 1, 1810, David Ramsay Papers, David M. Rubenstein Rare Book and Manuscript Library, Duke University, Durham, NC (hereafter RBML, Duke); Thaddeus Osgood to JM, April 28, 1811, Jedidiah Morse Papers, RBML, Duke.

102. Morse, *A Sermon, Delivered before the American Board of Commissioners for Foreign Missions*, 7, 29, 30.

103. Porterfield claims Dwight helped to create an American exceptionalism by tying millennial hopes to national purposes. If anything, Dwight by this time had strongly decoupled the kingdom of God and the American nation. Porterfield, *Conceived in Doubt,* 202–6.

3   Caleb Strong and the Politics of Personal Piety

1. Caleb Strong, *A Proclamation, for a Day of Public Fasting, Humiliation, and Prayer* (Boston: Russell and Cutler, 1812).

2. Ibid.; *Columbian Centinel,* June 27, 1812; *The New-England Palladium,* June 30, 1812; *Panoplist* 5 (June 1812): 47–48; Gribbin, *The Churches Militant,* 20.

3. Gribbin, *The Churches Militant,* 44–51, 66–69.

4. Quoted in Albert Matthews, "Uncle Sam," *Proceedings of the American Antiquarian Society* 19 (1909): 30.

5. Despite his historical importance as a central figure in Massachusetts Federalism and public service, which stretched over forty years, Strong has received only minimal historical treatment. Two eulogies for Strong were delivered after his death: Joseph Lyman, *A Sermon, Delivered at Northampton, Nov. 11, 1819, at the Interment of the Hon. Caleb Strong, L.L.D. Late Governor of the Commonwealth of Massachusetts* (Northampton, MA: Thomas W. Shepard, 1819), and Alden Bradford, *Biography of the Hon. Caleb Strong* (Boston: West, Richardson, and Lord, 1820). Later in the nineteenth century, Henry Cabot Lodge devoted a chapter to his career. Lodge, *Studies in History* (Boston: Houghton, Mifflin, 1884), 224–62. In the twentieth century, Strong has most often been noticed by antiquarians. See James Russell Trumbull, *History of Northampton, Massachusetts, from Its Settlement in 1654,* 2 vols. (Northampton, MA: Gazette Printing, 1898–1902), 2:593–604, and Emily L. Myers, "Caleb Strong" (M.A. thesis, Smith College, 1938). Only a few academic historians have discussed Strong at any length. James Banner, in *To the Hartford Convention,* places him within Massachusetts Federalism but notes the need for further study of Strong. Banner, *To the Hartford Convention,* 378. To Ronald Formisano, Strong succeeded through his centrist appeal. Formisano, *The Transformation of Political Culture: Massachusetts Parties, 1790s–1840s* (New York: Oxford University Press, 1983), 62–63. Still, neither Banner nor Formisano fully reckon with Strong's combining of religious and political concerns.

6. Bradford, *Biography of the Hon. Caleb Strong,* 29.

7. For Edwards in Northampton, see Marsden, *Jonathan Edwards,* 114–374, and Patricia Tracy, *Jonathan Edwards, Pastor: Religion and Society in Eighteenth-Century Northampton* (New York: Hill and Wang, 1979). Lyman, *A Sermon, Delivered at Northampton,* 19; Trumbull, *History of Northampton, Massachusetts,* 2:97, 100, 328, 607.

8. J. L. Sibley et al., *Sibley's Harvard Graduates,* 18 vols. to date (Cambridge, MA: Harvard University Press, and Boston: Massachusetts Historical Society, 1933–99), 15:239–59, 448–73; 16:94–110.

9. Edward Dwight, "Caleb Strong," *Congregational Quarterly* 2 (April 1860): 171. For Harvard, see J. David Hoeveler, *Creating the American Mind: Intellect and Poli-*

tics in the American Colonial Colleges (Lanham, MD: Rowman and Littlefield, 2002), 213–81.

10. Lyman, *A Sermon, Delivered at Northampton*, 20. On Hawley's law practice, see Trumbull, *History of Northampton, Massachusetts*, 2:536–38.

11. Marsden, *Jonathan Edwards*, 357–74; Tracy, *Jonathan Edwards, Pastor*, 171–94; Trumbull, *History of Northampton, Massachusetts*, 2:202–34; Joseph Hawley Papers (microfilm), NYPL. The collection contains multiple pieces of Hawley's correspondence with and about Jonathan Edwards.

12. Lyman, *A Sermon, Delivered at Northampton*, 21.

13. George Bliss, "Address to the Members of the Bar, September 1826," quoted in Trumbull, *History of Northampton, Massachusetts*, 2:595.

14. *Independent Chronicle*, February 16–19, 1801. Robert Treat Paine answered the strongest charges in a letter to the editor of the *Columbian Centinel*, March 28, 1801. For another defense of Strong, see *The Question Answered—Where Was and What Was, CALEB STRONG, in the "Dark Hours of Adversity"?* (Boston: N.p., 1807).

15. Joseph Hawley Papers, NYPL, reel 1. For a narrative of the period, see Myers, "Caleb Strong," 14–22. Myers is more convincing than Lodge, who denied that Strong would have ever considered signing such addresses. Lodge, *Studies in History*, 231–33; Trumbull, *History of Northampton, Massachusetts*, 2:349–54.

16. Sarah Hooker to Clarissa Strong, May 19, 1802, Dwight Family Papers, Yale, Series 1, Box 1; Banner, *To the Hartford Convention*, 180.

17. *Journal of the Convention for Framing a Constitution of Government for the State of Massachusetts Bay, from the Commencement of Their First Session, September 1, 1779, to the Close of Their Last Session, June 16, 1780* (Boston: Dutton and Wentworth, 1832), 30, 40.

18. Ibid., 223.

19. Myers, "Caleb Strong," 23–27. See Timothy Pickering to Caleb Strong, December 14, 1804, Timothy Pickering Papers, MHS, reel 14; Caleb Strong Manuscripts, Stephen C. Strong Collection, Forbes Library, Northampton, MA, 18.

20. Trumbull, *History of Northampton, Massachusetts*, 2:481; Leonard Richards, *Shays's Rebellion: The American Revolution's Final Battle* (Philadelphia: University of Pennsylvania Press, 2002).

21. Caleb Strong Manuscripts, Stephen C. Strong Collection, Forbes Library, Northampton, MA, 98–108; Robert Feer, *Shays's Rebellion* (New York: Garland, 1988), 411–12.

22. Strong to Theodore Sedgwick, January 4, 1797, Sedgwick Family Papers, MHS, Box 3.

23. William Pierce, "Journal," in Max Farrand, ed., *The Records of the Federal Convention of 1787*, 4 vols. (New Haven, CT: Yale University Press, 1911–37), 3:88.

24. Farrand, ed., *The Records of the Federal Convention of 1787*, 2:7–8.

25. Jack Rakove, *Original Meanings: Politics and Ideas in the Making of the Constitution* (New York: Vintage Books, 1996), 77–80.

26. Farrand, ed., *The Records of the Federal Convention of 1787*, 1:72, 360; 2:232, 293, 297.

27. Ibid., 2:100.

28. Theophilus Parsons, "Notes on Convention Debates," January 24, 1788, in Merrill Jensen et al., eds., *The Documentary History of the Ratification of the Constitution*, 26 vols. to date (Madison: State Historical Society of Wisconsin, 1976–), 6:1342.

29. For instance, Nathan Dane to Strong, October 10, 1787, in ibid., 4:62–63; Henry Van Schaack to Strong, October 10, 1787, in ibid., 4:63–64; "Instructions to Caleb Strong and Benjamin Sheldon from Northampton and Easthampton," in ibid., 5:997; Nathaniel Gorham to Caleb Strong, December 31, 1787, in ibid., 5:558.

30. Two accounts of the Massachusetts convention that notice Strong's contributions are Rakove, *Original Meanings*, 118–21, and Maier, *Ratification*, 155–213.

31. Jensen et al., eds., *Documentary History of the Ratification of the Constitution*, 6:1189, 1246–47, 1338–39; Benjamin Lincoln to George Washington, January 20, 1788, in ibid., 7:1542; "Comment," *Massachusetts Gazette*, January 15, 1788, in ibid., 5:727; George Benson to Nicholas Brown, February 3, 1788, in ibid., 7:1567.

32. Theophilus Parsons, *Memoir of Theophilus Parsons, Chief Justice of the Supreme Judicial Court of Massachusetts* (Boston: Ticknor and Fields, 1859), 171. Portraits of Strong's "honest face" hang in the Forbes Library, Northampton, Massachusetts, and Faneuil Hall, Boston.

33. "The Convention Debates," 16 January 1788, in Jensen et al., eds., *Documentary History of the Ratification of the Constitution*, 6:1216.

34. John Forbes to John Quincy Adams, January 19, 1788, in ibid., 7:1532; Jeremy Belknap to Ebenezer Hazard, 20 January 1788, in ibid., 7:1533–34; George Benson to Nicholas Brown, 30 January 1788, in ibid., 7:1558–59; Winthrop Sargent to Henry Knox, February 3, 1788, in ibid., 7:1573; Bradford, *Biography of the Hon. Caleb Strong*, 15–16.

35. Myers, "Caleb Strong," 46; Trumbull, *History of Northampton, Massachusetts*, 2:596; Maeva Marcus, ed., *Documentary History of the Supreme Court of the United States, 1789–1800*, 8 vols. (New York: Columbia University Press, 1985–2007), 4:366, 387–88, 395–99, 474, 532, 550.

36. Congressional Records, April 7, 1789, in Thomas Hart Benton, *Abridgment of the Debates of Congress, from 1789 to 1856*, 16 vols. (New York: D. Appleton, 1860–61), 1:10.

37. Lodge, *Studies in History*, 239; Myers, "Caleb Strong," 51–52; Strong to Samuel Phillips, July 30, 1790, Phillips Family Papers (1704–1858), MHS, Box 1. See also the entry for April 8, 1790, in William Maclay's diary in Linda Grant De Pauw et al., eds., *Documentary History of the First Federal Congress of the United States of America, March 4, 1789–March 3, 1791*, 20 vols. to date (Baltimore: Johns Hopkins University Press, 1972–), 9:239.

38. May 26, 1789, in ibid., 9:53–55.

39. Congressional Records, January 6, 1796, in Benton, *Abridgment of the Debates of Congress*, 1:597–98.

40. Strong to Theodore Sedgwick, May 15, 1794, Sedgwick Family Papers, MHS, Box 3; Elkins and McKitrick, *The Age of Federalism*, 388–96; Charles King, ed., *The Life and Correspondence of Rufus King*, 6 vols. (New York: G. P. Putnam's Sons, 1894–1900), 1:517–20.

41. Strong to Dwight Foster, June 13, 1795, Alexander Calvin and Ellen Morton

Washburn Autograph Collection, MHS; Strong to William Cushing, April 12, 1796, William Cushing Papers, MHS.

42. Strong to Timothy Pickering, August 22, 1795, Timothy Pickering Papers, MHS, reel 20.

43. Strong to William Cushing, April 12, 1796, William Cushing Papers, MHS.

44. Strong to Theodore Sedgwick, January 4, 1797, Sedgwick Family Papers, MHS, Box 3.

45. Strong to Phillips, June 1, 1796, Caleb Strong Manuscripts, Stephen C. Strong Collection, Forbes Library, Northampton, MA, 66.

46. James Hillhouse to Strong, January 16, 1798, Caleb Strong Manuscripts, Stephen C. Strong Collection, Forbes Library, Northampton, MA, 71; Strong to Theodore Sedgwick, April 17, 1798, Sedgwick Family Papers, MHS, Box 3; Strong to Theodore Sedgwick, June 19, 1798, Sedgwick Family Papers, MHS, Box 3; Strong to Theodore Sedgwick, July 7, 1798, Sedgwick Family Papers, MHS, Box 3.

47. Strong to Theodore Sedgwick, March 28, 1798, Sedgwick Family Papers, MHS, Box 3.

48. Banner, *To the Hartford Convention*, 216–25.

49. Strong to Timothy Pickering, March 14, 1806, Timothy Pickering Papers, MHS, reel 27.

50. Strong, *Patriotism and Piety*, 60, 69, 78. See also Strong to Timothy Pickering, March 14, 1806, Timothy Pickering Papers, MHS, reel 27.

51. Strong, *Patriotism and Piety*, 16; Allen, *Reason the Only Oracle of Man*.

52. Strong, *Patriotism and Piety*, 41.

53. Ibid., 40–41, 113.

54. Ibid., 97–98.

55. Ibid., 98–100.

56. Caleb Strong, "1814 Fast Day Proclamation," Miscellaneous Manuscripts S, NYHS.

57. Samuel Adams, *A Proclamation for a Day of Public Fasting, Humiliation and Prayer. Thursday, the Second Day of April Next* (Boston: Thomas Adams, 1795); John Hancock, *A Proclamation for a Day of Public Thanksgiving. Thursday, the Twenty-Ninth Day of November Next* (Boston: Thomas Adams, 1792); Increase Sumner, *A Proclamation for a Day of Public Thanksgiving. Thursday, the Twenty-Ninth of November Next* (Boston: Young and Minns, 1798).

58. Strong, *Patriotism and Piety*, 24, 46, 76, 77, 84, 97, 106–7, 122, 133, 146, 153.

59. Ibid., 161.

60. Ibid., 152–53.

61. Ibid., 58, 146–47. For partisan antipartisanship, see Waldstreicher, *In the Midst of Perpetual Fetes*, 201–7.

62. *An Appeal to the Old Whigs of Massachusetts* (N.p.: N.p., 1806), 7–9, 11.

63. Strong, *Patriotism and Piety*, 60, 61.

64. Ibid., 189–200.

65. Formisano, *The Transformation of Political Culture*, 47–49, 57–83, 149–70.

66. For other young Federalists, see Koschnik, *"Let a Common Interest Bind Us Together,"* 41–89, 153–83.

67. *Columbian Centinel,* May 27, 1807. The address and Strong's reply are reproduced in *Patriotism and Piety,* 200-202. *Columbian Centinel,* May 30, 1807.

68. Strong, *Patriotism and Piety,* iii.

69. Caleb Strong to Clarissa Strong, July 5, 1808, Dwight Family Papers, Yale, Box 1; Caleb Strong to Clarissa Strong Dwight, August 10, 1810, Dwight Family Papers, Yale, Box 1. For the Hillhouses, see Karen Kauffman, "James and Rebecca Hillhouse: Public and Private Commitments in the Early Republic," *Connecticut History* 38 (Fall 1999): 105-26.

70. Lyman, *A Sermon, Delivered at Northampton,* 21.

71. Andover Theological Seminary, *The Constitution and Associate Statutes of the Theological Seminary in Andover* (Andover, MA: Flagg and Gould, 1817), 21, 38.

72. *Address to the Free and Independent People of Massachusetts* (Boston: N.p., 1812), 3.

73. John Jay to Caleb Strong, May 29, 1812, Caleb Strong Papers, MHS, Vol. 2, p. 9.

74. For the War of 1812, see J. C. A. Stagg, *Mr. Madison's War: Politics, Diplomacy, and Warfare in the Early American Republic* (Princeton, NJ: Princeton University Press, 1983), and Donald Hickey, *The War of 1812: A Forgotten Conflict* (Urbana: University of Illinois Press, 2012).

75. *The Strong Fast; or, Hypocrisy in the Suds* (Boston: Nathaniel Coverly, 1812). For the defense of American "tars," see Paul Gilje, "'Free Trade and Sailors' Rights': The Rhetoric of the War of 1812," *Journal of the Early Republic* 30 (Spring 2010): 1-23.

76. *The Bulwarks of Religion* (Boston: Nathaniel Coverly, 1812).

77. For an extended treatment of this discussion, see Caleb Strong, *The Speech of His Excellency Governor Strong, Delivered before the Legislature of Massachusetts, October 16, 1812, with the Documents Which Accompanied the Same* (Boston: Russell and Cutler, 1812).

78. Caleb Strong, Address to the Massachusetts Legislature, May 28, 1813, in *Columbian Centinel,* May 29, 1813.

79. For Strong's complaints to family and friends during 1814, see Strong to Clarissa Dwight, October 19, 1814, Dwight Family Papers, Yale, Series 1, Box 1, as well as Strong to Timothy Pickering, October 7, 1814, Timothy Pickering Papers, MHS, reel 30.

80. Quoted in James Walker, "Memoir of Hon. Daniel Appleton White," *Proceedings of the Massachusetts Historical Society* 6 (1862-63): 289.

81. Such an interpretation fits well with James Banner's description of the Massachusetts Federalists who made the convention as moderate men more interested in containing radicals than threatening the Union. Banner, *To the Hartford Convention,* 294-350.

82. Strong to Theodore Dwight, November 19, 1803, Caleb Strong Manuscripts, Stephen C. Strong Collection, Forbes Library, Northampton, MA, 84; Theodore Dwight to Strong, August 7, 1812, Caleb Strong Manuscripts, Stephen C. Strong Collection, Forbes Library, Northampton, MA, 91; Strong to Timothy Pickering, February 13, 1815, Timothy Pickering Papers, MHS, reel 44.

83. Quoted in Bradford, *Biography of the Hon. Caleb Strong,* 25.

84. Sibley et al., *Sibley's Harvard Graduates,* 16:99.

85. Lyman, *A Sermon, Delivered at Northampton,* 21.

86. Samuel Bayard to Elias Boudinot, August 3, 1816, Bayard-Boudinot-Pintard Papers, American Bible Society, New York (hereafter ABS).

87. American Bible Society, *Constitution,* 7; American Bible Society, *American Bible Societies Auxiliary* (New York: N.p., 1818).

88. Lyman, *A Sermon, Delivered at Northampton,* 22–23; *Hampshire Gazette,* November 16, 1819, quoted in Trumbull, *History of Northampton, Massachusetts,* 2:601.

89. Bradford, *Biography of the Hon. Caleb Strong,* 28–29.

4   Advocating "Public Righteousness"

1. Elias Boudinot (hereafter EB) to Susan Boudinot, October 30, 1782, Stimson Collection, Rare Books and Special Collections, Firestone Memorial Library, Princeton University, Princeton, NJ (hereafter RBSC, Princeton), Box 1.

2. Marsden, *Jonathan Edwards;* Mark Noll, *The Rise of Evangelicalism: The Age of Edwards, Whitefield, and the Wesleys* (Downers Grove, IL: InterVarsity Press, 2003); Fred J. Hood, *Reformed America: The Middle and Southern States, 1783–1837* (University: University of Alabama Press, 1980).

3. New Side was the Mid-Atlantic colonies' equivalent of New Lights in New England. George Adams Boyd, *Elias Boudinot: Patriot and Statesman* (Princeton, NJ: Princeton University Press, 1952), 7–8. On the First Great Awakening, see Thomas S. Kidd, *The Great Awakening: The Roots of Evangelical Christianity in Colonial America* (New Haven, CT: Yale University Press, 2007).

4. Marsden, *Jonathan Edwards,* 490–98.

5. EB to William Tennent III, November 22, 1758, William Tennent III Letter Album, South Caroliniana Library, University of South Carolina, Columbia; EB to Hannah Stockton, August 6, 1758, Stimson Collection, RBSC, Princeton, Box 1.

6. Boyd, *Elias Boudinot,* 15–17.

7. Ibid., 17; Elias Boudinot, *Journal or Historical Recollections of the American Events during the Revolutionary War* (1894; reprint New York: Arno Press, 1968), 3–8; Jeffry Morrison, *John Witherspoon and the Founding of the American Republic* (Notre Dame, IN: University of Notre Dame Press, 2005), 71–92.

8. EB to James Searle, April 5, 1779 (later copy), Boudinot Family Papers, Special Collections and University Archives, Rutgers University, New Brunswick, NJ.

9. Boudinot, *Journal,* 9–10; EB to Hannah Boudinot, March 11, 1778, Stimson Collection, RBSC, Princeton, Box 1.

10. Boyd, *Elias Boudinot,* 33–67. For Boudinot's correspondence during this time, see William A. Oldridge Collection of George Washington's Headquarters Staff Writings, Library of Congress, Washington, DC; Papers of Elias Boudinot, Library of Congress.

11. EB to Hannah Boudinot, July 22, 1777, Stimson Collection, RBSC, Princeton, Box 1.

12. Reflecting on the war from many years after its completion, Boudinot stressed the providential success of the revolution. Boudinot, *Journal,* 53–55, 84.

13. EB to Hannah Boudinot, July 7, 1778, in Paul Smith, ed., *Letters of Delegates to*

Congress, 26 vols. (Washington, DC: Library of Congress, 1976–2000), 10:232; EB to Hannah Boudinot, July 9, 1778, in ibid., 10:241; EB to Hannah Boudinot, August 13, 1778, Stimson Collection, RBSC, Princeton, Box 1.

14. Chauncey Worthington Ford et al., eds., *Journals of the Continental Congress, 1774–1789,* 34 vols. (Washington, DC: Government Printing Office, 1904–37), 25:699–701; Barbara Clark, *EB: the Story of Elias Boudinot IV, His Family, His Friends, and His Country* (Philadelphia: Dorrance, 1977), 286–87. This was in accord with the practice of the Confederation Congress. James Hutson, *Church and State in America: The First Two Centuries* (New York: Cambridge University Press, 2008), 95–104.

15. EB to Elisha Boudinot, November 14, 1782, Stimson Collection, RBSC, Princeton, Box 1.

16. EB, April 10, 1783, in Smith, ed., *Letters of Delegates to Congress,* 20:159; Boyd, *Elias Boudinot,* 98–126.

17. EB to George Washington, March 17, 1783, Smith, ed., *Letters of Delegates to Congress,* 20:30–34.

18. EB to Elisha Boudinot, June 23, 1783, Thorne Collection of Elias Boudinot, RBSC, Princeton, Box 1.

19. Boyd, *Elias Boudinot,* 127–37; Varnum Lansing Collins, *The Continental Congress at Princeton* (Princeton, NJ: Princeton University Library, 1908); EB to George Washington, June 21, 1783, Smith, ed., *Letters of Delegates to Congress,* 20:349–50; EB to General Livingston, June 23, 1783, in Smith, ed., *Letters of Delegates to Congress,* 20:350, 357.

20. EB to Hannah Boudinot, October 27, 1786, Stimson Collection, RBSC, Princeton, Box 1.

21. EB to Hannah Boudinot, April 2, 1789, Stimson Collection, RBSC, Princeton, Box 1; EB to Hannah Boudinot, April 24, 1789, Elias Boudinot Collection, RBSC, Princeton; Boyd, *Elias Boudinot,* 138–67.

22. Ibid., 154–222; De Pauw et al., eds., *Documentary History of the First Federal Congress,* 12:378–410, 14:431–41; *Annals of Congress, 2nd Congress* (Washington, DC: Gales and Seaton, 1849), 814–22, 947–55; Elkins and McKitrick, *The Age of Federalism,* 142, 230–32.

23. De Pauw et al., eds., *Documentary History of the First Federal Congress,* 10:74; Boyd, *Elias Boudinot,* 159–60.

24. Elias Boudinot, Speech, February 12, 1790, in De Pauw et al., eds., *Documentary History of the First Federal Congress,* 12:299; Elias Boudinot, "Subject of Slavery," in Jane J. Boudinot, *The Life, Public Services, Addresses and Letters of Elias Boudinot, LL.D.: President of the Continental Congress,* 2 vols. (Boston: Houghton Mifflin, 1896; reprint New York: Da Capo Press, 1971), 2:218–29, 220 (quotation).

25. De Pauw et al., eds., *Documentary History of the First Federal Congress,* 11:1500–1501; Boudinot, *The Life, Public Services, Addresses and Letters of Elias Boudinot,* 2:353–55.

26. Elias Boudinot, *An Oration, Delivered at Elizabeth-Town, New Jersey, Agreeably to a Resolution of the State Society of Cincinnati, on the Fourth of July, M.DCC. XCIII* (Elizabethtown, NJ: Sheperd Kollock, 1793), 10, 12–14.

27. Ibid., 13, 14, 27.

28. EB to Elisha Boudinot, February 20, 1794, Thorne Collection of Elias Boudinot, RBSC, Princeton, Box 1.

29. That millennial ideas influenced this period will not surprise early American historians, but Boudinot's life adds additional layers missing from the work of other historians, by demonstrating the impact of millennialism on the laity. Hatch, *The Sacred Cause of Liberty*; Bloch, *Visionary Republic*; Susan Juster, *Doomsayers: Anglo-American Prophecy in the Age of Revolution* (Philadelphia: University of Pennsylvania Press, 2003).

30. *Annals of Congress, 3rd Congress* (Washington, DC: Gales and Seaton, 1849), 302–10, 571–75; Elias Boudinot, "Non-Intercourse with Great Britain," in Boudinot, *The Life, Public Services, Addresses and Letters of Elias Boudinot*, 2:335–45.

31. EB to Samuel Bayard, October 17, 1795, William H. Bradford Princeton Collection, RBSC, Princeton, Box 1.

32. EB to Samuel Bayard, November 5, 1795, Berol Manuscript Collection, Rare Book and Manuscript Library, Columbia University, New York.

33. EB to Samuel Bayard, October 17, 1795, William H. Bradford Princeton Collection, RBSC, Princeton, Box 1.

34. EB to Elisha Boudinot, May 13, 1796, Thorne Collection of Elias Boudinot, RBSC, Princeton, Box 1.

35. For the mint, see Elias Boudinot, *Orders and Directions for Conducting the Mint of the United States, Established by Elias Boudinot, Director of Said Mint. November 2, 1795* (Philadelphia: John Fenno, 1796); Boyd, *Elias Boudinot*, 240–50; and Carl Prince, "The Passing of the Aristocracy: Jefferson's Removal of the Federalists, 1801–1805," *Journal of American History* 57 (December 1970): 563–75.

36. EB to Elisha Boudinot, May 13, 1796, Thorne Collection of Elias Boudinot, RBSC, Princeton, Box 1. For the significance of print for politics phenomenon, see Pasley, *"The Tyranny of Printers."*

37. EB to Elisha Boudinot, November 28, 1796, Thorne Collection of Elias Boudinot, RBSC, Princeton, Box 1.

38. EB to Samuel Bayard, 14 December 1796, quoted in Boudinot, *The Life, Public Services, Addresses and Letters of Elias Boudinot*, 2:119.

39. EB to Elisha Boudinot, June 12, 1798, Thorne Collection of Elias Boudinot, RBSC, Princeton, Box 1.

40. EB to Samuel Bayard, April 22, 1797, Stimson Collection, RBSC, Princeton, Box 1.

41. This significant book has received very little attention. One short and unsatisfactory attempt at understanding the work comes in Richard Popkin, *"The Age of Reason* versus *The Age of Revelation:* Two Critics of Tom Paine: David Levi and Elias Boudinot," in J. A. Leo Lemay, ed., *Deism, Masonry, and the Enlightenment: Essays Honoring Alfred Owen Aldridge* (Newark: University of Delaware Press, 1987), 158–70.

42. Elias Boudinot, *The Age of Revelation; or, The Age of Reason Shewn to Be an Age of Infidelity* (Philadelphia: Asbury Dickins, 1801), xii, iv.

43. Ibid., xx, xxii, 131–32.

44. Ibid., 26, 27.

45. Ibid., 45–60, 71–79, 90–99, 164–77, 221–27, 249–57.

46. As Sophia Rosenfeld has demonstrated, this battle over "common sense" was part of a longer eighteenth-century struggle. Rosenfeld, *Common Sense: A Political History* (Cambridge, MA: Harvard University Press, 2011).

47. Boudinot, *Age of Revelation*, 30.

48. Ibid., 68, 177, 197–201, 210–13, 277.

49. EB to Elisha Boudinot, January 7, 1801, Thorne Collection of Elias Boudinot, RBSC, Princeton, Box 1; EB to Elisha Boudinot, February 19, 1801, Thorne Collection of Elias Boudinot, RBSC, Princeton, Box 1.

50. EB to Elisha Boudinot, January 7, 1801, Thorne Collection of Elias Boudinot, RBSC, Princeton, Box 1.

51. EB to Elisha Boudinot, December 22, 1800, Thorne Collection of Elias Boudinot, RBSC, Princeton, Box 1.

52. Nicholas Guyatt describes the "push" out of politics succinctly in *Providence and the Invention of the United States*, 154–56, but misses the "pull."

53. Milton Halsey Thomas, ed., *Elias Boudinot's "Journey to Boston" in 1809* (Princeton, NJ: Princeton University Library, 1955), 12–16.

54. Ibid., 65–70; EB to Elisha Boudinot, August 9, 1809, Thorne Collection of Elias Boudinot, RBSC, Princeton, Box 1; EB to Rev. Edward D. Griffin, October 24, 1809, Miscellaneous Manuscripts, Boudinot, Elias, NYHS.

55. Thomas, ed., *Elias Boudinot's "Journey,"* 21–22, 37–40, 46, 56–57.

56. EB to John Jay, November 5, 1819, John Jay Papers, Rare Books and Manuscripts Library, Columbia University, New York, Box 5.

57. EB to Elias E. Boudinot, November 27, 1819, Stimson Collection, RBSC, Princeton, Box 1.

58. EB to Elias E. Boudinot, December 15, 1819, Stimson Collection, RBSC, Princeton, Box 1; Garry Wills, *Negro President: Jefferson and the Slave Power* (Boston: Houghton Mifflin, 2003).

59. EB to John Pintard, January 9, 1820, Elias Boudinot Papers, ABS.

60. Boudinot had known Tennent and attended his church. Elias Boudinot, *A Memoir of the Rev. William Tennent, Minister of Freehold, Monmouth County, N.J.* (Springfield, NJ: G. W. Callender, 1822), 22, 26. Boudinot's effort apparently succeeded: the piece was reprinted a number of times in various parts of the North. Extant versions exist from Trenton, New Jersey (published by Oram, 1810); Kingston, New York (Covel, 1813); Salem, New York (Stevenson, 1814); Philadelphia (Rakestraw, 1814); Poughkeepsie, New York (Potters, 1815); Wilmington, Ohio (Van Vleet, 1815); Philadelphia (Meyer, 1816); New York (Duyckinck, 1818); Wilmington, Delaware (Porter, 1819); Philadelphia (Dickinson, 1819); and Chambersburg, Pennsylvania (Harper, 1819). On Christian print culture, see Brown, *The Word in the World*, and David Paul Nord, *Faith in Reading: Religious Publishing and the Birth of Mass Media in America* (New York: Oxford University Press, 2004).

61. Elias Boudinot, *The Second Advent; or, Coming of the Messiah in Glory, Shown to Be a Scripture Doctrine, and Taught by Divine Revelation, from the Beginning of the World* (Trenton: D. Fenton and S. Hutchinson, 1815), iii–iv, 551.

62. Ibid., 531–37, 531 (quotation).

63. Elias Boudinot, *An Address Delivered before the New-Jersey Bible Society* (Burlington, NJ: David Allinson, 1811), 2, 3–5, 8–10.

64. EB to Rev. Alexander Proudfit, June 9, 1815, Elias Boudinot Papers, ABS.

65. Elias Boudinot, *An Answer to the Objections of the Managers of the Philadelphia Bible-Society, against a Meeting of Delegates from the Bible Societies in the Union, to Agree on Some Plan to Disseminate the Bible in Parts without the United States* (Burlington, NJ: David Allinson, 1815), 10.

66. EB to William Jay, April 6, 1816, Elias Boudinot Papers, ABS.

67. American Bible Society, *Constitution*, 3–7.

68. On the growth of the ABS, see Peter Wosh, *Spreading the Word: The Bible Business in Nineteenth-Century America* (Ithaca, NY: Cornell University Press, 1994), 7–88; Brown, *The Word in the World*, 27–78; Nord, *Faith in Reading*, 61–88.

69. EB to William Jay, April 6, 1816, Elias Boudinot Papers, ABS; William Jay to EB, May 15, 1816, Elias Boudinot Papers, ABS; EB to Theodore Dwight, April 9, 1818, Boudinot Papers, ABS; Samuel Bayard to EB, August 3, 1816, John Marsden Pintard Papers, ABS.

70. Donald Mathews, "The Second Great Awakening as an Organizing Process, 1780–1830," *American Quarterly* 21 (Spring 1969): 23–43; Johann Neem, "Civil Society and American Nationalism, 1776–1865," in Elisabeth Clemens and Doug Guthrie, eds., *Politics and Partnerships: The Role of Voluntary Associations in America's Political Past and Present* (Chicago: University of Chicago Press, 2010), 30–38; Theda Skocpol, *Diminished Democracy: From Membership to Management in American Civic Life* (Norman: University of Oklahoma Press, 2003), 12, 23–40; Liam Riordan, *Many Identities, One Nation: The Revolution and Its Legacy in the Mid-Atlantic* (Philadelphia: University of Pennsylvania Press, 2007), 184.

71. During Boudinot's term as president, correspondence came from, among others, the Baltimore Society; the Missionary Society of Bethlehem, Pennsylvania; the Charleston (South Carolina) Bible Society; the Dartmouth College Bible Society; the Nassau Hall Bible Society; and the Winchester, Kentucky, Bible Society. Elias Boudinot Papers, ABS. Johann Neem examines other grassroots religious mobilization in *Creating a Nation of Joiners*, 81–113.

72. Skocpol, *Diminished Democracy*, 85, 93; Riordan, *Many Identities, One Nation*, 173–74. Political scientist Robert Putnam has written about community formation and functioning in *Bowling Alone: The Collapse and Revival of American Community* (New York: Simon and Schuster, 2000), and "*E Pluribus Unum*: Diversity and Community in the Twenty-First Century," *Scandinavian Political Studies* 30 (June 2007): 137–74.

73. On moral reform, see Mark Hanley, *Beyond a Christian Commonwealth: The Protestant Quarrel with the American Republic, 1830–1860* (Chapel Hill: University of North Carolina Press, 1994), and Richard Carwardine, *Evangelicals and Politics in Antebellum America* (New Haven, CT: Yale University Press, 1993).

74. Neem, "Civil Society and American Nationalism," 36–37; Riordan, *Many Identities, One Nation*, 195.

75. Boudinot received correspondence from the Cincinnati, Ohio, Female Bible

Society and the Stones River Auxiliary Bible Society in Rutherford County, Tennessee. Elias Boudinot Papers, ABS.

76. Maria Jay Banyer to John Jay, May 9, 1823, JJP, Box 3; George Washington Doane, *Bishop Doane's Words at the Burial of Mrs. Bradford* (Burlington, NJ: John Rodgers, 1854); Riordan, *Many Identities, One Nation,* 200; Bruce Dorsey, *Reforming Men and Women: Gender in the Antebellum City* (Ithaca, NY: Cornell University Press, 2002), 33.

77. Riordan, *Many Identities, One Nation,* 192–203; Alisse Theodore Portnoy, "'Female Petitioners Can Lawfully Be Heard': Negotiating Female Decorum, United States Politics, and Political Agency, 1829–1831," *Journal of the Early Republic* 23 (Winter 2003): 573–610; Mary Hershberger, "Mobilizing Women, Anticipating Abolition: The Struggle against Indian Removal in the 1830s," *Journal of American History* 86 (June 1999): 15–40.

78. "Extracts from the Address of Dr. E. Boudinot President of the American & New Jersey Bible Society, Delivered before the Managers & Members of the Latter Society on Wednesday the 26 August 1817," William H. Bradford Princeton Collection, RBSC, Princeton, Box 1.

79. Elias Boudinot, "Address to the American Bible Society," May 1821, Elias Boudinot Papers, ABS.

5   Unitarian Politics and the Splintering of the Federalist Coalition

1. Quoted in Arthur M. Schlesinger, Jr., ed., *History of American Presidential Elections,* vol. 1 (New York: Chelsea House, 1985), 124.

2. A Christian Federalist, *A Short Address to the Voters of Delaware* (Dover?: William Black?, 1800), 3–7.

3. The touchstone for understanding Unitarian morality is Daniel Walker Howe, *The Unitarian Conscience: Harvard Moral Philosophy, 1805–1861* (Cambridge, MA: Harvard University Press, 1970), 1–23, 45–68, 93–120.

4. John Adams to JM, May 15, 1815, in James Hutson, *The Founders on Religion: A Book of Quotations* (Princeton, NJ: Princeton University Press, 2005), 220.

5. Conrad Wright, *The Beginnings of Unitarianism in America* (Boston: Beacon Press, 1955), 28–199; Conrad Wright, *The Liberal Christians: Essays on American Unitarian History* (Boston: Beacon Press, 1970), 1–21.

6. Richard Welsh, Jr., *Theodore Sedgwick, Federalist: A Political Portrait* (Middletown, CT: Wesleyan University Press, 1965), 239–52; Lucinda Damon-Bach and Victoria Clements, eds., *Catharine Maria Sedgwick: Critical Perspectives* (Boston: Northeastern University Press, 2003); J. Rixey Ruffin, *A Paradise of Reason: William Bentley and Enlightenment Christianity in the Early Republic* (New York: Oxford University Press, 2008).

7. In this paragraph, I follow Conrad Wright's argument in "American Unitarianism in 1805," *Journal of Unitarian Universalist History* 30 (2005): 3–22.

8. Ibid., 23–24; Howe, *The Unitarian Conscience,* 121–48, 205–26, connects Unitarian concepts of morality, society, and politics.

9. General studies of Adams include Joseph Ellis, *Passionate Sage: The Character and Legacy of John Adams* (New York: Norton, 1993); James Grant, *John Adams: Party of One* (New York: Farrar, Strauss, and Giroux, 2005); and Richard Ryerson, ed., *John Adams and the Founding of the Republic* (Charlottesville: University of Virginia Press, 2001).

10. For Adams as party leader, see Manning Dauer, *The Adams Federalists* (Baltimore: Johns Hopkins University Press, 1953), and Steven Kurtz, *The Presidency of John Adams: The Collapse of Federalism, 1795-1800* (Philadelphia: University of Pennsylvania Press, 1957). Both ignore the role of religion in Adams's politics.

11. This section is less concerned with defining Adams's personal beliefs (which have been explored elsewhere) than about describing his public uses of religion, which have not been sufficiently delineated. Holmes, *The Faiths of the Founding Fathers*, 73-78; Gregg Frazer, *The Religious Beliefs of America's Founders: Reason, Revelation, and Revolution* (Lawrence: University Press of Kansas, 2012), 107-24.

12. On Adams's political thought, the classic work is John Howe, Jr., *The Changing Political Thought of John Adams* (Princeton, NJ: Princeton University Press, 1966). A recent reassessment comes from C. Bradley Thompson, *John Adams and the Spirit of Liberty* (Lawrence: University Press of Kansas, 1998).

13. Ellis, *Passionate Sage*, 52; Edmund Morgan, "John Adams and the Puritan Tradition," *New England Quarterly* 34 (1961): 518-29.

14. John Adams, "A Dissertation on the Canon and Feudal Law," in C. Bradley Thompson, ed., *The Revolutionary Writings of John Adams* (Indianapolis: Liberty Fund, 2000), 23.

15. Ibid., 23, 24, 25.

16. Ibid., 28.

17. John Adams, "Governor Winthrop to Governor Bradford," January 26, 1767; February 9, 1767; and February 16, 1767, in Thompson, ed., *Revolutionary Writings*, 59, 62, 63.

18. For Adams's account of a specific clash in 1774, see John Adams, Diary, October 14, 1774, quoted in Norman Cousins, ed., *The Republic of Reason: The Personal Philosophies of the Founding Fathers* (New York: Harper and Row, 1988), 86-89.

19. John Adams, "The Report of a Constitution; or, Form of Government, for the Commonwealth of Massachusetts," in Thompson, ed., *Revolutionary Writings*, 298. With the addition that it is a "right as well as a Duty," the convention accepted this language.

20. For Adams's role in the Massachusetts Constitutional Convention, see John Witte, Jr., "One Public Religion, Many Private Religions: John Adams and the 1780 Massachusetts Constitution," in Daniel Dreisbach, Mark Hall, and Jeffry Morrison, eds., *The Founders on God and Government* (Lanham, MD: Rowman and Littlefield, 2004), especially 27-30. See also John Witte, Jr., "'A Most Mild and Equitable Establishment of Religion': John Adams and the Massachusetts Experiment," in James Hutson, ed., *Religion and the New Republic: Faith in the Founding of America* (Lanham, MD: Rowman and Littlefield, 2000), 1-40.

21. Adams, "The Report of a Constitution," in Thompson, ed., *Revolutionary Writings*, 307-17.

22. Ibid., 298.

23. For an illustration of this alliance, see Daniel Dreisbach, "Mr. Jefferson, a Mammoth Cheese, and 'The Wall of Separation between Church and State': A Bicentennial Commemoration," *Journal of Church and State* 43 (2001): 725–45.

24. Adams to William D. Williamson, February 25, 1812, quoted in Witte, "One Public Religion," 29.

25. John Adams, "Inaugural Speech to Both Houses of Congress," in *The Works of John Adams, Second President of the United States,* ed. Charles Francis Adams, 10 vols. (Boston: Little, Brown, 1850–56), 9:105, 111.

26. Ibid., 9:109–10.

27. Adams, "Speech to Both Houses of Congress," November 23, 1797, in Ibid., 9:121–22.

28. Adams, *"Proclamation for a National Fast,"* in Ibid., 9:169.

29. Ashbel Green, *The Life of Ashbel Green, V.D.M.* (New York: Robert Carter and Brothers, 1849), 270–71.

30. Many of these addresses and the president's answers were published in 1798 in *A Selection of the Patriotic Addresses, to the President of the United States, Together with the President's Answers* (Boston: John W. Folsom, 1798). David Waldstreicher observes that Adams used the addresses and replies as political weapons. Waldstreicher, *In the Midst of Perpetual Fetes,* 156–64.

31. John Adams, "To the Grand Jurors of the County of Hampshire, Massachusetts," in Adams, *Works,* 9:227.

32. John Adams, "To the American Academy of Arts and Sciences," in ibid., 9:181; John Adams, "To the Inhabitants of the Town of Hartford, Connecticut," in ibid., 9:192; John Adams, "To the Soldier Citizens of New Jersey," in ibid., 9:196; John Adams, "To the Legislature of Massachusetts," in ibid., 9:201.

33. John Adams, "To the Students of New Jersey College," in ibid., 9:206.

34. John Adams, "To the Inhabitants of Washington County, Maryland," in ibid., 9:214; John Adams, "To the Inhabitants of Arlington and Sandgate, Vermont," in ibid., 9:202; John Adams, "To the Inhabitants of the Borough of Harrisburgh, Pennsylvania," in ibid., 9:193. For Adams's opposition to innovation, see Zoltán Haraszti, *John Adams and the Prophets of Progress* (Cambridge, MA: Harvard University Press, 1952).

35. Adams, "To the Inhabitants of the Borough of Harrisburgh, Pennsylvania," in Adams, *Works,* 9:193.

36. John Adams, "To the Grand Jury of Morris County, New Jersey," in ibid., 9:231. This address was organized by Elias Boudinot's brother Elisha—another indication of Federalist coordination.

37. John Adams, "To the Officers of the First Brigade of the Third Division of the Militia of Massachusetts," in ibid., 9:228–29.

38. On Ware's biography, see Jonathan Den Hartog, "Henry Ware," in John Shook, ed., *Dictionary of Early American Philosophers* (New York: Thoemmes Continuum, 2012), 1080–84.

39. Henry Ware, *The Continuance of Peace and Increasing Prosperity a Source of Consolation and Just Cause of Gratitude to the Inhabitants of the United States. A Ser-*

mon, Delivered February 19, 1795; Being a Day Set Apart by the President, for Thanksgiving and Prayer through the United States (Boston: Samuel Hall, 1795), 9, 21.

40. Ibid., 15, 16, 22, 28.

41. Ibid., 8, 14, 17, 26, 30.

42. Henry Ware, *A Sermon, Occasioned by the Death of George Washington, Supreme Commander of the American Forces during the Revolutionary War; First President, and Late Lieutenant-General and Commander in Chief of the Armies of the United States of America; Who Departed This Life at Mount Vernon, December 14, 1799, in the 68th Year of His Age* (Boston: Samuel Hall, 1800), 6, 16, 17, 18, 20, 21, 24.

43. Henry Ware, *A Sermon, Delivered at Hingham, Lord's-Day, May 5, 1805* (Boston: E. Lincoln, 1805); Conrad Wright, "The Election of Henry Ware: Two Contemporary Accounts," *Harvard Library Bulletin* 17 (July 1969): 245–78; Field, *The Crisis of the Standing Order,* 111–79; Marc Arkin, "The Force of Ancient Manners: Federalist Politics and the Unitarian Controversy Revisited," *Journal of the Early Republic* 22 (Winter 2002): 575–610.

44. Eliphalet Porter, *A Sermon, Preached at the Ordination of the Rev. Charles Lowell to the Pastoral Care of the West Church and Congregation in Boston, January 1, 1806* (Boston: Belcher and Armstrong, 1806), 27. On Unitarian biblical interpretation, see Michael J. Lee, *The Erosion of Biblical Certainty: Battles over Authority and Interpretation in America* (New York: Palgrave Macmillan, 2013).

45. Bruce Kuklick collected the entire exchange in *The Unitarian Controversy, 1819–1823* (New York: Garland, 1987). On Leonard Woods, see Jonathan Den Hartog, "Leonard Woods," in Shook, ed., *Dictionary of Early American Philosophers,* 1185–88. Noll, *America's God,* 284–87.

46. Henry Ware, *An Eulogy, Pronounced July 20, 1810, at the Interment of the Rev. Samuel Webber, D.D.* (Cambridge, MA: Hilliard and Metcalf, 1810), 14.

47. Henry Ware, *A Sermon, Delivered before His Excellency John Brooks, Esq., Governor, His Honor William Phillips, Esq., Lieutenant Governor, the Honorable Council, and the Two Houses Composing the Legislature of Massachusetts, on the Anniversary Election, May 30, 1821* (Boston: Russell and Gardner, 1821), 4, 8, 9, 12, 14, 15, 16.

48. Ibid., 22.

49. Jedidiah Morse, *The True Reasons on Which the Election of a Hollis Professor of Divinity in Harvard College Was Opposed at the Board of Overseers, February 14, 1805* (Charlestown, MA: N.p., 1805), 16–25, 28.

50. JM to Joseph Lyman, June 15, 1805, quoted in Field, *The Crisis of the Standing Order,* 124.

51. Eliphalet Pearson Manuscripts, in Wright, "The Election of Henry Ware," 277.

52. "Constant Reader," *The Centinel,* January 16, 1805.

53. Arkin, "The Force of Ancient Manners," 580, 581.

54. JM to Joseph Lyman, February 9, 1805, quoted in Field, *The Crisis of the Standing Order,* 124.

55. JM to Joseph Lyman, June 15, 1805, quoted in Arkin, "The Force of Ancient Manners," 596.

56. JM to Joseph Lyman, February 9, 1805, quoted in ibid., 599–600.

57. Eliphalet Pearson Manuscripts, in Wright, "The Election of Henry Ware," 276.

58. Since Morse and his allies were also valuable parts of the Federalist coalition, their place in the party ought not to be forgotten. Thus I differ from Arkin's treatment, which only identifies the High Federalists who cooperated with the Unitarians as Federalists.

59. On Andover Seminary, see Andover Theological Seminary, *The Constitution and Associate Statutes.*

60. An example of this attack was the article by Jedidiah Morse and Leonard Woods, "Survey of the New England Churches," *Panoplist* 2 (October 1806): 212. Field, *The Crisis of the Standing Order*, 151–71.

61. For Hannah Adams, see Gary D. Schmidt, *A Passionate Usefulness: The Life and Literary Labors of Hannah Adams* (Charlottesville: University of Virginia Press, 2004).

62. Hannah Adams, *A Summary History of New-England, from the First Settlement at Plymouth, to the Acceptance of the Federal Constitution* (Dedham, MA: H. Mann and J. H. Adams, 1799).

63. Jedidiah Morse and Elijah Parish, *A Compendious History of New England: Designed for Schools and Private Families* (Charlestown, MA: Samuel Etheridge, 1804).

64. For Adams's perspective, see Hannah Adams, "A Memoir of Miss Hannah Adams," unpublished manuscript, 1832, Hannah Adams Papers, MHS. For the background, see Schmidt, *A Passionate Usefulness*, 154–87, 157 (quotation), and Phillips, *Jedidiah Morse*, 151–57.

65. Hannah Adams, *An Abridgement of the History of New-England, for the Use of Young Persons* (Boston: Newell, 1805).

66. Schmidt, *A Passionate Usefulness*, 164. For Higginson's involvement, see "Remonstrance, Signed S.H., Jr. for Miss H.A.," May 1809, Hannah Adams Papers, MHS.

67. Typescript of Judgment, May 11, 1809, Hannah Adams Papers, MHS; Schmidt, *A Passionate Usefulness*, 187–222.

68. JM to Hannah Adams, November 18 and November 30, 1812, Hannah Adams Papers, MHS; The Referees to JM, April 27, 1813, Hannah Adams Papers, MHS.

69. Jedidiah Morse, *An Appeal to the Public, on the Controversy Respecting the Revolution in Harvard College, and the Events Which Have Followed It; Occasioned by the Use Which Has Been Made of Certain Complaints and Accusations of Miss Hannah Adams, against the Author* (Charleston, MA: For the Author, 1814); Hannah Adams, *A Narrative of the Controversy between the Rev. Jedidiah Morse, D.D., and the Author* (Boston: Cummings and Hilliard, 1814); Schmidt, *A Passionate Usefulness*, 223–74.

70. JM to Hannah Adams, January 31, 1814, quoted in Schmidt, *A Passionate Usefulness*, 265.

71. For another interpretation, see Conrad Wright, *The Unitarian Controversy: Essays on American Unitarian History* (Boston: Skinner House Books, 1994), 59–82.

72. [Sidney Morse], *Remarks on the Controversy between Doctor Morse and Miss Adams, Together with Some Notice of the Review of Dr. Morse's Appeal* (Boston: Samuel T. Armstrong, 1814), 15–16, 22. A second, enlarged edition came out within the year.

73. Ibid., 25.

74. Jedidiah Morse, *Review of American Unitarianism* (Boston: Samuel T. Armstrong, 1815), 1. Morse drew on Thomas Belsham, *Memoirs of the Life of the Rev. Theophilus Lindsey* (London: N.p., 1812; reprint Boston: Nathaniel Willis, 1815).

75. Morse, *Review of American Unitarianism*, 7–10, 20, 27.

76. William Ellery Channing, *A Letter to the Rev. Samuel C. Thacher, on the Aspersions, Contained in a Late Number of* the Panoplist, *on the Ministers of Boston and the Vicinity, by William E. Channing, Minister of the Church of Christ in Federal Street, Boston. Third Edition, with Additional Remarks* (Boston: Wells and Lilly, 1815).

77. Wright, *The Unitarian Controversy*, 82.

6   Religion and Federalism with a South Carolina Accent

1. Henry William De Saussure (hereafter HWDS) to JM, February 11, 1788, Miscellaneous Manuscripts, De Saussure, Henry W., NYHS; HWDS to JM, October 1, 1793, Miscellaneous Manuscripts, De Saussure, Henry W., NYHS.

2. HWDS to JM, June 27, 1800, Henry William De Saussure Collection, South Caroliniana Library, Columbia (hereafter SCL).

3. On Federalist party development, the two classic works are Lisle Rose, *Prologue to Democracy: The Federalists in the South, 1789–1800* (Lexington: University of Kentucky Press, 1968), and James Broussard, *The Southern Federalists, 1800–1816* (Baton Rouge: Louisiana State University Press, 1978).

4. Broussard, *Southern Federalists*, 393–94.

5. This chapter might have considered other South Carolina Federalists including William Loughton Smith, David Ramsay, Thomas Pinckney, and James Louis Petigru. De Saussure and Cotesworth Pinckney, however, offer clear and unappreciated insights into this question of religion and Southern Federalism.

6. Jon Butler, *Awash in a Sea of Faith: Christianizing the American People* (Cambridge, MA: Harvard University Press, 1990), 258–67.

7. "Henry William De Saussure," in Allen Johnson et al., eds., *Dictionary of American Biography*, 25 vols. (New York: Charles Scribner's Sons, 1928–36), 3:253–54; William Harper, *Memoir of the Life, Character, and Public Services, of the Late Hon. Henry Wm. De Saussure, Prepared and Read on the 15th of February, 1841. At the Circular Church, Charleston, by Appointment of the South Carolina Bar Association* (Charleston: W. Riley, 1841), 12–13.

8. Sally Hadden, "DeSaussure and Ford: A Charleston Law Firm of the 1790s," in Daniel Hamilton and Alfred Brophy, eds., *Transformations in American Legal History: Essays in Honor of Professor Morton Horwitz* (Cambridge, MA: Harvard Law School, 2009), 85–108; DeSaussure and Ford Cash Book, 1786–95, Ford Papers, South Carolina Historical Society, Charleston (hereafter "SCHS"); DeSaussure and Ford Cash Book, 1797–1801, Ford Papers, SCHS.

9. Harper, *Memoir of the Life*, 14–19.

10. HWDS to John Coburn, June 17, 1786, De Saussure Papers, SCHS; HWDS to JM, February 11, 1788, Miscellaneous Manuscripts, De Saussure, Henry W., NYHS.

11. HWDS to M. De Saussure Monay, October 1804, De Saussure Papers, SCHS; De Saussure Genealogy, Henry William De Saussure Papers, RBML, Duke; Harper,

Memoir of the Life, 6–8; Jon Butler, *The Huguenots in America: A Refugee People in New World Society* (Cambridge, MA: Harvard University Press, 1983), 91–143; Bertrand Van Ruymbeke, *From New Babylon to Eden: The Huguenots and Their Migration to Colonial South Carolina* (Columbia: University of South Carolina Press, 2006).

12. Circular Congregational Church (Charleston, SC) Constitution, By-laws, and Articles of Faith, 1814, SCHS; Circular Congregational Church Church Histories, 1853, 1892, SCHS; David Ramsay, *The History of the Independent Congregational Church in Charleston, S. Carolina* (Charleston: J. Maxwell, 1815); George Edwards, *A History of the Independent or Congregational Church of Charleston, South Carolina, Commonly Known as the Circular Church* (Boston: Pilgrim Press, 1947), 45.

13. Isaac Keith to Ashbel Green, October 11, 1797, Circular Congregational Church Records, SCHS; Andrew Flinn, *A Funeral Discourse, Commemorative of the Rev. Isaac Stockton Keith, D.D., One of the Ministers of the Independent Congregational Church in Charleston, S.C. Delivered in the Circular Church, Jan. 4, 1814, at the Request of the Board of Managers of the Charleston Bible Society* (Charleston?: N.p., 1814?).

14. HWDS to Timothy Ford, November 15, 1815, Ford-Ravenal Family Papers, SCHS.

15. Bill Palmer, Jr., "A Manuscript History of the First Presbyterian Church, Columbia, S.C.," n.d., 12, 20, 25, 47, Records: Presbyterian Church, Richland County, Columbia First, SCL; First Presbyterian Church Columbia History, 1795–1821, Records: Presbyterian Church, Richland County, Columbia First, SCL.

16. Harper, *Memoir of the Life*, 33.

17. HWDS to Thomas Waties, October 13, 1821, De Saussure Papers, SCHS.

18. HWDS to John E. Calhoun, January 20, 1806, Henry William De Saussure Collection, SCL.

19. On the Southern Reformed tradition, see Robert Calhoon, *Evangelicals & Conservatives in the Early South, 1740–1861* (Columbia: University of South Carolina Press, 1988), and Hood, *Reformed America*.

20. Harper, *Memoir of the Life*, 21, 22, 37. On Federalist patronage, see Rose, *Prologue to Democracy*, 22–39, 45–46.

21. HWDS to unknown, November 20, 1795, De Saussure Papers, SCHS.

22. *Letter from the Secretary of State: Enclosing the Reports of the Late and Present Director of the Mint, Exhibiting the State of That Establishment, and Shewing the Necessity of Some Further Legislative Provisions to Render It More Efficient and Secure* (Philadelphia: Francis and Robert Bailey, 1795); Edmund Randolph to HWDS, June 6, 1795, De Saussure Papers, SCHS; Edmund Randolph to HWDS, July 1, 1795, De Saussure Papers, SCHS; Timothy Pickering to HWDS, October 15, 1795, De Saussure Papers, SCHS; HWDS to George Washington, October 27, 1795, De Saussure Papers, SCHS.

23. Walter Edgar provides a general overview of developments in *South Carolina: A History* (Columbia: University of South Carolina Press, 1998), 226–87. Rachel Klein offers a more focused study on the regional tensions within South Carolina politics in *Unification of a Slave State: The Rise of the Planter Class in the South Carolina Backcountry, 1760–1808* (Chapel Hill: University of North Carolina Press, 1990), 178–268.

24. De Saussure borrowed the pseudonym Phocion from an Athenian statesman noted for his wisdom, despite resisting the Athenian majority. De Saussure was suggesting that for politics, wisdom should trump numbers.

25. On representation in South Carolina, see James Haw, "Political Representation in South Carolina, 1699–1794: Evolution of a Low-country Tradition," *South Carolina Historical Magazine* 103 (2002): 106–29.

26. Timothy Ford, writing as Americanus, made similar claims. Ford, *The Constitutionalist; or, An Inquiry How Far It Is Expedient and Proper to Alter the Constitution of South Carolina* (Charleston: Markland and M'Iver, 1794).

27. Henry William De Saussure, *Letters on the Questions of the Justice and Expediency of Going into Alterations of the Representation in the Legislature of South-Carolina, as Fixed by the Constitution* (Charleston: Markland and M'Iver, 1795), 4, 5.

28. Ibid., 6, 9, 25, 27.

29. Ibid., 7.

30. HWDS to Jacob Read, July 14, 1798, Henry William De Saussure Collection, SCL.

31. HWDS to Timothy Pickering, November 26, 1798, Timothy Pickering Papers, MHS, reel 23.

32. HWDS to Jacob Read, July 14, 1798, Henry William De Saussure Collection, SCL; Henry William De Saussure, *An Oration, Prepared, to Be Delivered in St. Phillip's Church, before the Inhabitants of Charleston, South-Carolina, on the Fourth of July, 1798. In Commemoration of American Independence* (Charleston: W. P. Young, 1798), 15, 23, 41, 43.

33. Ibid., 27.

34. Ibid., 44, 45.

35. Ibid., 18, 45.

36. HWDS to Timothy Pickering, November 10, 1798, Timothy Pickering Papers, MHS, reel 23.

37. HWDS to unknown, November 20, 1795, De Saussure Papers, SCHS; HWDS to Jacob Read, July 14, 1798, Henry William De Saussure Collection, SCL; HWDS to John Rutledge, Jr., August 14, 1800, John Rutledge, Jr., Papers, Southern Historical Collection, Louis Round Wilson Special Collections Library, University of North Carolina at Chapel Hill (hereafter UNC).

38. HWDS to JM, June 27, 1800, Henry William De Saussure Collection, SCL.

39. HWDS to John Rutledge, Jr., August 14, 1800, John Rutledge, Jr., Papers, UNC.

40. Henry William De Saussure, *Answer to a Dialogue between a Federalist and a Republican: First Inserted in the News-papers in Charleston, and Now Republished at the Desire of a Number of Citizens* (Charleston: W. P. Young, 1800), 3, 7

41. Henry William De Saussure, *Address to the Citizens of South-Carolina, on the Approaching Election of President and Vice-President of the United States* (Charleston: W. P. Young, 1800), 6.

42. De Saussure, *Answer to a Dialogue*, 14–15.

43. In this attack, De Saussure echoed the attacks made by other Federalists. Kerber, *Federalists in Dissent*, 67–94.

44. De Saussure, *Address to the Citizens of South-Carolina*, 10.

45. De Saussure, *Answer to a Dialogue*, 31.

46. De Saussure, *Address to the Citizens of South-Carolina*, 28, 33.

47. In contrast to the claim by Lisle Rose in *Prologue to Democracy*, 234–82, that rivalries weakened South Carolinian Federalists' support for Adams, De Saussure's writings and efforts demonstrate efforts on behalf of both candidates.

48. De Saussure, *Address to the Citizens of South-Carolina*, 17.

49. Marvin Zahniser, *Charles Cotesworth Pinckney: Founding Father* (Chapel Hill: University of North Carolina Press, 1967), 224–33.

50. HWDS to John Rutledge, Jr., January 12, 1801, John Rutledge, Jr., Papers, UNC.

51. HWDS to John Rutledge, Jr., August 25, 1801, John Rutledge, Jr., Papers, UNC; HWDS to John Rutledge, Jr., November 2, 1801, John Rutledge, Jr., Papers, UNC.

52. HWDS to John Rutledge, Jr., August 25, 1801, John Rutledge, Jr., Papers, UNC; HWDS to John Rutledge, September 11, 1801, John Rutledge, Jr., Papers, UNC.

53. HWDS to John Rutledge, Jr., September 10, 1802, John Rutledge, Jr., Papers, UNC; HWDS to John Rutledge, Jr., September 21, 1802, John Rutledge, Jr., Papers, UNC.

54. HWDS to Josiah Quincy, December 7, 1808, and HWDS to Josiah Quincy, January 21, 1809, quoted in Edmund Quincy, *Life of Josiah Quincy* (Boston: Fields, Osgood, 1869), 189–91.

55. Harper, *Memoir of the Life*, 27–29, 37–38; Henry William De Saussure, *An Oration Delivered by Chancellor De Saussure, on the Fourth of July, Being the Fiftieth Anniversary of American Independence* (Columbia: D. E. Sweeney, 1826).

56. Bible Society of Charleston, Treasurer's Book, 1821–62, SCL.

57. HWDS to Timothy Ford, July 9, 1816, Ford-Ravenal Family Papers, SCHS.

58. Circular Congregational Church, Society Records, The Society for Elderly and Disabled Ministers, SCHS; Edwards, *A History of the Independent or Congregational Church*, 128.

59. Receipt from Isaac Keith, De Saussure Papers, SCHS.

60. Harper, *Memoir of the Life*, 27.

61. Henry William De Saussure, *Memoir of the Life, and Eulogy on the Character, of the Late Judge Waties* (Columbia: David W. Sims, 1828), 12, 22, 23, 24.

62. Maier, *Ratification*, 241–53.

63. The standard work on Pinckney's life is Zahniser's biography, *Charles Cotesworth Pinckney*. Also helpful is Frances Leigh Williams, *A Founding Family: The Pinckneys of South Carolina* (New York: Harcourt Brace Jovanovich, 1978).

64. Charles Cotesworth Pinckney (hereafter CCP) to Timothy Pickering, February 1, 1797, quoted in Zahniser, *Charles Cotesworth Pinckney*, 147.

65. CCP to Thomas Pinckney, February 22, 1798, quoted in Zahniser, *Charles Cotesworth Pinckney*, 178n33.

66. CCP to Timothy Pickering, May 19, 1800, Timothy Pickering Papers, MHS, reel 13; CCP to Timothy Pickering, June 19, 1800, Timothy Pickering Papers, MHS, reel 26.

67. CCP to Theodore Sedgwick, February 12, 1801, Sedgwick Family Papers, MHS, Box 4.

68. CCP to John Rutledge, Jr., January 17, 1803, John Rutledge, Jr., Papers, RBML, Duke.

69. CCP to John Rutledge, Jr., September 8, 1808, John Rutledge, Jr., Papers, UNC.

70. Zahniser, *Charles Cotesworth Pinckney,* 9; Christopher E. Gadsden, *A Sermon, Preached at St. Philip's Church, August 21, 1825, on the Occasion of the Decease of General Charles Cotesworth Pinckney* (Charleston, SC: A. E. Miller, 1825), 19; "Sermon Notes in Cotesworth Pinckney's Handwriting," Pinckney-Means Family Papers, SCHS.

71. Zahniser, *Charles Cotesworth Pinckney,* 30; St. Philip's Episcopal Church Records, Vestry Records, 1761–95, Charleston County Public Library, Charleston.

72. Protestant Episcopal Diocese of South Carolina Records, Records of the Protestant Episcopal Society for the Advancement of Christianity in South Carolina, SCHS, Box 21; Gadsden, *A Sermon,* 20.

73. Bible Society of Charleston, Treasurer's Book, 1821–62, SCL; CCP to Hudson & Goodwin, December 1, 1810, Charles Cotesworth Pinckney Papers, SCL; *The Constitution of the Bible Society of Charleston, (S.C.) Adopted June 18, 1810. With the Address of Their Committee to the Public* (Charleston: J. Hoff, 1810); Charleston Bible Society Records, SCHS; Alexander Garden, *Eulogy on Gen. Chs. Cotesworth Pinckney, President-General of the Society of the Cincinnati* (Charleston, SC: A. E. Miller, 1825), 30, 42–43; Zahniser, *Charles Cotesworth Pinckney,* 271–72.

74. Garden, *Eulogy on Gen. Chs. Cotesworth Pinckney,* 30.

75. Harvey T. Cook, "A Biography of Richard Furman," 1913, reprinted in G. William Foster, Jr., ed., *Life and Works of Dr. Richard Furman, D.D.* (Harrisonburg, VA: Sprinkle, 2004), 44, 47–48, 59–60.

76. De Saussure, *Letters on the Questions of the Justice and Expediency,* 8, 14.

77. De Saussure, *Address to the Citizens of South-Carolina,* 15, 16.

78. Henry William De Saussure, *A Series of Numbers Addressed to the Public, on the Subject of the Slaves and Free People of Color* (Columbia: State Gazette Office, 1822), 5.

79. Ibid., 6. For the proslavery religious argument generally, see Noll, *America's God,* 386–401. For a close examination of how this same argument was made in Virginia, see Charles Irons, *The Origins of Proslavery Christianity: White and Black Evangelicals in Colonial and Antebellum Virginia* (Chapel Hill: University of North Carolina Press, 2008). For cruelty in the slavery debate, see Margaret Abruzzo, *Polemical Pain: Slavery, Cruelty, and the Rise of Humanitarianism* (Baltimore: Johns Hopkins University Press, 2011).

80. De Saussure, *A Series of Numbers Addressed to the Public,* 5, 7, 8, 11.

81. Ibid., 14, 17.

82. Ibid., 6, 18, 19.

83. Larry Tise suggests De Saussure's appeals had a reasonable chance at success. Tise, *Proslavery: A History of the Defense of Slavery in America, 1701–1840* (Athens: University of Georgia Press, 1987), 238–307.

84. For the comparison, see Minkema and Stout, "The Edwardsean Tradition and the Antislavery Debate, 1740–1865," 47–74, and Peter Hinks, "Timothy Dwight, Con-

gregationalism, and Early Antislavery," in Steven Mintz and John Stauffer, eds., *The Problem of Evil: Slavery, Freedom, and the Ambiguities of American Reform* (Amherst: University of Massachusetts Press, 2007), 148–61.

85. CCP to Harriet Horry, May 14, 1787, Pinckney-Means Family Papers, SCHS; Bills and Receipts, 1788–1819, Charles Cotesworth Pinckney Papers, RBML, Duke; CCP to Edward Rutledge, January 1796, Edward Rutledge Papers, RBML, Duke.

86. Henry William Harrington to CCP, August 17, 1785, Henry William Harrington Collection, UNC; CCP to Henry William Harrington, August 29, 1785, Henry William Harrington Collection, UNC; "List of Mr. Stead's Negroes," March 24, 1803, Charles Cotesworth Pinckney Papers, RBML, Duke.

87. Quoted in Jeffrey Robert Young, *Domesticating Slavery: The Master Class in Georgia and South Carolina, 1670–1837* (Chapel Hill: University of North Carolina Press, 1999), 94.

88. Zahniser, *Charles Cotesworth Pinckney,* 82–92; Rakove, *Original Meanings,* 85–88.

89. CCP to unknown (Andrew Pickens?), March 31, 1790, Charles Cotesworth Pinckney Papers, SCL. On the Quaker petition, see Ellis, *Founding Brothers,* 81–119.

90. Jeffrey Robert Young, *Proslavery and Sectional Thought in the Early South, 1740–1829* (Columbia: University of South Carolina Press, 2006), 239–40.

7   Peter Augustus Jay

1. Johann Neem has examined how voluntary societies had to justify their existence in early national Massachusetts, showing that a civil society developed out of political conflict between Federalists (later Whigs) and Democrats. Neem, *Creating a Nation of Joiners,* 81–139. Albrecht Koschnik has described how many voluntary societies in Philadelphia had Federalist origins. Koschnik, *"Let a Common Interest Bind Us Together,"* 153–227. This chapter goes beyond merely noting connections between Federalism and voluntarism by examining motivations and cultural meanings through the lens of Peter Augustus Jay's efforts. Further, linking the religious, moral, and political components demonstrates the complexities of motivations in these significant historical developments.

2. John L. Brooke demonstrates the interplay of political and social authority in *Columbia Rising: Civil Life on the Upper Hudson from the Revolution to the Age of Jackson* (Chapel Hill: University of North Carolina Press, 2010), 1–12, 234–45, 452–58. See also Johann Neem, "Creating Social Capital in the Early American Republic: The View from Connecticut," *Journal of Interdisciplinary History* 39 (Spring 2009): 471–95.

3. Peter Augustus Jay (hereafter PAJ) to John Jay, April 29, 1792, JJP, Box 31.

4. John Jay, *Memorials of Peter A. Jay, Compiled for His Descendents* (Holland: G. J. Thieme, 1929), 16; PAJ to Sarah Livingston Jay, June 20, 1794, JJP, Box 31.

5. For instance, Wilberforce loaned Jay a book acquainting him with the conditions of Sierra Leone, which he judged "shameful." Jay, *Memorials,* 18; PAJ to Dr. I. Kemp, February 25, 1795, JJP, Box 31.

6. PAJ to Sarah Jay, March 7, 1795, JJP, Box 31; PAJ to Sarah Jay, March 13, 1795, JJP, Box 31.

7. PAJ to John Jay, November 26, 1797, JJP, Box 31.

8. PAJ to Peter Jay Munro, February 19, 1798, JJP, Box 31; PAJ to John Jay, March 17, 1798, JJP, Box 31; PAJ to John Jay, June 7, 1798, JJP, Box 31.

9. Koschnik, *"Let a Common Interest Bind Us Together,"* 90–183, has examined the mobilization of "young Federalists" in Philadelphia. Jay's experience suggests similar developments were occurring in New York City and provides insight into the actions and motivations of one particular "young Federalist."

10. PAJ to John Jay, April 26, 1798, JJP, Box 31.

11. PAJ to John Jay, May 6, 1798, JJP, Box 31.

12. Peter Augustus Jay, "Address to the President of the United States," JJP, Box 31.

13. PAJ to John Jay, May 13, 1798, JJP, Box 31; PAJ to John Jay, August 10, 1798, JJP, Box 31.

14. PAJ to John Jay, November 27, 1800, JJP, Box 31.

15. PAJ to John Jay, May 13, 1798, JJP, Box 31; PAJ to John Jay, June 7, 1798, JJP, Box 31; PAJ to John Jay, August 1, 1798, JJP, Box 31.

16. PAJ to Elias Woodward, March 28, 1798, JJP, Box 31.

17. PAJ to Elias Woodward, February 17, 1799, JJP, Box 31.

18. PAJ to Elias Woodward, March 28, 1798, JJP, Box 31.

19. PAJ to Elias Woodward, August 10, 1798, JJP, Box 31.

20. PAJ to John Jay, May 3, 1800, JJP, Box 31.

21. PAJ to Maria Jay Banyer, May 10, 1801, JJP, Box 31.

22. Jay, *Memorials,* 25, 32; Peter Augustus Jay, "To the Law Society," John Jay Ide Papers, NYHS, Box 3.

23. PAJ to Elias Woodward, November 30, 1800, JJP, Box 31.

24. Jay, *Memorials,* 40–54, 58; PAJ to Elias Woodward, July 18, 1802, Jay Family Papers, Yale, Box 1; PAJ to Elias Woodward, August 23, 1802, Jay Family Papers, Yale, Box 1; PAJ to Elias Woodward, August 16, 1805, Jay Family Papers, Yale, Box 1.

25. PAJ to Elias Woodward, June 17, 1801, Jay Family Papers, Yale, Box 1.

26. PAJ to Augustus William Harvey, March 28, 1806, JJP, Box 32; PAJ to Dr. Jowitt, March 28, 1806, JJP, Box 32.

27. PAJ to Charles Caldwell, April 14, 1810, JJP, Box 32.

28. Jay, *Memorials,* 62, 64, 71.

29. PAJ to Mary Rutherfurd Jay, late 1809?, JJP, Box 32; PAJ to John Jay, January 12, 1810, JJP, Box 32.

30. PAJ to William Barker and Benjamin Isaacs, March 19, 1807, JJP, Box 32; PAJ to William Coleman, May 1, 1807, JJP, Box 32.

31. PAJ to Maria Jay Banyer, April 26, 1808, JJP, Box 32.

32. PAJ to Maria Jay Banyer, May 1, 1812, JJP, Box 32.

33. PAJ to John Jay, May 1, 1812, JJP, Box 32; PAJ to John Jay, May 8, 1812, JJP, Box 32; PAJ to John Jay, February 5, 1813, JJP, Box 32.

34. PAJ to John Jay, February 12, 1813, JJP, Box 32; Caleb S. Riggs to PAJ, June 18, 1813, Miscellaneous Manuscripts, Jay, Peter Augustus, NYHS; Jay, *Memorials,* 71–72.

35. PAJ to Maria Jay Banyer, December 31, 1813, JJP, Box 32.

36. PAJ to John Jay, June 26, 1812, JJP, Box 32; PAJ to John Jay, July 10, 1812, JJP, Box 32.

37. PAJ to John Jay, September 11, 1812, JJP, Box 32; PAJ to John Jay, September 17, 1812, JJP, Box 32.

38. PAJ to Judge William Miller, January 20, 1815, JJP, Box 33.

39. Jay, *Memorials,* 82–85; PAJ to William Van Ness, February 7, 1816, JJP, Box 33.

40. Peter Augustus Jay, "To the Electors of the State of New York," quoted in Jay, *Memorials,* 89, 90.

41. PAJ to John Jay, January 28, 1819, JJP, Box 33; PAJ to John Jay, May 20, 1819, JJP, Box 33.

42. PAJ to William Van Ness, January 14, 1820, JJP, Box 33; Jay, *Memorials,* 99–102. On the final disappearance of the Federalist party structure, see Livermore, *The Twilight of Federalism.*

43. PAJ to Mary Rutherfurd Jay, September 14, 1821, JJP, Box 33; PAJ to John Jay, October 3, 1821, JJP, Box 33; Jay, *Memorials,* 104–10. For the full records of the convention, see Nathaniel H. Carter and William L. Stone, *Reports of the Proceedings and Debates of the Convention of 1821: Assembled for the Purpose of Amending the Constitution of the State of New-York: Containing All the Official Documents Relating to the Subject, and Other Valuable Matter* (Albany: E. and E. Hosford, 1821).

44. PAJ to John Jay, October 10, 1821, JJP, Box 33; PAJ to John Jay, October 28, 1821, JJP, Box 33.

45. PAJ to John Jay, November 15, 1821, JJP, Box 33.

46. Peter Augustus Jay, Convention Speech, September 19, 1821, in David N. Gellman and David Quigley, eds., *Jim Crow New York: A Documentary History of Race and Citizenship, 1777–1877* (New York: New York University Press, 2003), 112, 140, 179.

47. PAJ to Mary Rutherfurd Jay, November 8, 1821, JJP, Box 33.

48. PAJ to John Jay, November 22, 1821, JJP, Box 33; PAJ to John Jay, January 11, 1822, JJP, Box 33.

49. PAJ to Mary Rutherfurd Jay, November 8, 1821, JJP, Box 33.

50. PAJ to William Livingston, January 30, 1781, in Freeman, North, and Wedge, eds., *Selected Letters,* 99; William Livingston to Sarah Livingston Jay, January 8, 1783, in ibid., 128; Kitty Livingston to John Jay, December 30, 1783, in ibid., 162.

51. PAJ to Maria Jay, July 13, 1799, John Jay Ide Collection, NYHS, Box 1.

52. Peter Augustus Jay, "Arguments for Belief in a Deity and the Scriptures," John Jay Ide Collection, NYHS, Box 3; William Paley, *Natural Theology; or, Evidence of the Existence and Attributes of the Deity, Collected from the Appearance of Nature* (London: R. Faulder, 1802; reprint New York: Evert Duyckinck, 1814).

53. Jay, *Memorials,* 65, 161–62, 176, 181; PAJ to Maria Jay Banyer, October 11, 1806, JJP, Box 32; PAJ to Mary Jay, September 8, 1815, JJP, Box 33; PAJ to Bishop John Henry Hobart, December 7, 1820, John Jay Ide Collection, NYHS, Box 1; PAJ to Maria Jay Banyer, March 30, 1837, JJP, Box 34.

54. PAJ to Maria Jay Banyer, May 9, 1837, John Jay Ide Collection, NYHS, Box 1; PAJ to Maria Jay Banyer, July 20, 1838, JJP, Box 34.

55. Jay, *Memorials,* 209; PAJ to Mary Rutherfurd Jay, August 5, 1826, Jay Family Papers, Yale, Box 1; PAJ to Elizabeth Clarkson Jay, November 9, 1838, John Jay Ide Collection, NYHS, Box 1; PAJ to Peter Augustus Jay, Jr., January 28, 1839, JJP, Box 34.

56. Peter Augustus Jay, "Address to the American Bible Society," May 13, 1816, John Jay Ide Collection, NYHS, Box 3.

57. Jay, *Memorials*, 116; PAJ to Adolphe Louis Frederic Theodore, November 5, 1833, JJP, Box 34.

58. Jay, "Address to the American Bible Society."

59. Jay, *Memorials*, 65, 77, 123, 125, 156, 163, 194, 201.

60. Peter Augustus Jay, "Address to the Temperance Society," John Jay Ide Collection, NYHS, Box 3.

61. PAJ to John Jay, October 31, 1822, JJP, Box 33; PAJ to E. W. King, January 9, 1826, JJP, Box 34.

62. PAJ to William Jay, October 16, 1840, JJP, Box 35.

63. Quoted in Jay, *Memorials*, 191.

64. PAJ to John Jay, December 4, 1823, JJP, Box 33; PAJ to John Jay, November 26, 1824, JJP, Box 34; PAJ to James Fenimore Cooper, May 26, 1829, JJP, Box 34.

65. PAJ to James Fenimore Cooper, November 22, 1830, JJP, Box 34.

66. On Indian removal, see Anthony F. C. Wallace, *The Long, Bitter Trail: Andrew Jackson and the Indians* (New York: Hill and Wang, 1993).

67. PAJ to James Fenimore Cooper, February 21, 1832, JJP, Box 34; PAJ to Henry Lee, December 24, 1832, JJP, Box 34; PAJ to Anne Jay, January 7, 1833, JJP, Box 34. On the Nullification Crisis, see William Freehling, *The Road to Disunion, volume 1, Secessionists at Bay, 1776–1854* (New York: Oxford University Press, 1990), 253–86.

68. PAJ to James Fenimore Cooper, May 14, 1833, JJP, Box 34.

69. PAJ to James Fenimore Cooper, November 22, 1830, JJP, Box 34.

70. PAJ to P. G. Stuyvesant, February 23, 1839, JJP, Box 34.

71. PAJ to William Jay, October 16, 1840, JJP, Box 35; PAJ to William Jay, October 23, 1840, JJP, Box 35. On the Whigs, see Howe, *The Political Culture of the American Whigs*, and Michael Holt, *The Rise and Fall of the American Whig Party: Jacksonian Politics and the Onset of the Civil War* (New York: Oxford University Press, 1999).

72. PAJ to William Jay, November 23, 1840, JJP, Box 35.

73. PAJ to James J. Roosevelt, January 16, 1843, JJP, Box 35.

74. The contours of Victorian, middle-class America have been limned in Daniel Walker Howe, ed., *Victorian America* (Philadelphia: University of Pennsylvania Press, 1976), and Stuart Blumin, *The Emergence of the Middle Class: Social Experience in the American City, 1760–1900* (New York: Cambridge University Press, 1989).

8   William Jay

1. Timothy Dwight to John Jay, January 4, 1803, JJP, Box 8; Bayard Tuckerman, *William Jay and the Constitutional Movement for the Abolition of Slavery* (New York: Dodd, Mead, 1894), 1–4.

2. Douglas Sweeney, *Nathaniel Taylor, New Haven Theology, and the Legacy of Jonathan Edwards* (New York: Oxford University Press, 2003), 15–65; Taylor, *William Cooper's Town*, 338–45.

3. William Jay (hereafter WJ) to Timothy Dwight, 1818, quoted in Tuckerman, *William Jay*, 7.

4. WJ to Thomas Fessenden, John A. Underwood, and Samuel Tindal, December 5, 1840, JJP, Box 38.

5. William Jay, *Prize Essays on the Institution of the Sabbath. The Former, by William Jay, Esquire, to Whom Was Awarded the Premium of One Hundred Dollars, by a Committee of the Synod of Albany. The Latter, by Rev. Samuel Nott, Jun. Pastor of the Church in Galway, N.Y.* (Albany: Websters and Skinners, 1827), 18, 34.

6. Ibid., 13, 31. Jay made particular reference to Dwight's discussion of the Sabbath in sermons 105–9 of *Theology: Explained and Defended in a Series of Sermons*, 5 vols. (Middletown, CT: Clark and Lyman, 1818–19), 4:1–85.

7. William Jay, *An Essay on Duelling* (Savannah: Savannah Anti-Duelling Association, 1829). Cf. Timothy Dwight, *A Sermon on Duelling: Preached in the Chapel of Yale College, New-Haven, September 9th, 1804, and in the Old Presbyterian Church, New-York, January 21st, 1805* (New York: Collins, Perkins, 1805). Dwight delivered this sermon while Jay was in New Haven.

8. WJ to Minot Mitchell, May 1843, quoted in Tuckerman, *William Jay*, 122.

9. WJ to Rev. John McVickar, March 27, 1815, JJP, Box 37.

10. A Citizen of the State of New-York [William Jay], *A Memoir on the Subject of a General Bible Society for the United States of America* (New Jersey: N.p., 1816); WJ to EB, March 25, 1816, Elias Boudinot Papers, ABS; Robert Trendel, *William Jay: Churchman, Public Servant and Reformer* (New York: Arno Press, 1982), 65–80.

11. [Jay], *A Memoir on the Subject of a General Bible Society*, 3, 9–11, 15.

12. EB to WJ, April 6, 1816, Elias Boudinot Papers, ABS; WJ to EB, April 23, 1816, Elias Boudinot Papers, ABS, Box 1.

13. American Bible Society, *Constitution*, 4, 5, 9–12.

14. WJ to EB, May 15, 1816, Elias Boudinot Papers, ABS, Box 1.

15. WJ to John Jay, July 26, 1816, JJP, Box 37; WJ to John Jay, July 4, 1816, JJP, Box 37.

16. A Churchman [William Jay], *Dialogue between a Clergyman and a Layman. On the Subject of Bible Societies* (New York: For the Author, 1817). For additional context, see Kyle Bulthuis, "Preacher Politics and People Power: Congregational Conflicts in New York City, 1810–1830," *Church History* 78 (June 2009): 263–70.

17. The exchange included multiple pamphlets, starting with William Jay, *A Letter to the Right Reverend Bishop Hobart: With Remarks on His Hostility to Bible Societies, and His Mode of Defending It, and Also on His Vindication of the Reverend Mr. Norris's Late Pamphlet, by a Churchman* (New York: John P. Haven, 1823). R. Bruce Mullin offers the best discussion of the conflicting ideals in this debate. Mullin, *Episcopal Vision/American Reality: High Church Theology and Social Thought in Evangelical America* (New Haven, CT: Yale University Press, 1986), 50–59.

18. WJ to PAJ, December 13, 1826, JJP, Box 37.

19. WJ to Anna Jay, April 11, 1839, JJP, Box 38.

20. WJ to PAJ, January 5, 1828, JJP, Box 37; WJ to John Jay (son), May 16, 1831, JJP, Box 37; WJ to John Jay (son), January 14, 1848, JJP, Box 39.

21. WJ to John Jay (son), April 16, 1831, JJP, Box 37; WJ to John Jay (son), July 2, 1831, JJP, Box 37; WJ to John Jay (son), February 4, 1832, JJP, Box 37.

22. WJ to Edward Delavan, December 24, 1834, JJP, Box 38.

23. WJ to John Jay (son), June 20, 1835, JJP, Box 38; WJ to A. Woodruff, June 29, 1839, JJP, Box 38.

24. On Jay and the peace societies, see Stephen P. Budney, *William Jay: Abolitionist and Anticolonialist* (Westport, CT: Praeger, 2005), 85–111; William Jay, *War and Peace: The Evils of the First and a Plan for Preserving the Last* (New York: Wiley and Putnam, 1842), 71–75.

25. Jay's efforts on behalf of abolition have been chronicled elsewhere. See Tuckerman, *William Jay, passim;* Trendel, *William Jay,* 171–416; Budney, *William Jay,* 27–84, 113–34. As a result, this passage interprets several themes in Jay's activities, rather than providing a comprehensive account of those actions.

26. For other historians who have noted connections between Federalist fathers and abolitionist sons, see Marc Arkin, "The Federalist Trope: Power and Passion in Abolitionist Rhetoric," *Journal of American History* 88 (June 2001): 75–98, and Cleves, *The Reign of Terror in America,* 230–75.

27. WJ to EB, 1819, quoted in Tuckerman, *William Jay,* 28. Jay quoted Numbers 16:48 and II Corinthians 6:2.

28. WJ to Joel Doolittle, February 11, 1836, JJP, Box 38.

29. WJ to Joseph C. Hornblower, July 17, 1851, JJP, Box 39. Note the reference to Galatians 6:9.

30. WJ to Henry G. Ludlow, October 25, 1834, JJP, Box 38; WJ to the Pennsylvania Convention, November 25, 1836, Nina Iselin Collection, John Jay Homestead, Bedford, NY; WJ to Samuel Webb and Mr. Scott, January 3, 1838, JJP, Box 38.

31. William Jay, "Introductory Remarks to the Reproof of the American Church Contained in the Recent 'History of the Protestant Episcopal Church in America' by the Bishop of Oxford," in *Miscellaneous Writings on Slavery* (New York: John P. Jewett, 1853), 421, 451.

32. Ibid., 441.

33. WJ to Joseph C. Hornblower, July 11, 1851, JJP, Box 39.

34. William Jay, "On the Condition of the Free People of Color in the United States," in *Miscellaneous Writings on Slavery,* 371–96; Jay, "Introductory Remarks to the Reproof of the American Church," 440–52; William Jay, "An Address to the Anti-Slavery Christians of the United States. Signed by a Number of Clergymen and Others," in *Miscellaneous Writings on Slavery,* 628–30, 637; WJ to Lewis Tappan, November 6, 1840, JJP, Box 38; John H. Hewitt, "Unresting the Waters: The Fight against Racism in New York's Episcopal Establishment, 1845–1854," *Afro-Americans in New York Life and History* 18 (January 1994): 7–30.

35. William Jay, "A Letter to the Right Rev. L. Silliman Ives, Bishop of the Protestant Episcopal Church in the State of North Carolina," in *Miscellaneous Writings on Slavery,* 486–88.

36. WJ to Hiram Jeliff, quoted in Tuckerman, *William Jay,* 145, 146; William Jay to unknown, 1846, quoted in ibid., 116.

37. Jay argued against the "come-outer" mentality that advocated leaving the churches. He still believed the churches were the best means of salvation. WJ to a Young Man, 1854, quoted in ibid., 147–48.

38. William Jay, *Inquiry into the Character and Tendency of the American Colo-*

nization, and American Anti-Slavery Societies (New York: Leavitt, Lord, 1835). The literature of abolitionism is vast. See especially David Brion Davis, *The Problem of Slavery in the Age of Revolutions, 1770–1823* (Ithaca, NY: Cornell University Press, 1975); James Brewer Stewart, *Holy Warriors: The Abolitionists and American Slavery* (New York: Hill and Wang, 1976); Thomas Bender, ed., *The Anti-Slavery Debate: Capitalism and Abolitionism as a Problem in Historical Interpretation* (Berkeley: University of California Press, 1992); Abzug, *Cosmos Crumbling*; Lewis Perry, *Radical Abolitionism: Anarchy and the Government of God in Antislavery Thought* (Knoxville: University of Tennessee Press, 1995); and Jonathan Earle, *Jacksonian Antislavery and the Politics of Free Soil, 1824–1854* (Chapel Hill: University of North Carolina Press, 2004). Jay's life particularly helps to illuminate issues of religion and politics raised in James Brewer Stewart, "Reconsidering the Abolitionists in an Age of Fundamentalist Politics," *Journal of the Early Republic* 26 (Spring 2006): 1–23.

39. Abzug, *Cosmos Crumbling*, 204–229; Budney, *William Jay*, 55–61.

40. WJ to Walker Todd, January 8, 1828, Nina Iselin Collection, John Jay Homestead, Bedford, NY; WJ to Aaron Brown, March 22, 1830, JJP, Box 37.

41. WJ to Lewis Tappan, March 28, 1838, JJP, Box 38.

42. WJ to Joseph Pierce, June 22, 1839, JJP, Box 38.

43. WJ to Abel Lipolt, December 14, 1838, JJP, Box 38; WJ to the Executive Committee of the American Anti-Slavery Society, June 3, 1837, Nina Iselin Collection, John Jay Homestead, Bedford, NY.

44. WJ to Angelina Grimké, February 1, 1837, Nina Iselin Collection, John Jay Homestead, Bedford, NY; WJ to Lewis Tappan, August 23, 1839, JJP, Box 38; WJ to James C. Jackson, June 8, 1840, JJP, Box 38.

45. WJ to Joseph Pierce, December 14, 1839, JJP, Box 38.

46. WJ to John Quincy Adams, July 9, 1839, JJP, Box 38; WJ to John Jay (son), November 22, 1837, JJP, Box 38; WJ to Minott Mitchell, January 27, 1838, JJP, Box 38; David Grimsted, *American Mobbing, 1828–1861: Toward Civil War* (New York: Oxford University Press, 1998).

47. WJ to Anna Jay and Maria Jay Banyer, March 11, 1837, JJP, Box 38; WJ to John Jay (son), May 4, 1846, JJP, Box 39.

48. WJ to Rev. Oliver Wetmore, September 26, 1836, Nina Iselin Collection, John Jay Homestead, Bedford, NY.

49. WJ to Samuel Webb and Mr. Scott, January 3, 1838, JJP, Box 38.

50. WJ to Rev. Oliver Wetmore, September 26, 1836, Nina Iselin Collection, John Jay Homestead, Bedford, NY.

51. WJ to Joel Doolittle, February 11, 1836, JJP, Box 38; WJ to Joseph Pierce, December 14, 1839, JJP, Box 38; WJ to Lewis Tappan, September 22, 1840, JJP, Box 38.

52. WJ to Hickson W. Field, December 16, 1840, JJP, Box 38.

53. William Jay, *The Creole Case and Mr. Webster's Dispatch* (New York: Office of the New York American, 1842); WJ to John Jay (son), October 11, 1847, JJP, Box 39; WJ to Joseph C. Hornblower, July 11, 1851, JJP, Box 39.

54. WJ to John Jay (son), September 31, 1848, JJP, Box 39; WJ to Ella Jay, October 1, 1848, JJP, Box 39; Trendel, *William Jay*, 352–62; Budney, *William Jay*, 72–76.

55. William Jay to unknown, 1846, quoted in Tuckerman, *William Jay*, 121.

56. WJ to John Jay (son), June 7, 1845, JJP, Box 39; WJ to John Jay (son), May 12, 1846, JJP, Box 39; William Jay, *A Review of the Causes and Consequences of the Mexican War* (Boston: Benjamin B. Mussey, 1849).

57. WJ to John Jay (son), August 4, 1852, JJP, Box 39; WJ to Maria Jay Banyer and Sarah Louisa Jay, June 21, 1856, JJP, Box 40; WJ to John Jay (son), June 26, 1856, JJP, Box 40.

58. WJ to John Jay (son), September 2, 1856, JJP, Box 40. On Jay's death, see Frederick Douglass, *Eulogy, of the Late Hon. Wm. Jay, by Frederick Douglass, Delivered on the Invitation of the Colored Citizens of New York City, in Shiloh Presbyterian Church, New York, May 12, 1859* (Rochester, NY: A. Strong, 1859).

Epilogue

1. Foletta, *Coming to Terms with Democracy*, 4.

2. The phrase is from Butler, *Awash in a Sea of Faith*, 225–88. Note that the early stages of the Second Great Awakening occurred in Federalist-dominated areas. Kling, *A Field of Divine Wonders*.

Index

Italicized page numbers refer to illustrations.